Living Water for Thirsty Souls

Unleashing the Power of Exegetical Preaching

Living Water for Thirsty Souls

Unleashing the Power of Exegetical Preaching

MARVIN A. McMICKLE

JUDSON PRESS
PUBLISHERS SINCE 1824
VALLEY FORGE, PA

Living Water for Thirsty Souls: Unleashing the Power of Exegetical Preaching
© 2001 by Judson Press, Valley Forge, PA 19482-0851
All rights reserved.

Scripture quotations in this volume are from the King James Version of the Bible.

Library of Congress Cataloging-in-Publication Data

McMickle, Marvin Andrew.
    Living water for thirsty souls : unleashing the power of exegetical preaching / Marvin A. McMickle.
    p. cm.
    Includes bibliographical references.
    ISBN 0-8170-1358-X (pbk. : alk. paper)
    1. Preaching. 2. Bible—Homiletical use. 3. Sermons, American. 4. Baptists—Sermons.
    I. Title.

BV4211.3 .M37 2001
251–dc21   00-060334

Printed in the U.S.A.

10 09 08

3 4 5 6 7 8 9 10

To Dr. Kenneth V. Mull, professor emeritus of religion and archaeology at Aurora University in Aurora, Illinois. You were the first and truest scholar and pastor I ever encountered. Whatever has become of my life as a scholar and a pastor is because, at a critical juncture, you took the time to care. Thank you.

Contents

Foreword

What should one expect from the hands of one gifted in his own right and who sat at the feet of both Jesus and Gamaliel? If such a combination seems unthinkable in modern times, consider Marvin A. McMickle. Favored by God, he was placed at the feet of giants in American preaching such as William Augustus Jones, the late Samuel DeWitt Proctor, and Gardner Calvin Taylor, men of "rare and winsome" giftedness, to borrow a phrase from Taylor. Not to mention a stellar education at Union Theological Seminary and Princeton Theological Seminary to boot.

Some people, however, go through life not only squandering God-given gifts, but God-ordained intersections, opportunities, and ministries. Such was not the case with Marvin McMickle. I first met Marvin McMickle at the insistence of Gardner Taylor. When Gardner Taylor speaks everybody listens; when he insists, you feel pulled by the orbit of the divine. It has not only been my privilege and delight, but part of my destiny to yield to that orbital pull. As providence would direct it, McMickle would be the one to preach my ordination sermon and Gardner Taylor would preach my installation sermon. I don't believe that such intersections in life's orbital pull are accidental.

I have not only experienced McMickle's preaching, in a variety of venues and occasions—funeral, anniversary, ordination, retreat, seminary, church, banquet hall—but I have observed first-hand his teaching both hermeneutics (or biblical interpretation) and homiletics. Moreover, I have seen him, "up close and personal," in the arenas of life—public servant, social activist, ecumenical leader, academic colleague to name a few—always with integrity, intelligence, and inspiration. Such a pilgrimage speaks to his preeminent giftedness and qualification for the task at hand.

Surely, someone will inquire, "Do we need another book on preaching? Are not such volumes legion?" My answer is yes and yes. Some books are a collection of sermons only, others are theoretical, exegetical or methodological approaches to preaching only, and still others are historical or analytical analyses of preaching only. Some are for the giraffes, others for the sheep. Few are combinations, and fewer still are for all. McMickle realizes that both sheep and giraffes need food and water for their thirsty souls. His objective is to present a guidebook that is accessible to every preacher, irrespective of his or her present training. What recommends this book over many others is not that it includes excellent sermons in final form and an exegetical and tools tourguide for the uninitiated, but that it carefully presents a model that is simple, systematic, memorable, and comprehensive that all can use.

McMickle's model is constructed on an alliterative system common among ancient rhetorician and especially beloved in the black church tradition. His system consists of what he calls the *8 Ls:—Limits, Literature, Language, Location, Leads, Links, Lessons, Life Application.* In order for a text not to become a pretext to say whatever one wants to say, McMickle believes that all preaching must be steeped in sound exegetical inquiry. To do less is to truncate a word from the Lord, a word that is precious water to thirsty souls.

Not only does McMickle take one through a step-by-step procedure for getting through the 8Ls, but he also illustrates the model with each sermon. Along the way he offers some insightful and helpful ideas for diminishing the Saturday scramble and anxiety for choosing a text, thus leaving more time for preparation. Some examples are preaching a series of sermons from a word, a phrase, a verse, a book or sections of the Bible, the lectionary, the liturgical calendar, national holidays, and a rotation of theological doctrines. He places great emphasis on the series approach by including a variety of sermons he preached at his own church, a series entitled "Conversations at Calvary," based on the text Luke 23:33-49. Such a series, broken into Part I and Part II, would be useful to those who must endure multiple morning services every Sunday but do not want to preach the same sermon twice. (Perhaps the Trinity can help those who have three morning services.)

Proponents of literary, social-scientific, cultural studies, and social location perspectives to biblical interpretation will readily note that McMickle's model is steeped in the historical critical perspective, dominant through the 1970s but taking it on the chin in the 80s and 90s. I myself insist that my students in New Testament studies be proficient in at least two of these paradigms and know something about the others. Yet, there is something not only simple and subtle, but also elastic about the *8Ls* model that will inspire creative preachers to use their imagination to draw upon the exegetical perspectives of these other paradigms. Having stepped through the open door to exegetical preaching based on the *8Ls* model, the user may be further encouraged to tear the door off its hinges so that an even broader word may be spoken by God to the people.

This is possible for at least two reasons: First, although some of the Ls are more relegated to historical critical inquiries, others are open to literary critical inquiries as well. Second, McMickle does not mandate which *L* must be given the greater emphasis. In fact, his own sermons on the same text illustrate how emphasis can shift from one *L* to another.

Location is the setting for literary critics using the narrative critical approach. However, in response to Mark's record, "But go, tell his disciples and Peter, He is going ahead of you into Galilee. There you will see him. . ." (16:7), a historical critic would inquire about the geographical, cultural, and political significance of northern Palestine in the first century. In contrast, a narrative critic emphasizing the significance of setting would offer the additional insight that Galilee is wherever Jesus goes ahead of you, because there you will see him. In fact, there is no other way to see him, unless you follow him as he goes ahead of you.

Leads highlight the significance of characters for a narrative critic. Such a shift in emphasis on the dynamics between characters offers rewarding insights in a text, wonderfully illustrated by McMickle when he makes this shift in the second sermon ("Lord, Remember Me") from the same Lucan text.

I want to highlight one final *L*, **Language**. McMickle is well aware of the power of one word. Here lies another emphasis shift among the *Ls* which allows me to offer one final illustration about the elasticity of the *8Ls* in this model. For Mark the heavens are not merely "opened" (*anoigo*) as with the other Synoptics; they are "torn," "ripped apart" (*schizo*) at Jesus' baptism in the wilderness. A door opened can be closed, but a door torn from its hinges leaves access not just for entrance from the outside, but also exit from the inside. God is on the loose in your space. Such is the case with other words. "Mountain" for the historical critic is Mt. Sinai, but it is the place where God commissions, commands, and communes for the literary critic. The "wilderness" may be located in the Negev for the historical critic, but it is the place where God's provisions are made manifest for the literary critic. Gennesaret, in northern Galilee may be a geographical location for the historical critic, but it is the location where the power of God is manifested in, on, and around the "sea" for the literary critic, the place between the two sides— political, religious, ethnic.

The value of this model, and indeed this book, is not that all will use it, but that all *can* use it. The "burdensome joy" (to borrow a phrase from James Earl Massey's book on preaching) of presenting a word from the Lord for thirsty souls demands that we draw from springs that run deep and wide. Here lies such a spring.

William H. Myers, Ph.D.
Professor of New Testament & Black Church Studies
Ashland Theological Seminary, Ohio
Thanksgiving 2000

Acknowledgments

This book would not have been possible without the unending support of the officers and members of the Antioch Baptist Church of Cleveland, Ohio. Their willingness to afford me the time required to do this work is greatly appreciated. I have never doubted their love and support while I was often hidden away doing the research and writing that has resulted in this book.

My wife, Peggy, and my son, Aaron, are also to be thanked for what has resulted in these pages. Often, even after my time at the church office has ended, I bring my research and writing home and am consumed by them for an additional period of time. My family has either patiently waited or lovingly intruded into my work. Both responses are deeply appreciated.

Finally, my homiletics students at Ashland Theological Seminary are the reason this book was written. All of the principles and ideas found here were first used in classes at Ashland. It was out of my desire to be a better teacher that I worked to produce this volume. The end result is not the book, but the continuing blessing that I hope the book will be to students and preachers who may find here some help as they seek faithfully to preach from the Bible. I hope and pray that their sermons, and my own, will truly become *Living Water for Thirsty Souls!*

Introduction

It is the central premise of this book that preaching should be grounded and centered in the truths, insights, and subtle lessons found in the Bible. The voices of those whose own preaching is recorded in the pages of Scripture remind us that our words must be based upon God's words as revealed in the Bible. That is the message found in such phrases as, "Thus saith the Lord," "The spirit of the Lord is upon me," "Hear the word of the Lord," and "He who has ears to hear let him hear what the Spirit says to the churches."

Today's preachers should remember that the word we preach is not of ourselves. We stand on the firmest possible ground when we are passing on to our hearers not what we think, or our own views on any given issue about which we feel passionately. Our preaching becomes most authentic, and most useful, when we too can declare, "Hear the word of the Lord."

During my first pastorate in Montclair, New Jersey (1976–1986), one of the deacons would ask me the same question every Sunday morning. Borrowing from the language of Jeremiah 37:17, he would inquire, "Reverend, is there any word from the Lord?" Implicit in his question is the point I want to underscore at the beginning of this book: The voice that people want to hear is not really the voice of the preacher. The voice that people really *need* to hear is not that of the preacher. The message the people have assembled to receive is not whatever wit or wisdom may be on our mind on any given Sunday. After all of the intervening years, I can still hear the voice of that deacon haunting me as I write my sermons and then stand to deliver them: "Reverend, is there any word from the Lord?"

Another way to express this same point is by describing the pulpit of the Concord Baptist Church of Brooklyn, New York, where Dr. Gardner C. Taylor served as pastor for over forty years. There is a small carpet that is placed behind the pulpit that is visible to the preacher as he or she approaches the congregation. Once behind the pulpit, the preacher literally stands on the words from John 12:21: "Sir, we would see Jesus." Having stood there on several occasions, my greatest concern was not attempting to preach in the presence of the greatest preacher America has produced in the last one hundred years. The even greater anxiety came in response to the challenge of those words. I was reminded during the entire sermon that it was a word from the Lord, not an opinion from me, that people needed and wanted to hear.

How to use nonbiblical sources

This book is designed to help preachers engage in a disciplined and deliberate study of biblical materials so that they can faithfully declare the phrase, "Hear the word of the Lord." It is not being suggested here that nonbiblical materials cannot and should not be drawn upon for use in preaching. To the contrary, sermons should make regular use of ideas and insights drawn from current events, historical and biographical works, and observations from the natural order and human nature. In addition, preaching can be strengthened by the use of themes and issues communicated through the various arts and entertainment media. Likewise, the reflections of theologians, biblical scholars, secular writers, and even those formative events from the life of the preacher can be quite useful in giving depth and texture to the sermon.

The preacher can learn a great deal about the questions that concern people by paying attention to Letters to the Editor and the Op/Ed page of the local newspaper. Similarly, preachers should take note of the reviews of films, novels, television programs, and stage plays. Many of the pressing issues of the day, as well as many of the lingering concerns of the past, are dealt with in those formats. In short, the pulpit does not control the flow of ideas that swirl around those who hear our sermons, so we need to tap in and know what others are saying and thinking.

In his book, *Biblical Preaching*, Haddon Robinson points to this need for the preacher to pay attention to what is going on in the world around him or her. He says:

> The expositor must also be aware of the currents swirling across his own times, for each generation develops out of its own history and culture and speaks its own language. A minister may stand before a congregation and deliver exegetically accurate sermons, scholarly and organized, but dead and power-less because they ignore the life-wrenching problems and questions of the hearers.[1]

Paying attention to the ideas, writings, and comments that can be heard throughout society greatly assists the preacher in tapping into those "life-wrenching problems and questions" that are gathered in the pews on any given Sunday morning.

Making the Bible our ultimate source of authority

While the sources listed above can serve as building blocks for a sermon, no one of them, nor all of them taken together, can serve as an adequate substitute for a sermon that has as its foundation some serious reflection upon a portion of Scripture. The preacher needs to approach this process with a clear sense of what views and opinions he or she will feel ultimately accountable to. Must our sermons be shaped and influenced by the comments and opinions of some media mogul or Hollywood celebrity? Is something true and worth passing on to our congregation simply because it was spoken by a movie star, a superstar athlete, or a high-profile public intellectual?

The views of these people may certainly be drawn upon in preaching. Quite often, however, the preacher will choose to do so only for purposes of refutation, as Paul does in Acts 17 with the things he observed in Athens. Nothing is deserving of the central place in a sermon simply because it was spoken by Michael Jordan or written by Cornel West. Like Paul, we must hold our sermons and ourselves accountable to the revelations of Scripture. No preacher should drift away from the words of Jeremiah 37:17, "Is there any word from the Lord?"

Our authority for preaching truth to power

The Bible is full of incredible moments when preachers stand before the highest levels of political and ecclesiastical authority and speak truth to power without flinching or hesitating. What was the source for those sermons? What accounts for the courage and boldness exhibited by Moses when he stood before Pharaoh? What accounts for the decision of Nathan to confront David about his sins involving Bathsheba and Uriah? How do you explain the zeal with which Amos confronted the sins of Jeroboam, or with which Jeremiah spoke about Jehoiakim?

This same spirit is present in the New Testament as well. What motivated John the Baptist to challenge Herod Antipas about his unlawful marriage, or Peter and John to defy the ruling of the Sanhedrin that they cease preaching about Jesus? What motivated Paul to turn his trial before Felix and Agrippa into an evangelistic service? One thing is certain. None of these preaching moments was the result of any insights that any of those preachers stumbled upon in some desperate Saturday night search for a sermon idea. Each of those preachers stood upon the assurance that they were delivering a word that came to them from the Lord.

We may or may not have the challenge of preaching to the same sort of audience (heads of state and entrenched denominational leadership) as our spiritual forebears. However, we will have ample opportunity to speak to issues that can only be resolved at that level. Such opportunities may involve affordable and accessible healthcare or an end to the testing of nuclear weapons on the political side, and the ordination of women or the ethical investment of church resources on the ecclesiastical front. They may involve the abuse of power or sexual misconduct, whether such abuses involve a political or denominational leader. Regardless, the preacher is in a much stronger position to speak, no matter to which audience, when he or she can honestly say, "Thus saith the Lord."

How should the Bible be used in preaching?

It has been stated that sermons should be based upon biblical materials, and that our authority to preach even to persons at the highest levels of power becomes more unassailable when that is the case. That leads to the question of how the biblical material should be approached so that its message is neither misinterpreted nor misapplied. For the last twenty-five years I have been actively engaged in pastoral ministry. During those years I have not only faced the challenge of preparing two or more sermons each week, but I have also had the opportunity to work with clergy colleagues in conferences, conventions, and local associations. How to make the best and most exegetically honest use of the Bible in preaching has been my chief objective in all of those settings.

For the last fifteen years, I have also had the added privilege of teaching homiletics at four different theological seminaries. In that context I have been able to formulate an approach to biblical exegesis for preaching that is easy for students to learn and useful for pastors to employ long after their student days are done. The methodology to be presented is based upon an eight-step process called the *8 Ls.*

As a preacher who appreciates the use of alliteration, my using eight words that all begin with the same letter assists with ease of memorization and recall. The eight steps are *Limits, Literature, Language, Location, Links, Leads, Lessons,* and *Life Application.* These eight steps clearly reflect the traditional methodology for doing biblical exegesis. And when these eight steps are taken in order, preachers will be better prepared to deliver a sermon that thoroughly examines a biblical text and presents its message in a way that is relevant for the intended audience, whoever they are and wherever they are gathered.

Model sermons for the 8 Ls methodology

As a way of demonstrating how this approach to textual analysis can result in materials suitable for preaching, this book will also include sample sermons at the end of each chapter that seek to illustrate some aspect of what has been discussed in that chapter. For the most part, the sermons are taken from a single biblical passage, Luke 23:32-47, which records Jesus' encounter with the two criminals who were hanged with him, and the final moments of Jesus' life. The first lesson to be drawn from this exercise is that there is typically more in a biblical passage than can adequately be examined in a single sermon.

I want to encourage preachers to benefit from all they will discover about a text through this *8 Ls* methodology. In order to do that, they need to be willing to do more in the area of developing a sermon series where a single text is considered from many different perspectives over a period of many weeks. This takes away the constant anxiety of "what to preach," and allows the fruits of exegetical study to be shared with the congregation. It will be shown that from that single passage in Luke can be drawn enough sermon material to illustrate every principle being discussed in this book.

However, sermons based upon other passages will also be included in some chapters so as to offer the reader the widest possible illustration of how the *8 Ls* methodology can lead the preacher through the transition from text to sermon. The sermons are not to be viewed as separate and apart from the book itself. Rather, they are meant to be teaching tools that demonstrate that thorough and disciplined biblical exegesis, employing a methodology that is not beyond the reach of most pastors, can yield a rich harvest of preaching material.

1
Biblical Exegesis: A Prelude to Preaching

In this chapter, I want to discuss briefly the importance of doing biblical exegesis as a necessary first step in preparing to preach. It is not enough to simply read a passage of Scripture, quickly envision three things that can be said about the passage, link that together with some illustrative materials from hymns, poems, or personal experiences, and call that a biblical sermon. The premise of this book is that sermons should be based upon the meaning of a passage of Scripture. The purpose of this book is to help preachers unlock that meaning and thereby enrich their sermons.

The pros and cons of an "exegetical" methodology
I use the word *exegesis* with much caution because over the years that word has come to carry a great deal of baggage. Not only that, but in some preaching circles the word exegesis goes unspoken and unrecognized. Insistence upon the use of an *exegetical* methodology in preparation for preaching may ring of a certain intellectual elitism among those preachers who have built successful careers in ministry without having had access to any formal theological training. Moreover, it may presume library resources and foreign language skills that these pastors do not possess. How do we make the concept of doing biblical exegesis nonthreatening to preachers who fit this profile?

Those of us who teach in and have graduated from theological schools should remember that a considerable number of our colleagues have not shared in that experience. Such preachers are neither to be pitied nor scorned, however, because many of them have done much more with what they have than many of those who bring the finest theological credentials. I have seen the fruits of the labor of these unlettered preachers across the years. They have brought glory to God not only in their small, store-front congregations, but in magnificent buildings with thriving ministries born out of their piety and their deeply held personal conviction that God has called them to preach.

However, if there is a way that theological resources can be made available and accessible to those with no formal theological training so that their preaching can take on even more depth, that can only strengthen the work in which such persons are already engaged. Part of the intention of this book is to shape and share an approach to doing biblical exegesis that can be used by persons who have had little or no formal theological training.

Exegesis and the question of biblical authority

There are others who do not embrace the concept of doing biblical exegesis, but for an entirely different reason. They may well be seminary graduates who took courses in hermeneutics and biblical criticism as part of their degree programs. They bought the books, learned the languages, and mastered the methodology. However, today they do not use any of those tools. Why?

Did they find the procedure too complicated? Did they not really understand how to make the shift from textual analysis to sermon development? Does their time management as ministers leave them rushed and unable to do any thorough sermon preparation? Or do they fundamentally distrust the process of biblical criticism? I suspect that this last observation is the case in far too many instances. Too many preachers remain soured by their perception that when they were introduced to the critical method, it was primarily used to disprove and devalue aspects of the biblical record that those preachers, and their faith communities, held as sacred and sacrosanct. These concerns can range from the virgin birth, to the bodily resurrection of Jesus, to the facticity of the miracles, to whether or not the earthly Jesus existed, and who he was.

I fear there are far too many preachers who hold this position. They do not employ the critical methodology because they are suspicious of its intentions. As a result of some exposure to a professor who was more interested in the Bible as literature than in the Bible as living Word, they were offended by a lack of reverence for the Word of God. They sense only a determination to raise as many doubts as possible about the authorship and authority of Scripture.

Such issues may have fueled many a late night discussion in some campus lounge where students gathered at the end of the day. But what does one do with these issues and insights when burdened with the responsibilities of parish ministry? Under the weight of the load, and uncertain of the value of the exercise in the first place, many preachers may choose to randomly select a verse or two of Scripture. They may then hastily pair that with the lines of a hymn or an illustration taken from some anthology. Equipped with that "fast food" diet, they then go forth to feed the flock of God.

8 Ls as a bridge over troubled waters
The purpose of this book is to present an approach to doing biblical exegesis for preaching that is accessible to those with little or no theological training. Secondly, the purpose of this book is to present a nonthreatening methodology to those preachers who may remain suspicious of exegesis because they believe it undercuts the authority of Scripture. Finally, the purpose of this book is to present an effective and reliable methodology for those preachers who have long been familiar and comfortable with the steps and procedures associated with doing biblical exegesis.

Engaging in a disciplined analysis of Scripture is a required step in the preparation of a sermon. Therefore, the challenge of this book is not to discount the worth of the exercise, or to encourage those preachers looking for an excuse not to do the most thorough biblical analysis of which they are capable. Rather, this book seeks to lay out an approach to doing that biblical analysis that is useful for preachers no matter what level of formal theological training they bring to the process.

The 8 Ls Methodology
The exegetical methodology being presented in this book is based upon the use of an eight-step process called, only for alliterative purposes, the *8 Ls*. The eight steps are described below.

1. **Limits** Exegesis is the systematic analysis of a portion of biblical material. Thus, the first step is to determine how much of that material is to be reviewed in preparation for a sermon based upon that material. This step involves determining the precise length of the biblical passage to be reviewed. Presuming that a sermon is based upon some portion of biblical material, the first decision that must be made with respect to the Bible is how few or how many verses will be considered. What are the natural boundaries of the pericope or passage of biblical material? Can a sermon be based upon an entire book of the Bible, or on materials that cover several chapters? Can the preacher make use of just a single verse, a single phrase, or even a single word found in the Scriptures? Part of this process is a matter of text selection. Where does one look for materials so as not to be stuck with a narrow range of issues, doctrines, and books of the Bible? *Limits* not only suggests how to make the decision concerning how much biblical material can and should be used, but how to select that material in the first place.

2. **Literature** The preacher needs to determine the type or genre of literature under review. The Bible is not just a book; it is better understood as a library composed of many different types of literature. There are legal, historical, biographical, and poetic materials. The Bible includes prophetic, apocalyptic, wisdom, parabolic, and genealogical information. The preacher will need to take these differences in literary genre into account, because obviously one cannot understand and then preach from a parable in the same way that one would from poetry or prophecy.

3. **Location** Every biblical text has a contextual identity. The events recorded and the words spoken were written or spoken and heard or read within a certain social, political, and historical setting. The preacher needs, as nearly as possible, to understand those dynamics. Only then can the text be understood and authentically directed to the preacher's own time and place. The text will also quite frequently make mention of specific physical locations that can have great bearing on the

meaning of that text. Thus, the preacher must also become familiar with the geographical setting in which the text is set.

4. Language The Bible was not written in English. It was not written with an awareness of the social dynamics of the twenty-first century. The Bible is a book whose earliest writings are nearly four thousand years old. It reflects the values, beliefs, and expressions of several very ancient cultures. That suggests that, as a prelude to preaching, great care must be given to understanding the true meaning of the words and phrases that appear in any text that is being studied. It cannot be assumed that modern readers of the Bible, or those contemporary audiences who listen to sermons based upon biblical material, will have an adequate understanding of the words that might be key to a proper understanding of any passage. The preacher must take the time to consider whether or not he or she understands the meaning of the words found in the passage. Having done that, the preacher needs to preach in such a way as to enable the congregation to attain that same level of understanding.

5. Links One of the things that exegesis reveals is how frequently one passage of Scripture can be dependent upon, informed by, or even in tension with other texts in the Bible. This step suggests that preachers need to consider what other passages come to mind while the primary passage is being studied. What are the passages to which the preacher is referred by the biblical scholars whose work is considered as part of doing exegesis? Where else in the Bible do the words appear that are present in the passage under review? Are the words in the passage direct quotations from other portions of Scripture? If so, has the purpose or meaning of that older source shifted in any way? No preacher can be too aware of how his or her pericope is informed and influenced by other portions of Scripture. Pointing out this interplay among and between various texts only strengthens the final product, which is the sermon.

6. Leads Who are the major characters in the biblical passage under review? That can be a person, the community of

Christians in a certain city, or any group whose actions are being discussed and described. Leads can be protagonists or antagonists (the heroes and the villains). Leads can be major characters from whose perspective the text has frequently been considered, or some minor character from whose perspective the text can yield fresh insights. This step is an opportunity to do more with a text than preach one sermon and then move on. It should be determined from how many perspectives any text can legitimately be preached. That being done, every possible angle into and from that text should be examined both in exegesis and, hopefully, in preaching. Throughout this book, great emphasis will be given to the use of the sermon series. This step opens the door to that practice.

7. **Lessons** Before the preacher can say what the biblical text means to his or her contemporary congregation, some attempt must be made to determine what the message of the text was to the first audience that heard or read those words, and to the audiences scattered around the world and across nearly two thousand years that have heard and interpreted the passage that we are now considering. Who was the first audience? What were the issues that Amos addressed in Bethel or that Paul addressed in Athens? Beyond that, how have preachers and theologians used the passage across the years? What is the history of the interpretation of the passage that is being studied? Gathering this information may take a little time and will require the use of certain books and other resources. However, all of this information can be gained, and once acquired it not only enriches the sermon but permanently enriches the preacher as well.

8. **Life Application** At this point, the actual form and content of the sermon comes into focus. What is the message that the preacher wants to communicate to the listeners on that day? How does the biblical text speak to the lives and pressures of people living two thousand years after the most recent portions of the Bible were written? This step in the process will unlock the creativity of the preacher. While everyone who studies a passage could come to the same exegetical conclusions,

it is at the point of *Life Application* that each preacher's context and cultural setting, as well as his or her personality and gifts, will come into play. One of the wonders of preaching is the fact that two preachers can take the same text, use the same scholarly resources, ask the same hermeneutic questions, and then end up preaching entirely different sermons.

8 Ls as an updated version of the critical method

Anyone familiar with the historical/critical methodology for doing biblical exegesis will recognize that what I am proposing is informed, at almost every step, by that classical approach to biblical analysis. However, while that methodology has often served as a series of steps that laid bare the origins, authorship, and editorial history of any given passage, the *8 Ls* is designed to set before the preacher the information necessary to preach a thoroughly informed biblical sermon.

The *8 Ls* is not designed to challenge the authorship of biblical materials as an end in itself. It is not designed to undermine the confidence that the church can and should have in the Bible. It is not designed to simply study the Bible as a piece of ancient literature, or to use the Bible merely as a way of gaining a better understanding of the people and cultures of the ancient world.

Rather, the *8 Ls* methodology is designed to provide the preacher with a concise and systematic approach to studying a portion of Scripture, with an eye toward using that information as the core of a sermon. Better preaching from better-informed preachers is the goal that is being sought. A computer analogy might prove to be helpful at this point. If you program in the right information, you can expect to get the results that you are seeking. If you ask the right question you will get the right answer. That principle applies just as well in doing biblical analysis as a prelude to preaching from that text. If we ask the right questions of the biblical text, we will receive the information that will greatly enhance our understanding of the Bible and greatly enrich the sermons that we preach.

Preaching that is informed by journalism

One way to understand the benefit of biblical exegesis is to compare writing a sermon to writing an article or news release for a newspaper. I worked for some years in the printing industry, and as a result of that experience I had some training in journalistic writing. I can remember being told about the six key questions in journalism: *who, what, when, where, why,* and *how.* A good journalist writes in such a way that each of those six questions is not just answered, but answered as soon as possible in the story.

The *8 Ls* is a way to get the preacher to bring those same questions to bear on the biblical text. Who did what in this story? Who are the characters, and what are their relationships to one another? What has happened? What events have occurred? What words have been spoken? What actions have been recorded? When and where did these events take place, and is there anything especially important or interesting about that physical location? Is any reason offered as to why things happened as they did? How did the events occur one after the other?

From what to "So what?"

Preachers need to approach a biblical text like an investigative reporter approaches a news story. There is, however, one step that is not required of reporters but that is demanded of the preacher. We must move from the simple issue of "what happened" to the more critical, and perhaps more subjective, issue of "so what?" What difference does it make in my life, for my community, as regards the future of the planet that such words were spoken or that such deeds were done? The discipline of a good journalist involves withholding any personal views on the issue under discussion. A reporter simply gives "the facts" and lets the reader or viewer reach whatever conclusions they choose.

That is not our task as preachers, so far as doing exegesis is concerned. The words of Harry Emerson Fosdick, over sixty years ago, remain true to this day: "People do not come to church anxious to learn what happened to the ancient Jebusites."[1] But people do want to know, or will listen while someone attempts to tell them, how the experiences of those ancient societies recorded in Scripture serve as mirrors and models for our lives today. Preaching is greatly aided when the information gathered in biblical exegesis is thoughtfully applied to the *Life Application* of the congregation. That is the function of the "so what" component in preaching.

The resurrection of Jesus is not just a what, it is a "so what." 1 Corinthians 15 says, "For as in Adam all die, even so in Christ shall all be made alive." The feeding of the multitude with two fishes and five loaves of bread is not just a what, it is a "so what." The same God in whose hands little became much on a hillside in Galilee is the source of hope and courage for millions around the world today who wonder about the source of their next meal. The purpose of exegesis for preaching is not just to lay out what happened, but to make a passionate case for why that happening is important for a contemporary congregation.

"So what" as the heart of all public speaking

In *Public Speaking as Listeners Like It*, Richard Borden notes that the ultimate goal of all public speaking is to address the issue of "so what." He argues that those who speak must overcome four challenges on the way to being heard by an audience. He calls those challenges:

1. **Ho Hum,** by which he means the speaker has to make a quick and interesting connection with an audience that might otherwise not be interested in the topic.

2. **Why bring that up?** by which he means that the speaker must demonstrate how and why that topic is relevant, even important to the listener.

3. **For instance** - This is where the body of the argument is set forward.

4. **So what?** At this point, the speaker must indicate what next step the listeners should take. The question must be answered, "Where do we go from here?" [2]

This "so what" step is no less essential in preaching than it is in other forms of public speaking. In fact, one could argue that it is more important in the context of a sermon because of the issues that are being discussed and because of the eternal and spiritual outcome that hangs in the balance.

Robert McCracken adds further insight to the "so what" aspect of preaching in his book, *The Making of the Sermon.*[3] He suggests that there are four basic ways by which a preacher can set this issue before his or her listeners. The preacher can ask the people to think about a complex and troublesome issue. McCracken calls that first way *kindling the mind.* Next, the preacher can ask the people to engage in some specific action. He calls that way, *energizing the will.* Another "so what" way is to challenge people to repent of some sin or abandon some immoral or ungodly behavior. He calls that way *disturbing the conscience.* Finally, the preacher can lead people in praise of the grace and goodness of God whose mighty acts have just been celebrated in the sermon. That act of praise he calls *stirring the heart.*

Here is where exegesis and preaching meet, and where the good news of the gospel is most effectively declared. When a biblical text has been thoughtfully and systematically analyzed, and when the fruit of that study has been applied to the *Life Application* of a particular congregation, that "so what" moment becomes a blessing from God. The *8 Ls* process is designed to equip preachers to do precisely this on a regular basis.

Biblical preaching as the source of living water

In her book *Preaching from the Old Testament,* Elizabeth Achtemeier correctly identifies the challenge that confronts most preachers as they contemplate sermon preparation. She says:

> Most busy students or pastors will read through a biblical text in one English translation until they get a sermon idea. At that point the text and its context are left behind, and the preacher develops the idea into a supposedly "biblical" sermon. But the finished product may bear no relation to the meaning of the text and little relation to the biblical message as a whole.[4]

During my twenty-five years as a preacher and teacher of preaching, I have certainly heard enough sermons that followed this model of preparation. The biblical text became a pretext to discuss whatever the preacher had in mind that day. A Scripture passage was certainly read as a prelude to preaching, and it may even have been referenced a time or two during the sermon. But too often that text did not inform or define the sermon in any significant way.

When the Bible is used this way, the whole reason for using a text is trivialized. What can be expected from a sermon when a single biblical verse, phrase, or even word is lifted from its context without regard to its setting in the surrounding passage, or, even more importantly, its setting in historical time and place? Preaching that follows this approach is fundamentally flawed. The biblical text has not been carefully considered by the preacher during the preparation of the sermon, and thus that text will not be carefully presented to the congregation during the delivery of the sermon. Since the preacher has not been shaped or challenged by the text, he or she cannot use that text to shape and challenge the beliefs and behavior of the congregation. A message will no doubt be delivered, but it will more than likely be "the word of the preacher" rather than "the word of the Lord."

I remember a sober warning given by Gardner Taylor in a preaching class in 1973. He said, "A preacher can use a sermon either to prove that God is great or that the preacher is clever, but you cannot do both as a first priority."[5] The sermon that is most in danger of showcasing the talent and cleverness of the preacher is the one that gives the least attention to a serious analysis of the biblical text. That sermon may prove to be successful in demonstrating the ability of the preacher to stir an audience by the power of the spoken word. However, such a sermon is rarely successful in delivering a message that proves to be living water for thirsty souls who are pressing their way through barren land.

"Reverend, is there any word from the Lord?" Engaging in an ongoing, systematic analysis of biblical materials will enrich our preaching in ways that can scarcely be described. When Jesus spoke with the Samaritan woman at the well as recorded in John 4, he said to her, "Whoever drinks of the waters that I shall give him will never thirst. But the water that I shall give him will become in him a fountain of water springing up into everlasting life." Her response was, "Give me this water . . . " Every time we stand to preach the gospel of Jesus Christ, we need to reenact this scene. Imagine that the people gathered before you are speaking the words of this woman: "Give me this water." Now be sure that the words you are prepared to speak that day come as close as your skill, effort, and spiritual maturity can bring you to tapping into that water that springs up into everlasting life. The methodology described in this book can help preachers meet the needs of those who come each week with one desire: "Give me this water."

SERMON PREVIEW

I end this first chapter with a sermon based upon Luke 23:32-43. There is one principal reason why this sermon is included. It is one of several sermons based upon the same text that will appear in this book. Thus, it helps to illustrate how to develop a sermon series based upon an exhaustive treatment of a single portion of Scripture. As stated earlier in this chapter, sermons can be based upon portions of Scripture of varying lengths. More importantly, there is no obvious correlation between the length of the passage and the amount of sermonic material it might yield. When originally developed for use at Antioch Baptist Church of Cleveland, Ohio, this sermon series stretched over the months of July and August in the summer of 1998.

FATHER, FORGIVE THEM

LUKE 23:32-43

Standing at the very center of our faith as Christians is the issue of forgiveness. Like a two-edged sword, this matter of forgiveness slices its way through the New Testament in such a way that it is impossible not to notice it. In the Lord's Prayer, Jesus teaches us to pray these words, *"Forgive us our sins as we forgive those who sin against us. . . ."* With these words, Jesus links together our willingness to forgive others with God's willingness to forgive us. In Matthew 6:15, Jesus says quite explicitly, *"If you do not forgive others of their sins then God will not forgive you of your sins."* One of the surest marks of our maturity as Christians is our ever-expanding ability and easy willingness to show forgiveness. It must be so, for the very forgiveness of our own sins that we pray to God so earnestly for depends upon this two-part process. God will forgive us to the degree that we are ready, willing, and able to forgive others.

Please note in today's "Conversation at Calvary" that Jesus is practicing what he preaches. He does not ask us to do something that he is unwilling to do himself. Instead, he shows us to what extremes he is willing to extend forgiveness to those who have sinned against him. Thus, we can measure ourselves not only against the words of Jesus, but against his deeds as well. Listen to our Lord as he hangs upon that cruel cross at Calvary. Listen to the first words out of his mouth: "Father, forgive them; for they know not what they do." This comes from a man who has been falsely accused, unfairly condemned in a hastily arranged trial, beaten and battered with whips and fists, brutally nailed to a cross with spikes that shattered his ankles and wrists. It comes from a man mocked by his enemies, betrayed and abandoned by his closest friends, and now left to suffer the cruelest form of death the Roman Empire could devise. Listen again to the first words spoken by the man who has just endured all of the physical and psychological anguish that has just been described. He said, "Father, forgive them; for they know not what they do."

This sermon was preached by the author on August 23, 1998, at Antioch Baptist Church in Cleveland, Ohio, as part of the sermon series, "Conversations at Calvary." It was first published in *The African American Pulpit* 2, no. 2 (1999), 43-49. Used by permission.

Whom do you suppose Jesus had in mind when he spoke these words? Better yet, whom would you imagine he did not include in his call for forgiveness from God? Were the disciples being forgiven by Jesus? All of them certainly needed to be forgiven. Judas denied him, just as Jesus had predicted. Peter denied Jesus three times, just as the Lord had predicted. All of the disciples ran away and left Jesus to face his persecution by himself, also as had been predicted. Yet, I believe that when the Lord says, "Father, forgive them . . . ," that the disciples are included in that number. Jesus extends to each of them a second chance, and having received that forgiveness from Jesus, his disciples go into all the world and begin to turn it upside down (Acts 17:6).

I have argued in the past that even Judas could have received this gracious forgiveness and a second chance in the service of Christ, if he had not failed to understand the message of Jesus. The tragedy of Judas is not what he did to Jesus, but what he did to himself. He took his own life. He committed suicide. He hanged himself by the neck until he was dead, all because he never understood what Jesus was saying in those parables about the lost sheep, the lost coin, and the lost son. The very essence of God's mercy and grace is giving undeserving sinners a second chance. Judas could have been forgiven. If he couldn't be forgiven, then neither can we. For who among us has not, on more than one occasion, betrayed Jesus in word or deed?

Do you suppose that Jesus was forgiving the Jewish leaders who worked and schemed so hard to bring about his death? In large measure, the suffering that Jewish people have endured over the last two thousand years has come as a result of the Gentile assumption that it was Jews who killed Jesus. All across Europe and Russia, Jews have been driven from their homes, beaten and tormented, even killed in mass actions called pogroms, because they were all being held responsible for the death of Jesus nearly two thousand years ago.

This ignores the fact, of course, that it was the Roman governor, Pontius Pilate, who condemned Jesus to the cross on a charge of sedition, which meant disloyalty to the Roman State. It was a detachment of Roman soldiers who whipped Jesus, and then placed a crown of thorns upon his head, and then nailed him to his cross at Calvary. It was those Roman soldiers who gambled for his coat, gave him vinegar to drink, and thrust a sword into his side.

All of that notwithstanding, some people hate Jews to this day because

14

they hold them responsible for the death of Christ. What then do they do with these words from Jesus, "Father, forgive them . . ."? Surely the Jewish leaders who delivered Jesus into the hands of the Romans shared some blame in his death, but all of that seems to be set aside when the Lord speaks words of forgiveness to God from the cross. It was not just his disciples that Jesus was forgiving with these words, but those who actively worked to bring about his death. And with them, also the Romans who were the active agents in his execution. It was all of them that Jesus was intending to pardon. It was all of them that Jesus was attempting to shelter from the withering wrath of God that otherwise might have fallen upon them. It was everyone connected in any way with his death that Jesus was including under these words: "Father, forgive them; for they know not what they do."

When Jesus speaks to us about forgiveness, his are not just words spoken by someone who does not understand how difficult it is to forgive someone who has hurt or offended us. No one who hears or reads this sermon will ever have as much to forgive as Jesus did, forgiving both friends and enemies. Forgive being killed for crimes he did not commit. Forgive being the eternal Son of God who gave up a home in heaven to come down to earth, take on human form, and sacrifice his own life to achieve pardon and forgiveness for the sins for all humankind. Here is the essence of our faith: this central act of mercy and pardon, this act of forgiveness. That is what Jesus teaches us as he speaks his first words from the cross.

Now comes the question that you and I and this whole nation are going to have to ask ourselves concerning the recently reported behavior of our president, Bill Clinton. What has been reported about him is, of course, morally reprehensible. For the President of the United States to engage in sexual misconduct with a woman young enough to be his daughter, and to do this less than two hundred feet from where his daughter and his wife might have been at the time, is shameful. On top of all that, he intentionally misled his closest friends and this entire nation, failing to confess, until now, actions on his part that could have been confessed months ago, saving all of us a lot of time, money, and anguish. There is nothing that I can or will say to suggest that what our president is reported to have done is other than shocking and disgusting.

Having said all of that, let me now go on to say with Thomas Friedman

15

in last Tuesday's *New York Times* that the nation has three choices, and the president has one. The President can resign from office and face the fact that he has lost credibility not merely for what he did with Monica Lewinsky, but because he failed to tell the truth about it until the very end. On our side, we can demand that Congress impeach the president for what the U.S. Constitution calls *"high crimes and misdemeanors,"* or we can limp along with a wounded leader, and wonder whenever he does something positive if it is only done to distract us from his personal problems. (This has already been suggested in the rocket attacks last week on Afghanistan and Sudan.) Or, says Friedman, we can forgive him. This does not mean that we ignore what he has said and done. This does not mean that we attempt to diminish the magnitude of his misbehavior. It only means that, in the end, forgiveness does not stop when the offending party happens to be the President of the United States.

Let me make several points about why it is important that we be willing to forgive Bill Clinton. I do not mean to imply that we should approve what he has done, but that we should forgive him of his sins. First of all, we should forgive because most of the people in Washington who are leading the attack against him are really in no position to cast stones at him. How many of them could come up as clean as a whistle if a special prosecutor began digging into their sexual and financial lives, armed with almost unlimited investigative power and $45 million of the taxpayers' money?

Let me say again that I do not mean to suggest that the president's conduct should be excused. It is sinful conduct. Clinton believed the three great lies of the devil: *Everybody is doing it. Nobody will find out,* and *It won't hurt you.* In this case, everybody is not having a sexual relationship outside of their marriage. By a way he could never have imagined, people have found out about it. And the hurt that has been done to his family, his presidency, and this nation is almost incalculable. However, one can only wonder how many of those who are condemning Clinton the most are in a position themselves to "cast the first stone"?

Second, for better or for worse, we have created a climate of political life where anyone who attempts to run for or serve in office must undergo more scrutiny by the media than you and I can even comprehend. As a result, we have already driven many of the best people in our nation away from politics because they do not want to expose their families to the kind of scrutiny that is becoming commonplace these days.

Suppose you had a problem of some sort in your life some years ago. Now, suppose you want to enter public life. You have to know that whatever it was you said or did, no matter how many years ago it was and no matter what you have accomplished in your life since that time, will be spread across the front page of every newspaper in the country. Maybe you will just decide to stay away from public life.

That is the case here in Cleveland with Terry Butler at East Technical High School. Some twenty years ago he made a mistake that resulted in an arrest, imprisonment, and fine. He paid his debt to society. Then he wanted to get on with his life. He wanted to be a school administrator. He became one of the best principals in the Cleveland Public School System. But a reporter found out that he did not answer truthfully about his criminal record on a questionnaire. Butler has been suspended from his job, but is the school system better off or weaker without him? When will we realize that the media coverage and the persistent digging into people's pasts are driving people away from all sorts of public service?

Last week I heard a lecture delivered by a woman who once worked on the staff of General Colin Powell. She said that, beyond a doubt, Powell is the one person in America best equipped with experience and ability to be president of the United States. However, Powell has consistently removed himself from consideration because he does not want to drag himself and his family through that process of relentless scrutiny of things that are no one's business but his own. How many more people will we drive away from public service before we realize that whatever the president has done, talking about it in detail on radio and TV all day long does not make things any better? And the more that people are made to feel that every sordid detail of their past, even their distant past, will be dragged out for public inspection, the less likely it is that the people our nation most needs will make themselves available for public service. This is a sad outcome of the Kenneth Starr/Monica Lewinsky era.

Now we must return to the central issue at hand. Is what Clinton did and said the unpardonable sin, or can he seek, and will we as a nation grant, forgiveness? More importantly, will God withhold forgiveness from him for his words and deeds? All that I can say is that if he cannot be forgiven for his sins, then what makes us think that we can be forgiven for ours? Set aside the fact that you and I did not do exactly what the president is accused of doing. The fact remains that we have sinned. There are no exceptions to this. Romans 3 is quite clear about that: "For all have sinned, and come short of the glory of God." The difference between you and me and Bill Clinton is only in form, not in fact. Be careful, therefore, Christian, that you do not rush too quickly into judgment on this man. For it is only as you and I are willing and able to forgive the sins of others that our sins will be forgiven.

Of course, it is so much easier to take a posture of moral superiority and look down upon Clinton. That might be possible if sexual sins and lying were the only sins that existed. But over and over again, Paul expands the list of things that God finds unacceptable. In Galatians 5 Paul mentions not only illicit sex, but also selfishness, jealousy, anger, envy, drunkenness, and divisiveness. How many of us are left to cast stones when the circle of what constitutes sin is widened to that degree? The Ten Commandments mentions not only adultery, but also stealing, coveting, honoring the Sabbath day, and bearing false witness against our neighbor. Who now is left to cast a stone at the president? Who can say anything this morning except, "It ain't my mother, or my father, but it's me, O Lord, standing in the need of prayer"?

All across America, I can almost guarantee that Bill Clinton is being held up by the self-righteous of our society as the ultimate model of sin and degradation. How strange that is in a society that tolerates homelessness, that looks the other way while drugs destroy our nation's youth, and that smiles approvingly while movies and rap music celebrate the very behaviors for which the president is now being condemned. I only counsel the self-righteous, and those of us who are gathered here today, that we need to be cautious. Standing at the center of our faith is a man whose first words from the cross were "Father, forgive them; for they know not what they do." And that same man taught us to pray saying, "Forgive our sins as we forgive those who sin against us."

2
The 8 Ls:
Limits

In this chapter, I want to begin the discussion of each step in the *8 Ls* process, starting with a variety of methods by which the preacher can select a biblical text from week to week, and then looking at how to determine how much of that material can and should be used in any one sermon. The exegetical process begins only after a passage of Scripture has been selected for review. How to select that text can consume a great deal of time, so the preacher can benefit from a methodology that makes that process simpler. Then, having selected the text, this chapter will offer insights on how to consider the preaching possibilities of that passage, recognizing that more than one sermon may emerge from the process.

Selecting a text

Every pastor knows about the frightening regularity with which Sunday morning rolls around. With the approach of Sunday comes the attending expectation that the preacher will have something to say based upon some portion of Scripture. That being the case, the preacher needs some guidelines that can quickly resolve the question of "what text shall I choose." The less time that is spent deciding "what to preach" means the more time that is available to uncover the "Thus saith the Lord" in the passage.

The first step in doing exegesis for preaching is determining what material is to be considered. What are the beginning and ending points of that body of biblical material that will serve as the focal point of any given sermon? This decision can be quite flexible. The preacher can choose to consider as much or as little material as is desired, bearing in mind that the larger the volume of material to be analyzed the more general the analysis is likely to be.

In his book, *A Guide to Biblical Preaching*, James Cox notes that the limits or lengths of the preacher's focus can easily be defined.[1] One can preach on some theme that runs through the entire Bible, such as redemption, or covenant, or the people of God. One can focus on hefty sections of Scripture such as Moses in the Pentateuch, or Jesus in the Gospels, or Paul in the Epistles and Acts. One can focus on an entire book of the Bible, especially the shorter ones like Jonah, Obadiah, and Haggai in the Old Testament, or Jude and Philemon in the New Testament. Using this approach, the preacher seeks to set forth the central theme or proclamation, or to examine the life and spiritual journey of the central character.

Preaching on sections of the Bible

The preacher can also choose to focus on increasingly more limited portions of Scripture. A sermon can be based upon some notable and theologically rich chapter contained in a book of the Bible, including the story of Adam and Eve in Genesis 3, the story of Abraham and Isaac on Mt. Moriah in Genesis 22, or the call of Moses in Exodus 3. The list could go on to include the lengthy saga of David and Goliath in 1 Samuel 17, Elijah and the priests of Baal in 1 Kings 18, or Daniel in the lions' den in Daniel 7. These Old Testament texts can be matched with similar chapters in the New Testament. These could include 1 Corinthians 13 and the meaning of love, 1 Corinthians 15 and the doctrine of the resurrection, Hebrews 11 and those who died in faith, or Luke 15 and the parable of the lost things: sheep, coin, and son.

Another portion of Scripture that can serve as the basis of a sermon is the consideration of a single scene, conversation, or noteworthy encounter. Among these could be the discussion between Mordecai and Esther in Esther 4, or Paul before Agrippa in Acts 26, Jesus before Pilate in John 18, the call of Isaiah in Isaiah 6, Rahab and the spies in Joshua 2, or the encounter that Mary had with the risen Jesus in the garden in John 20. The list of such encounters and conversations is almost limitless. One can easily think of Jesus speaking to Peter about his denial or to Judas about his eventual betrayal. There is Ananias who reluctantly goes to minister to Saul of Tarsus following Saul's conversion when he is physically blinded. Moses before Pharaoh is another dramatic encounter, as is Amos and Amaziah in the temple in Bethel, Sarah laughing at the idea that she would soon bear a child, or Joseph hearing the word that Mary was to bear a child that he knew was not his. Taking the time to list as many of these encounters and conversations as easily come to mind would provide a preacher with preaching material for an entire year, probably with texts and ideas left over.

Preaching on a single verse, phrase, or word

There are marvelous preaching possibilities inside a single verse of Scripture, and preachers should not shy away from them because they appear to be too small. Who can doubt the value of preaching John 3:16? The first sermon I ever preached, at the age of sixteen, was based upon Luke 2:52, a verse that continues to challenge me today in terms of becoming a well-rounded and mature Christian. Any one of the Ten Commandments or any one of the Beatitudes are only one verse in length, but what power and wisdom are contained in those single verses. There is much that can be done with Isaiah 6:8: "Here am I; send me." The same can be said for Psalm 119:11: "Thy word have I hid in mine heart, that I might not sin against thee." Romans 6:23 is a source of rich preaching material: "For the wages of sin is death, but the gift of God is eternal life." So, too, is Revelation 3:20: "Behold I stand at the door, and knock: if any man hear my voice, and open the door, I will come in to him, and will sup with him, and he with me."

The attentive eye and the creative mind can also make great use out of those cryptic and piercing phrases, questions, and comments that are scattered throughout the Bible. In Genesis 3:9, God comes looking for Adam in the Garden of Eden and says, "Where are you?" In Joshua 24:15, we find these words, "As for me and my house, we will serve the Lord." In 2 Kings 5:1, we are told that Namaan was a mighty man of valor, "but he was a leper." Every Christian needs to confront the haunting question from the Upper Room as found in Matthew 26:22, "Lord, is it I?" Romans 8:35 asks, "Who shall separate us from the Love of God?" Hebrews 11:38 says there were some early disciples of Jesus who suffered a martyr's death, "of whom the world was not worthy." And in John

21

11:26, Jesus not only tells Mary and Martha that Lazarus will live again. He challenges them directly with this pointed question, "Do you believe this?" Any of these comments or questions opens the door to many preaching possibilities.

Consider finally the power of a single word set in the center of a sermon for congregational review. Hebrews 11:1 says, "*Faith* is the substance of things hoped for. . . ." 1 Corinthians 13:13 says, ". . . the greatest of these is *love.*" Isaiah 40:31 states, "They that *wait* upon the Lord. . . . " And in Matthew 4:19 Jesus says, "*Follow* me. . . . " Amos 5:24 says, "Let *justice* roll down like waters and *righteousness* like a mighty stream." Deuteronomy 6:4 says, "*Hear,* O Israel, the Lord our God, the Lord is *One.*" There is a great deal that a preacher can offer to a congregation when he or she chooses to limit the sermon to the consideration of a single word properly understood in the context of a passage of Scripture.

The value of using a lectionary

The approach to text selection I have just outlined has served me well for nearly thirty years. However, that approach may not work for everyone. For a good many preachers, the decision of what text to select as the basis of the sermon is made if they follow one of the many available lectionaries that provide a three-year guide to text selection. Eugene Lowry, in *Living With the Lectionary*, points to the primary benefits that come from the use of a lectionary.

> Two of the claims of the lectionary supporters are that, one, the lectionary covers the canon in a comprehensive way unlikely to happen without it, and two, that as a result, lectionary preachers offer a more balanced homiletical fare.[2] . . . . It (the lectionary) provides a thoughtful and well-established plan for our preaching.[3]

The use of a lectionary facilitates the process of getting started with sermon planning and works to guarantee that the preacher, and by default the listening congregation, do not get stuck in textual or topical ruts.

Many preachers fall victim to preaching repeatedly from a limited number of books of the Bible, frequently making little or no use of the Old Testament. They frequent the pages of 1 and 2

Corinthians, but rarely if ever touch upon Colossians. They preach from the Gospel of John, but not from the Epistles or the Revelation of John. They preach from Matthew but not Malachi; Ephesians but not Esther; James but not Joshua.

Merrill Abbey has written, "Left to our own devices, we necessarily make ourselves at home in the limited arc of the themes that fit our minds. The use of a lectionary, however, can stretch our minds to something more approximating the full circle of the gospel."[4] Most preachers I know need that stretching of the mind so our preaching can become more comprehensive. Every preacher should take very seriously the words of Paul in Acts 20:27, "For I have not shunned to declare unto you all the counsel of God." We cannot begin to live up to that standard of comprehensive preaching unless we find a way to be sure that our preaching is drawn from every portion of the Bible. The lectionary can assist in that effort.

Preaching through the liturgical calendar

There is an additional benefit that can be achieved by those preachers who do not want to follow the lectionary throughout the entire year. They can simply choose those texts that are appropriate for the different seasons of the Christian year. That means they would begin with Advent, and spend four weeks perhaps studying those prophetic texts in Isaiah and Micah that speak of the coming of the Messiah. The preacher might look at the genealogical material in Matthew or the announcement of the births of John and Jesus in Luke 1. Preachers might also look at those texts in Acts and 1 Thessalonians that refer to the Second Coming of Christ.

Then comes Christmas and the rich material that is available not only in Matthew 2 and Luke 2, but also in the Gospel of John 1:1-14, and that pregnant passage in Galatians 4:4 which appears to be the only passage where Paul refers to the birth of Christ. That is followed by Epiphany, and the celebration of the Magi in Matthew 2, who represent the appeal of Christ to the Gentile nations and the initial spread of the claims of the gospel to the ends of the earth. The preacher could also make use of the other stories that describe how the name of Jesus was spread beyond the boundaries of Judah and

Judaism. For instance, the story of the Samaritan woman at the well of Jacob in John 4, or the conversion of the Ethiopian eunuch in Acts 8 would be effective texts to use as part of an Epiphany observance.

So too would the troublesome passage in Luke 4 where Jesus returns to preach in his home synagogue in Nazareth. The congregation hardly responds when he implies that he is the fulfillment of the messianic prophecy in Isaiah 61. But when he implies that the love of God is as much available to the Syro-Phoenician woman in the days of Elijah, or the Syrian general named Namaan in the days of Elisha, people in his hometown nearly put him to death. Here, and in the Book of Jonah, the people of Israel seem not to want to share their salvation with the Gentiles. This point of tension would also make for an excellent text for Epiphany.

The season of Lent would be the next opportunity to take advantage of the themes of the liturgical calendar. This forty-day period from Ash Wednesday to Easter, not counting weekends, can be a time for the most helpful and healing preaching that can be done. These days give the preacher a chance to choose those texts that focus on such important themes as contrition, repentance, self-examination, spiritual renewal, addictions of all kinds that need to be broken, and our need for reconciliation with God and with each other. The psalms can be especially helpful during this season. "Search me, O God, and know my heart: try me, and know my thoughts . . ." (Psalm 139:23-24). "Create in me a clean heart, O God: and renew a right spirit within me" (Psalm 51:10). "As the hart panteth after the water brooks, so panteth my soul after thee, O God" (Psalm 42:1).

Needless to say, such notable days as Palm Sunday, Good Friday, Easter, and Pentecost are days on the liturgical calendar that should never be ignored. Not only do they have easily identifiable biblical texts that can be selected for those respective Sundays, but paying attention to these days, and the others that are part of the liturgical calendar, helps the congregation acquire a sense of "the whole counsel of God." Or as Merrill Abbey says, these texts and liturgical observances "stretch the mind to something more approximating the full circle of the Gospel."[5]

Preaching events in the life of the nation

While following the Christian calendar opens the door to multiple preaching ideas, so too does paying close attention to special days and observances on the national calendar. In the United States that means that the preacher might want to pay attention to such days as Martin Luther King Jr. Day, and use that as a time to invoke the words of Micah 6:8 or Amos 5:24. King Day is also a time to reflect on the issues of economic justice and the principles of nonviolence in addressing both domestic and international disputes. The United States is still a long way from being a genuinely inclusive and multicultural society. King Day is an ideal time to address the challenges that lie ahead.

Valentine's Day allows us a chance to consider the love we show toward each other, and the love that God has shown to us through Jesus Christ. It provides us with a chance to discuss *eros*, which seems to concern so many people in our society. That kind of love can then be contrasted with *agape*, which is that rich and selfless love that God displayed toward us in Christ and hopes we will demonstrate toward each other, as Jesus said in John 15:12. Valentine's Day is a good opportunity to discuss the skyrocketing divorce rate in American society, and the equally staggering number of young women having children out of wedlock, often due to the irresponsibility of the men involved. While these topics could just as easily be discussed at any other time of the year, they are especially suitable for Valentine's Day when so much attention is focused on the day. The topics of love and human relationships are far too important to allow them to be defined by florists and candy manufacturers. Valentine's Day is another time to invoke the words of Jeremiah 37:17, "Is there any word from the Lord?"

Independence Day can be contrasted to John 8:36, "If the Son shall make you free therefore, ye shall be free indeed." However, that day also affords the preacher the opportunity to reflect on the continuing forms of oppression and the lack of opportunity faced by many in this society. The Fourth of July does not have to be a celebration of the independence of those Americans who were able to "declare their independence" from Great Britain. It can also be a time to ponder how such a nation could allow slavery to exist for another ninety years, while marginalizing women and dehumanizing Native Americans at the same time.

Memorial Day, Labor Day, and Columbus Day can all be put to good use. Memorial Day is an appropriate time to remember those persons in our family, our churches, and our nation who have died. It is also a good time to be reminded of our own mortality, and of our readiness to face up to death and the judgment of God. Labor Day is a good time to remind people of the continuing struggle of working-class people, and of their need to be respected and protected from exploitation. On a broader level, such national policy concerns as the North American Free Trade Act (NAFTA) and the World Trade Organization (WTO) may greatly effect members of our congregations. It would not be inappropriate to refer to those issues when preaching on a text like Luke 10:7 which says, "the laborer is worthy of his hire." In some settings, focusing on the value of work over welfare would be an important theme, as would some emphasis on the dignity and value of all honest labor. There is also Paul's very explicit injunction in 2 Thessalonians 3:10: "If anyone will not work, neither shall he eat." People should not live on welfare if they are capable of being self-sufficient.

Columbus Day has become rather controversial lately, and that controversy should not be avoided. It is no longer a day to tell ourselves that in 1492 Columbus discovered America. The time is better spent considering what happened once Columbus and the other explorers arrived. This is a good time to talk about issues of intolerance and genocide such as were experienced by the Native Americans during the time of European exploration of the New World. More importantly, this is also a way to address the fact that these same practices of intolerance and genocide continue to be experienced by people around the world today. One need only think of such places as Kosovo, the Kashmir region of India, Rwanda, and the Kurds in Iraq.

Veterans' Day is an opportunity to reflect upon those who died in defense of freedom and in opposition to tyranny, and to be reminded that freedom is a very costly and precious thing. However, it is also time, especially in the nuclear era, to hear the words "Study war no more," as found in Micah 4:3 and Isaiah 2:4. Defense spending still represents the second largest expenditure in the budget of the federal government. What does that mean in terms of our continuing problems of homelessness, our inability to fight a meaningful war on drugs, and the fact that 45 million Americans are safe from the attack of a foreign army, but die due to lack of medical insurance?

Needless to say, Thanksgiving Day is rich with preaching possibilities both for the blessings God has extended to each of us as individuals, and for the blessings God has bestowed upon this nation. Drawing from the experience of the Pilgrims in the Plymouth colony in 1609, Thanksgiving is a good time to be thankful for the other people upon whom our lives are so dependent, as the lives of those Pilgrims were dependent upon the help that was given by the Native Americans.

However, we cannot simply spend that day with Psalm 106, "O give thanks unto the Lord; for he is good." We must also hear the challenging words of Luke 12:48, "To whom much has been given from him much will be required." In my book, *Preaching to the Black Middle Class*, I make the point that a special responsibility falls upon black middle-class churches. Such congregations, and their members severally, cannot simply go through life enjoying their new found prosperity, remaining oblivious to the poverty and squalor that exists right outside the doors of the inner-city churches they still attend.[6] Thanksgiving Day is a good time to talk about the responsibilities that go along with our prosperity as a nation, as congregations, and as individuals.

If a preacher were to make use of both the liturgical and national holidays, more than one-half of the Sundays of the year would be impacted, and a head start could be provided in terms of text selection. This would also have the effect of keeping the sermons fresh in terms of material and subject matter. This would still leave plenty of opportunities during the year for the preacher to consider whatever text he or she might prefer on a self-selected basis.

Preaching that flows out of Bible study settings

There are other ways by which texts can become the basis for a sermon; thus, these ways need to be carefully analyzed. Sermons can emerge out of personal or group Bible study, where the preacher wants to review from the pulpit something that first captured his or her attention in that other context. Many times my sermon on Sunday is informed by the discussion of a passage of Scripture in one of the two Bible classes I teach at Antioch each week.

Preaching from texts that have already been discussed in a study session has three distinct advantages. First, much of the rigorous exegetical work has already been done, thus giving the preacher a head start in sermon preparation. Second, the relevance and help-fulness of the biblical material to that congregation has already been tested and determined by the discussion that occurred in the class setting. Bible studies that strike a deep and responsive chord in the smaller group frequently can be of help to the larger congregation as well. Third, announcing that the sermon on Sunday grew out of the Bible study in the previous week can be a good recruiting tool for the Bible study class. People frequently want to be present when fresh spiritual ground is being broken.

Preachers should not hesitate to let their Bible study classes serve as one of the sources they rely upon for their sermon text selection. Of course, implicit in that statement is the notion that both the preacher and the congregation can benefit when the preacher also leads or shares in a Bible study in the church! I take special note of the fact that in Ephesians 4:11, Paul says that some are called to be "pastors and teachers." What God has joined together, let not man put asunder!

Preaching assigned texts on special occasions

One of the great challenges of preaching is to be invited to speak for a special event where the biblical text and, quite frequently, the theme have already been selected and the preacher is *urged* to focus on that assignment. This can occur in the life of a congregation dur-ing a revival or on an annual day for the church or one of its aux-iliaries. It can involve a community group, ranging from a civil rights gathering to a memorial service for a leading citizen. It can frequently happen within one's own denomination when all mem-ber churches are called upon to consider a particular emphasis either in a convened session or in their separate congregations.

The first time I was confronted with this was at the American Baptist Churches biennial, which met in Portland, Oregon, in 1985. The theme was "God's Call to Grow and to Care." The text, taken from Matthew 17, was the story of the transfiguration. It was not the easiest text and theme to match, but that was a good challenge to face. It reminded me of my homiletics class at Union Seminary in New York City with Edmund Steimle. Rather than allow us to pick the text or theme from which we would preach, he assigned one to us and challenged us to come up with a meaningful sermon. That may not happen often in the course of a year of preaching, but it should be viewed as an opportunity to sharpen one's skills.

Moving from topic to text
Samuel D. Proctor, for whom I worked at Abyssinian Baptist Church in New York City, offers yet another approach to the challenge of text selection, or "what to preach." In his book, *The Certain Sound of the Trumpet*, Proctor suggests that the preacher does not always have to begin with the search for a biblical text. He says, "There must be a sensitive awareness of the audience and its contextual situation.[7] . . . What should the word for them be on this day, in this place?"[8]

> One must be obsessed with this word, whether it is found in a scripture narrative or it gathers around a topic of Christian significance that trails through the Bible, or it is found in Christian tradition and experience. The preparation of the sermon must wait until a single proposition has reached for and grasped the preacher and has flooded her or his mind and soul, no matter where it originates.[9]

This is an important addition to the discussion on how to establish the limits of one's concerns in a sermon.

There may be times when the preacher will not start with a biblical text, but with an experience, a personal quandary, or an event that has shocked the nation and the world. From that event, the preacher goes out in search of a text that captures what he or she wants to say. This is perfectly acceptable once the text, having been found, is allowed to speak on its own terms, and is not twisted and misinterpreted to fit a conclusion that the preacher wishes to force upon it. This is where the other steps in this eight-step process will prove to be helpful.

Proctor proves to be helpful at another point. He advises the preacher not to limit himself or herself to a single focus or emphasis in preaching, such as a relentless obsession with social issues. While recognizing the need for and the importance of what is sometimes called "prophetic preaching," Proctor recognizes that no congregation can be adequately nourished on that diet alone. He says,

> Along with this social and prophetic word, the people need education in religious matters and comfort in life's crisis moments; they need to be given an impetus to serve, to participate, and to create alliances to address the issues that are so glaring in the pastor's sermons. So the social prophet must remember the total menu and the need for a complete diet in the weekly sermons.[10]

Choosing those texts that help the preacher address these topics that deal both with pressing social issues and with the struggles of daily life is the art and challenge of the preacher.

Preaching that follows a rotation of themes

Over the years, I have developed another method for beginning with a topic as opposed to a text. Under Proctor's approach, the question is open-ended: "What should the word be for them on this day?" I encourage students and pastors to organize their text selection and preaching around five rotating themes. You do not have to stick to that rotation week after week, but the system is there whenever it is needed. The themes are the *doctrines* of God, *Christ*, the *Holy Spirit*, *sin* and some aspect of the *human condition*, and the *local and global mission of the church*.

These are all nearly inexhaustible categories. It is unlikely that the greatest of preachers could exhaust all that could be said about any one of these topics in a year of preaching, much less all five topics added together. There is very little that can be discussed in a sermon that could not fit within one of these five theological doctrines: God, Christ, the Holy Spirit, the issues of sin and human behavior, and the work of the church both locally and globally. By rotating around these five themes, the preacher is providing a rich and varied diet, in accordance with Acts 20:28, where we are admonished to take heed to feed the flock of God.

What are the texts and who are the biblical characters that come

30

to mind when one begins to write down what could be said in a sermon about these five topics? Just under the doctrine of God alone, one quickly thinks of such themes as sovereignty, grace, love, and holiness. Added to these can be such things as the will of God, the attributes of God, the pre-existence of God, the power of God, God as creator, God as Holy Warrior, and God as lawgiver. There are the various names ascribed to God throughout the Bible. There are the "mighty acts of God" associated with the exodus and the deliverance of Israel from bondage in Egypt. There are the words of God drawn from those moments when God speaks, as to Moses from the burning bush, to Job out of the whirlwind, to Abraham on Mt. Moriah, or to Adam in the Garden of Eden.

This is only a partial listing of the preaching possibilities for the doctrine of God that can easily be matched with one or more biblical texts. The same can be done with the other four doctrinal areas listed above. If the preacher were simply to rotate from one category to the next, he or she would have an unlimited supply of fresh material that would be theologically centered and biblically grounded. If the preacher were to use this method of text selection only during those weeks when the lectionary, the liturgical calendar, or the holidays in the nation's life were not the primary guide, then the available material is even more ample. This is yet another way to "stretch the mind to something more approximating the full circle of the Gospel."[11]

In his book, *The Heart of Black Preaching*, Cleophus J. Larue suggests that there are five areas, or what he calls "domains of experience" that I would argue can also serve as the basis for a preaching rotation. His five areas are specifically designed as a way to understand preaching within the black church tradition. However, they are not entirely beyond the reach of all preachers. And they bear some mention here, especially for those black preachers who might benefit from this study. His categories are *personal piety, care of the soul, social justice, corporate concerns,* which would include matters of black self-help, and *maintenance of the institutional church* which would incorporate concerns on how to maintain various aspects of congregational life such as stewardship, discipline, and missions and evangelism.[12] While Larue was not offering these categories as methods of organizing a preaching rotation, I would add them to this list and suggest that they work perfectly well in such a fashion.

Maximizing the use of biblical materials

Establishing limits on the amount of material the preacher will use in a sermon is not merely an issue of how many verses are the optimal number. As has been suggested earlier, there are design techniques that can allow a preacher to handle as many or as few verses as might be desired. Of equal importance is to remember that all of the material uncovered during the exegetical process does not have to be compressed into a single sermon. If the analysis of the text is done thoroughly, the preacher ought to be left with more than enough ideas and insights for several sermons.

The preacher can decide to deliver a series of sermons over the course of several weeks. He or she can use the material in a revival with a different aspect of the text examined each evening of a given week. Of course, the preacher can simply decide to hold the material for use at some undesignated point in the future. Like money in the bank or food in the freezer, the extra insights gleaned from the exegetical study of a text will be there when you need them. This too is an issue of limits, not just concerning how many verses to consider, but over what period of time and including what number of sermons.

We sometimes choose very limited portions of Scripture to consider because we believe that we can handle no more than that in any given sermon. On the other hand, we sometimes overload a particular sermon with far more information than the listener can possibly absorb. We do that because we have convinced ourselves that we have to squeeze everything we have learned into that one sermon. The simple fact is, we would do well if we began to think not only about how to match one text with one sermon idea, but how to plan so that we get multiple sermons out of each exegetical effort.

Using one passage for a series of sermons

As an example, I once preached for ten weeks from a single passage of Scripture simply by shifting the focus of the sermon from one character or perspective to another. The text was Luke 23:33-49.

The narrative is about the events that surround the crucifixion of Jesus. The decision was to consider that event from the perspective of each identified person or group present at the scene. I have included most of the sermons from that series at the end of various chapters of this book as an example of this technique.

A separate sermon was preached from the perspective of Jesus and the three statements he made from the cross. Two sermons were preached reflecting the statements of the two malefactors who were hanged on either side of Jesus. Verse 35 says the people and rulers derided him, so two sermons were devoted to those persons. Two references were made to Roman soldiers who were assigned to the execution squad. The ones in verse 36 mocked Jesus along with the crowd. However, the centurion in verse 47 seems to reflect a very different attitude than his cohorts. Finally, verse 49 speaks of "all his acquaintance, and the women that followed him from Galilee." Consider the thoughts that passed through their minds different from everyone else who had gathered that day at Calvary.

The skill phase and creative phase of exegesis

In the book, *Biblical Sermons*, edited by Haddon Robinson, Joseph Stowell talks about exegesis and sermon design as the *skill phase* and the *creative phase* in the preparation of a sermon.[13] He says that doing biblical exegesis is equivalent to a person who goes grocery shopping and brings home a bag of ingredients. Anybody could have done that task. Anybody could have brought home flour, milk, eggs, sugar, butter, and other ingredients. But at that point, with groceries sitting on the counter, there are only ingredients. How to mix those ingredients into the desired dish sufficient to serve a certain number of persons is the creative challenge.

Depending upon how the ingredients are blended, and how much time is spent in the oven, you could end up with a pound cake, cookies, a loaf of bread, or biscuits. Exegesis is an exercise that does require some skill. The 8 Ls help to simplify the process. But unless the preacher also brings some creativity to the task, the full potential of the ingredients may not be tapped.

That is how preachers should view the material they have uncovered during their exegesis of a biblical text. Everything they have learned and every idea and insight that has been generated during that process does not need to, indeed it cannot possibly, all fit into one sermon. The preacher does not have to leave out most of what has been learned simply because it is too much for one sermon. By the same token, the preacher should not attempt to cram into one sermon everything that has been garnered from a thorough analysis of the text, knowing that justice is not being done to the material or to the nurturing of the congregation. Rather, the preacher should plan to spread that material out over several sermons. Such an approach is crucial when considering how to set the limits for what will be contained in any given sermon.

The point of this chapter is that the preacher can rely on one of a number of methods to aid in the process of text selection. The objective, however, is not just to find a text as quickly as possible. Of even greater importance is finding a way to present material to the congregation that is drawn from throughout the entire Bible, and that touches upon the widest possible number of theological doctrines and biblical truths. Sunday morning seems always to be right around the corner. Therefore, the preacher needs to be able to decide "what to preach" on the next Lord's day. However, it is hoped that the material presented will be as wide and varied as the scope of God's concerns and the breadth of the human experience.

SERMON PREVIEW

In the sermon that follows this chapter, I continue the series based upon Luke 23:32-43. Throughout this book, I want to underscore the importance of using the material discovered during exegesis for multiple sermons from a single passage of Scripture. This sermon examines the conversation between Jesus and the penitent man who was crucified with Jesus. The technique for preaching employed here is "listening to and employed learning from" conversations between two biblical characters. This technique can be used with literally hundreds of Bible passages.

LORD, REMEMBER ME

LUKE 23:32-43

Who was Jesus talking to when he gave the promise of paradise? Who was the person fortunate enough to know that before the end of that same day he would be walking around heaven with the Son of God? Do not look among the Lord's circle of friends or disciples because almost all of them were hiding from the same mob that had condemned Jesus to death on that cross. Do not look among the Pharisees because they were too busy standing beneath the cross of Jesus, mocking him and hurling insults at him. Do not look to the Romans who had the gruesome duty of carrying out this act of capital punishment because those battle-hardened veteran soldiers were preoccupied as they gambled to see which of them would walk away from Calvary with Jesus' outer garments. If you want to find the person who was promised a place in paradise with Jesus, look in the most unlikely place of all. Look at one of the men who was hanging on his own cross, next to Jesus.

The Bible tells us that three men died on Calvary that day. Two of them have traditionally been called thieves. However, there must be more to that word than is common to our understanding. Luke calls them malefactors. These men were not burglars or simple bandits. They may have been part of a band of men who attacked caravans, and perhaps killed people in the process. They may have been Zealots who were caught attempting to steal back some of the tax money that Rome had extorted from the Jews. Crucifixion was the worst punishment that Rome could impose upon a person. Just as American law does not allow us or require us to execute a thief, neither did Roman law. Whatever these two men had done, it was a great deal more than robbery. But whatever their offense, they were now being put to death as punishment for their crimes.

This text could very easily be used as the basis of a sermon on capital punishment. We could project into our own world whether or not it is ever right for the state to put persons to death as punishment for their crimes. This is one of the questions that grips and divides our nation.

This sermon was preached by the author on July 12, 1998, at Antioch Baptist Church in Cleveland, Ohio, as part of the sermon series, "Conversations at Calvary."

What does the Constitution mean by "cruel and unusual punishment"? It would certainly exclude crucifixion. But is death by electrocution any kinder, or by lethal injection? There is much this text could say to us about that subject.

We could consider, as in the case of Jesus, whether innocent people are subjected to capital punishment. We could ponder whether class and ethnic differences contribute to the decision concerning who does and does not face charges that result in capital punishment. Then and now, ancient Palestine and twenty-first century America, people are executed for their crimes. But in light of this story, we could ask if that practice is either fair or humane. There is much that could be said on the basis of this text, but we will only hint at it today and consider it more fully another time.

However, this story does tell us much that we need to consider today as we listen to the conversation between Jesus and one of those who died by his side. Notice first of all, that the sins of our past do not preclude the possibility of being saved in the future. God can and will look beyond our faults and see our needs. Second, what Jesus chooses to do for us can sometimes be done with amazing speed and swiftness. It does not take him forever to take care of us. Third, the path to paradise is paved by the three observations about Jesus made by that dying man on Calvary. In short, this story reveals to us something we need to know about the dying malefactor, about ourselves, and about Jesus.

The first thing we need to notice about this man is that he was willing to confess his sins before he asked for anything from Jesus. This makes me all the more certain that these men were not being killed for mere thievery, because the man who is promised a place in paradise says to his crucified comrade, "We are being justly punished for our crimes." I do not think he would face his execution so calmly or rationally if all he was guilty of was robbery. Instead of contesting his conviction, he seems to acknowledge his guilt. This is the way that every relationship with Jesus Christ must begin, not with requests but with confession and repentance. Not with what we want from him, but coming before him with penitent spirits and confessing our sins.

Let us listen again to the dying man. All around him are people who are hurling insults and curses at Jesus. The man hanging on the other side of Jesus is joining in the verbal bombardment. But somehow this man, despite the pain and suffering that he was undergoing, manages to say something else that catches the ear of Jesus. He declares who he believes Jesus to be. He says, *"Lord!"* I do not know where that word came from. It certainly did not arise from anything he saw in Jesus at that moment. What a sight the Lord must have been, with that crown of thorns thrust down upon his brow, with his body battered by the Romans who had whipped him the night before, with his wrists and ankles hammered to the cross. Jesus was a mass of blood, sweat, and tears. But through all of that, this man saw or heard something that caused him to turn to Jesus and say *"Lord!"*

It really does matter who we say Jesus is in our own lives. It really does matter what title we ascribe to him and what rank we give him in our own hearts. This man did not call him rabbi or teacher. That was not enough under the circumstances. A rabbi could not help him on that cross. He needed something more. *Lord!* He did not call him, Jesus. This was no time for a man–to–man conversation. It was not the earthly Jesus that he wanted; it was the eternal Son of God he was reaching out for in that hour. *Lord!* He did not call him a traitor or a seditionist, which were the crimes for which Jesus was being executed by Rome. That dying man used the one word that Jesus wants to hear all of his disciples use when they turn to him in prayer or praise; *LORD!*

Who is Jesus in your life? May he be nothing less than your Lord. Not your friend or your helper, but your Lord. Not some secondary relationship that is less important than many other people in your life. He wants to be our Lord. He wants to have first place in our hearts. He wants to share the throne of our souls with no one. O, may we all call Jesus by the same title used by that dying man, *"Lord!"*

Notice that this man does not take up a lot of time telling Jesus what to do, or informing Jesus of what he wanted. He makes a simple appeal, "When you come into your kingdom remember me." I do not know what caused the man to use just this combination of words. Was he asking Jesus to intercede with God so he would not have a lifetime of sin held against him? Was he concerned that Jesus, having known the man only as long as their time together on Calvary, might forget about him when Jesus went back to heaven to resume his life at God's right hand? Was this man, who may have been killed because of his opposition to the kingdom of Rome, seeking to become a willing subject in a kingdom headed by Jesus, be it in this world or beyond? It cannot be known what this man intended, but his is an important comment from Calvary.

Notice first of all, that this is a beautiful way to speak to God. Rather than laying out a long list of the things we think we want, we simply ask God to provide us with those things that God knows we need the most. Remember me! This is a faithful and trusting statement. It is like Jesus in Gethsemane, who, after he tells God what he wants, then places his life squarely in the hands of God and says, "Nevertheless, not my will, but thy will be done." Remember me! This prayer throws us wholly at the mercy of God, hoping that when God does remember us, it will be with grace and not with anger. This word from the cross of a dying criminal is impressive.

Notice in the second place, that what his comment produced was far more than he could ever have reasonably asked for or possibly expected. Jesus tells him, "Today, you will be with me in paradise." It must have given great comfort to that dying man that the pain and suffering through which he was passing at that moment were soon to be replaced by fellowship with the Son of God in paradise. And he would not have to wait long to enjoy such a blessing, for the promise of Jesus was for TODAY!

I do not know of anybody who can guarantee delivery TODAY except Jesus. FedEx and UPS can do it overnight when they are at their best and charging the highest rates. The U.S. Post Office claims that it has next day, second day, and third day delivery rates. But none of these companies can guarantee delivery TODAY.

Moreover, none of them delivers to the postal area code for paradise. I do not know how to address a letter intended for God in paradise. I used to write letters to Santa Claus when I was a child. I addressed the envelope, very simply, Santa Claus at The North Pole. I do not know where those letters went, but I at least knew how to address the letter. There is only one person who has travelling privileges in and out of paradise, and that is Jesus.

Philippians 2 tells us that Jesus left paradise in order to take on human form and become the atonement for our sins. As a result of that, God elevated him to a status even higher than he enjoyed before. Jesus told a rich man named Dives that a poor man named Lazarus did not have travelling privileges in and out of paradise, and therefore could not come with cool water to soothe his parched tongue (Luke 16:26). Only Jesus can deliver us into paradise. Only Jesus knows the route. Only Jesus can get us past the gates of glory. He tells us about this in John 14, when he says, "I am the way, the truth and the life: No man cometh unto the Father, but by me." What a blessing that dying man received: immediate delivery into paradise.

How you and I understand paradise may vary in certain details, but it is important to have some sense of this place called paradise. We know at least this much, that it is a place where we are in the constant presence of the Lord. That man is told, "You will be WITH ME in paradise." That might well be enough, just to be with Jesus forever. It is like a return to Eden. We are no longer forced to deal with God from a distance, and can once again stand before God without fear. Paul says in 1 Corinthians 13 that we will no longer "see through a glass darkly," but will see face to face.

Paradise is where death can no longer reach us, pain can no longer disturb us, fears can no longer haunt us, prejudice can no longer deter us, and Satan can no longer tempt or trouble us. Depending upon where you are in the world, paradise offers relief and release from something different. But no matter who or where you are, paradise is more than we could ever demand from God and will only be experienced by God's grace. That is the Good News in this text. Jesus offers this man something he could have enjoyed under no other circumstances. Today you will be with me in PARADISE.

This conversation at Calvary offers two glimmers of hope to you and me. The first is, if there is hope for that dying man on the cross then there is still hope for me. If the grace of God is sufficient to cover his sins, then I have grounds on which to hope that God will not forever hold my sins against me. If I approach Jesus as that dying man did, confessing him to be my Lord and trusting my soul into his care, then I too have the hope of heaven. If I can remember that the paradise that Jesus promised that dying man is awarded by Jesus and not earned by us through anything that we can ever do, then this story becomes a great blessing to my life.

Not only is there still hope for us, according to this story, but there is also still time. I wish that people would make a decision for Christ when they are young and would faithfully live as his disciples for the rest of their lives. But most people will not do that. Most people put off their decisions about Christ until the things they perceive to be more important have been taken care of. They have begun their careers, started their savings or retirement plans, entered into marriage, engaged in the social and political groups and causes that interest them. And except for an occasional wedding or funeral, they may not find themselves inside a church for most of the middle years of their lives. If they have children they may bring them to church, believing that a little Sunday School will not do their children any harm. But it does not yet seem to register that faith in Christ would do them and their children a great deal of good. My prayer is that even those who have strayed away or stayed away would realize that with God there is still time to be saved.

If a dying man nailed to his cross can reach out for forgiveness and receive it, surely there is still time for you and me. Do not use this man as a model for waiting until you are on your deathbed to get right with God. Instead, use this man as a gracious reminder that no matter what has kept you from turning to God in the past, it is not too late. In light of this Conversation at Calvary, I invite you to act while you still have time. The old gospel song states the matter plainly and powerfully, *COME TO JESUS!*

3
The 8 Ls:
Literature

This chapter will focus on the great variety of types of literature present in the Bible, and the challenges that are presented when they become the basis of a sermon. Following upon the discussion in Chapter Two regarding the ways to maintain balance and diversity in text and topic selection, preachers should also recognize that the same benefit can be acquired simply by recognizing the rich variety of literature contained in the Bible. It is important to observe that while the Bible may be the single most influential and continuously read book in history, it is not really a book at all. Rather, it is a collection of books, a virtual library of literature drawn from writings that were authored over a period of more than one thousand years.

The Bible as a library of literature

The Bible consists of creation stories that reflect the influence of Babylonian mythology. It contains legal materials that bear strong resemblance to the eighteenth century B.C. Code of Hammurabai. It contains stories about royal intrigue as people aspire for, occupy, and are subsequently removed from the thrones of Israel and Judah. By the same token, the Bible contains theological biographies concerning the life of Jesus of Nazareth. It includes the writings of Saul of Tarsus (Paul) addressed to churches and individuals scattered throughout the Roman Empire. And, of course, the Bible contains the books of Daniel and Revelation, both rich in their symbolism and intentionally obscure in their message.

Any preacher would be well advised to build this diversity of literature into his or her preaching rotation. More importantly, any preacher would be even better advised not to preach any biblical text without considering the type of literature. All books of the Bible are not the same in form or function. That observation is not incidental, it is fundamental.

One cannot preach prophecy and poetry in the same way, any more than one would seek to interpret Shakespeare and the abolitionist John Brown in the same way. By the same token, one cannot approach in the same way the Acts of the Apostles and the Prologue to John's Gospel any more than one would read in the same way a work of history and a treatise on philosophy. The Psalms and Proverbs stand next to one another in the Bible, but they have little else in common. The same could be said, by the way, about the Epistles of Hebrews and James.

It is, no doubt, largely because of this variety in literary style and content that the Bible has had such a profound influence on the intellectual and spiritual development of the human family. James Cox builds on this very point in his book, *A Guide to Biblical Preaching*. He says:

> Consider that the Bible is a part of our tradition, our heritage, our culture. Can you understand yourself as a Westerner, as an American, as a Christian, or as a Baptist without understanding something of the Bible? Our laws, our morals, our customs, our language, our literature—as well as our religious life—can be in many ways and in many degrees traced to the Bible. The Bible is the seen or unseen guest, the invited or uninvited guest in every home.[1]

Surely one of the reasons for the power and influence of the Bible is the fact that through its rich images and complex literary forms, it has been able to appeal to so many people across so many years.

This diversity of literary style is both the major cause of and one of the chief outcomes of the development of biblical criticism in the nineteenth century. It seemed apparent to biblical scholars operating under the influence of the scientific method of inquiry that the Bible was anything but the product of a single hand. The biggest event in the study of the Bible as literature may have come with *The Documentary Hypothesis* by Julius Wellhausen in 1876.[2] That critical approach to the literary sources of the Bible led to the question, "What was the origin of this literature?"

In many circles, that question also led to a rejection of the critical method by those who thought that the very asking of such questions could undermine the authority of the Scriptures and make it difficult for people to put their full faith in what the Bible says. Leander Keck, in *The Bible in the Pulpit*, observes that "The vast majority of the Protestant clergy have their roots in conservative piety where the Bible is revered as a holy book. For them the encounter with biblical criticism was sometimes painful."[3]

Did Moses write all five books of the Pentateuch? Or does that collection of materials include works from many writers, authored over a period of hundreds of years, and edited together at a later time? Was Daniel written during the Babylonian–Persian era? Or is it properly understood when viewed within the time frame of the Seleucid Empire after the break-up of the empire of Alexander the Great, some four hundred years later?

We have learned to appreciate each of the Epistles in light of their intended audience, be it a person (Timothy, Titus, or Onesimus), an issue or crisis (Judaizers in Galatians), or a place (Corinth, Ephesus, Philippi). If that is the case, should we not recognize that the four Gospels should be read in a similar fashion, in light of their intended audiences? We accept the fact that Mozart's *Requiem Mass* might have been finished by another composer and that parts of our sacred national texts, the Declaration of Independence and the Constitution of the United States, were more a committee assignment than they were the finished product of a single author.

However, when those same suggestions are applied to portions of the Bible, such as Isaiah or Ephesians, they are met with intense resistance in many circles. Keck continues,

> If Jesus did not say everything attributed to him by the Gospels — how can one preach the Bible convincingly? Not a few concluded that not only their preaching ministry was threatened but their faith as well.[4]

The second step in doing exegesis for preaching is to pay attention to the literary genre that shapes the biblical text under review. The challenge is to engage in that process without feeling that the authority of the Scriptures or the faith of the preacher or congregation is being undermined.

Haddon Robinson is helpful at this point as well. He suggests that preachers approach a text in three phases. He says:

> An expositor thinks in three areas. First, as an *exegete* he struggles with the meanings of the biblical writers. Then as a *man of God* he wrestles with how God wants to change him personally. Finally, as a *preacher* he ponders what God wants to say to his congregation.[5]

This is a useful approach because it allows the preacher to ask the tough exegetical questions in the context of his or her being both a believer who is searching for meaning, and as a preacher who is seeking to shape and strengthen the faith of others.

The first of the three areas is never to be avoided for fear that it may cause people to rethink their faith. Rather, that first area should be engaged in with the understanding that the results of the study may make the faith we share better understood and even more precious. It is being argued in this chapter that understanding how biblical texts worked in their own time may inform us on how to employ them in preaching in our own time.

Identifying the literary types in the Bible

Leonard L. Thompson, in *Introducing Biblical Literature*, observes that "three broad types of folk literature shape the language in the Bible. They are song, story, and saying."[6] While those three forms of oral communication are quite apparent throughout the Bible, it is possible to discuss biblical literature in terms of even smaller and more precise literary forms. The Bible includes history, hymnody, poetry, biography, and laws. It is presented in such varied forms as speeches and sermons, visions and dreams, diatribes and courtroom judgment scenes. The Bible also consists of prayers, proverbs, riddles, love songs, and epic sagas. The Bible is both prophecy and parable.

The Bible describes both the miraculous creation and the fiery destruction of the universe. It is the story of one people (Israel) chosen by God to begin the work of reconciliation, and it is the story of one person (Jesus) sent by God to bring that work to completion. In between lies a long line of patriarchs and matriarchs. Following them are judges and kings, prophets and priests, shepherds and soothsayers. Our preaching is enriched when these subtleties are made apparent, and when they are linked together as the various ways by which the biblical writers and editors sought to give expression to their faith.

The work of noticing these differences in literary content and form is technically referred to as form criticism. William Thompson, in *Preaching Biblically*, says:

> Just as the modern newspaper reader instinctively knows by the form that he or she is reading satire or the report of an accident or a travel column or an editorial or a reader's letter or a bit of gossip, so also can the form critic distinguish among historical narrative, parable, poetry, diatribe, and a host of other fixed forms.[7]

Why not be sensitive to the scope of biblical concern? And why not be attentive to the variety of ways by which those who wrote the books of the Bible sought to give expression to the meaning of their faith and to their experiences with God? Why not make use of those same devices, or at least call attention to them in the process of sermon design and delivery?

According to Leander Keck, paying attention to issues of form and function is precisely what constitutes biblical preaching. He says:

> . . . preaching is truly biblical when (a) the Bible governs the content of the sermon and when (b) the function of the sermon is analogous to that of the text. In other words, preaching is biblical when it imparts a Bible-shaped word in a Bible-like way.[8]

Sermons should not only be grounded and rooted in the content of a biblical passage; those same sermons should also seek to accomplish within the modern audience what those texts first sought to accomplish within the first ancient audiences.

Those outcomes can vary, and can include praise, lamentation or grieving, a stricter adherence to a code of conduct for the faithful, or recognition of some sinful conduct, and an act of repentance and a visible reconciliation principally with God. Other desired outcomes could be sheer wonder at the creative and destructive power of God and an equal amazement at the love and grace of that same God. The literary techniques employed throughout the Bible are used to aid in communicating all of these messages and many more.

Good preaching is not only aware of these literary devices, but is informed by them in both the preparation and delivery of the sermon. There are few, if any, poems or hymns any more beautiful than those contained in the Psalms. When they are treated as such, they open the mind of the preacher to rich images about God's relationship to the believing community. When they are preached as if they are historical or legal documents, specific with regard to date, authorship, or precise meaning, they lose much of their charm. By the same token, the prophetic calls for *justice* and *righteousness* are not poetic images, but clear challenges to the people of God to relate to one another in specific ways. The words of the prophets were not to be interpreted or analyzed. They were warnings and advisories meant to be taken seriously. Leander Keck's word bears repeating at this point, "A sermon is biblical when . . . the function of the sermon is analogous to that of the text."[9]

Of equal importance in this second step of doing biblical analysis is entering into the thought and cultural world of the Bible. Studying the literature invites the reader into the values, vocabulary, and theological assumptions of an ancient society not easily accessible to the preacher, and all but oblivious to the congregation. I can remember reading the English language classic, *Beowulf*, when I was a college student. It was all but impossible to comprehend, because the vocabulary, syntax, and cultural context were foreign to my twentieth–century mind.

How much more difficult is it to grasp the precise meaning of the Bible, which is the product of both another language, culture, and historical era? Paying close attention to the literary styles found in the Bible helps us to understand how the writers thought, what they feared and believed, and how those beliefs and understandings changed and were redefined over time. Thus, the Bible is not just a library of diverse literature; it is primarily a theological library wherein is found the continuing attempt of a community of faith to work out and give expression to its relationship to the God of all creation.

The mythological language of Genesis 1 and 2 may be different from the philosophical reflections found in John 1:1-11, but both seek to account for the origins of the universe. The understanding of being "the people of God" may be viewed differently in Acts than it was in Ezra, but the intention is the same: to define that relationship at a specific moment and place in time. The preacher needs to help the congregation regain a sense of that moment in time, and the literary devices used throughout the Bible are keys to doing precisely that. Having seen how being "the people of God" has been an evolving and changing concept over that period of time, the sermon based on either of those texts can rightly challenge some modern congregation on what that term may mean for them in the twenty-first century.

Using the of the diversity of biblical literature

In the process of doing biblical analysis, the preacher needs to consider how the form of the literature should influence the form of the sermon. Thomas G. Long, writing in *Preaching and the Literary Forms of the Bible*, touches on how to preach from five of the literary genres found in Scripture. He examines psalms, proverbs, narratives, parables, and epistles.[10] There is no need to repeat here what he already has so adequately detailed. What I will do is examine three additional types of biblical literature that are commonly employed in preaching, but were not touched upon by Long. The additional genres are (1) apocalyptic, (2) biography, and (3) prophecy.

(1) Apocalyptic

I have long been intrigued by this literary genre in the Bible. I believe it has to do with the fact that apocalyptic allowed for a form of expression that empowered oppressed groups who needed to find a way to communicate that was not readily understood by their oppressors. I belong to that school of thought that sees Daniel as a text from the time of the second century B.C. when Antiochus Epiphany ruled Palestine and tried to impose Hellenism on the Jewish people.[11] The faith of that community was strengthened, and their willingness to resist the power of Antiochus was reinforced by the stories of those who remained faithful in an earlier era in the face of the fiery furnace and the lions' den.

The Book of Revelation served a similar purpose within the Christian community in the first century A.D. as it sought to resist the power and corrupting influences of the Roman Empire. How can the faith become anchored when it is being so brutally and viciously persecuted by the Caesars? How can the values of this infant faith have an impact in a world so dominated by the pluralism and paganism of Rome? If Christ is Lord and Caesar's claims are false, how much longer will the power of Caesar be allowed to remain in force? Using a similar set of coded messages and visual devices, Revelation seeks to lift the hopes of the first-century followers of Christ. "He who has ears to hear, let him hear what the Spirit says to the churches."

African American slaves in the eighteenth and nineteenth centuries did precisely the same thing, especially with the Old Testament stories. First, they used the very images of the lions' den and the fiery furnace as symbols for their own bondage and slavery. In their music and preaching, often in the presence of the slaveowners and their overseers, they would assure themselves that God was still able to deliver his people.

I can recall growing up in a church that sang a song with these lyrics: "Didn't my Lord deliver Daniel, and why not every man?"[12] I can remember any number of sermons where the preacher drew comparisons between the plight of Shadrach, Meschach, and Abednego, and the plight of black people in America. We identified with those biblical characters and with the hope that the same God who intervened in their plight and brought deliverance could do likewise for us.

Second, the slaves themselves actually used a form of coded speech in their spirituals that allowed them to communicate with each other without revealing their true intentions to the masters and overseers. Such songs as "Swing Low Sweet Chariot" or "Steal Away to Jesus" had much less to do with death, than with verbal messages that indicated an escape attempt or, perhaps, some call to gather at a predisclosed location.[13]

Most important of all, however, was the fact that earthly political power, no matter how entrenched and apparently overwhelming, was no match for the power of God. Cut past all the strange images in Daniel and Revelation, and what you have are documents born from within a faith community that reminded itself that its God was greater than the secular political power that was attempting to crush its spirit and hush its witness. Preachers do not need to use texts from either of those two books just to talk about the parts of the language that are inscrutable and undecipherable. That was only part of their purpose. We need to find the Good News in these books. God is greater than the beast. "He who has ears to hear, let him hear what the spirit saith to the churches."

God can still lock the jaws of the consuming lions. The challenge for the preacher is to put a name and face to whatever force seeks to stand in the place of God. That can be repressive governments in China, India, Iraq, and Sudan that seek to persecute those who adhere to Christianity. God is still willing to stand with us inside the fires that burn around us, as we stand against a culture that has made the acquisition of money, the use of illegal drugs, and involvement in pornographic sex its new gods.

The beast that confronts us may not be the power of the Roman Empire, but it may well be the even greater power of health maintenance organizations (HMOs) and pharmaceutical companies who control the means of health care but operate it in ways that leave forty-five million Americans without any access to the system. Do these giant corporations also have "feet of clay," and will God eventually bring forth justice where greed and callousness presently reign supreme?

Do contemporary preachers have the courage to let the function of the text become the function of the sermon? If they do, they will become bold enough to observe that it may well be American society itself to which God may some day have to say, "Thou art weighed in the balances, and art found wanting" (Daniel 5:27). It may be our own national life, self-absorbed and self-secure, to which God may have to direct the words, "Babylon the great is fallen" (Revelation 18:2).

This is how a sermon using an apocalyptic text in the twenty-first century can be shaped. The precise identity of the oppressive force is different, but the idea that God will be with those who are willing to hold onto their faith rather than be corrupted by the prevailing value system of society is a message that needs to be declared.

Working from within the world's only remaining military and economic super power, the apocalyptic message is that God alone will prevail in the presence of those who imagine that their power will last forever.

(2) Biographical

When I was growing up in the 1950s, it might have been safe to assume that people knew many of the characters and story lines of the Bible. The preacher or Sunday school teacher could get away with saying, "Now all of you remember the story of Jacob's ladder . . . " No such assumptions can be made today. Biblical illiteracy is a major challenge with which we who work with the Scriptures must contend. The problem is not limited to those who sit in the pew. I remember sitting in the pulpit of Abyssinian Baptist Church in the presence of over 2500 worshipers and watching a visiting minister look in the index page to find the page number for the book of 1 Chronicles. The Bible is like the tire jack in the trunk of the car. Everybody has one, but most people do not know how to use it. Preaching biographical materials is a good way to reintroduce our listeners to the culture, questions, and conflicts of the biblical world.

The great benefit of biographical preaching is that it allows you to introduce people to the biblical text in the same manner in which people experience their own world, their sensory receptors. Sermons on biblical doctrine give you ideas and concepts to understand. Sermons on biblical characters give you things to see, hear, taste, touch, and smell. Such sermons take you into the far country with the prodigal son, leaving the preacher to describe the scenes to us as if he or she were a radio announcer describing a scene that the listeners could only see in their minds. It is the announcer's challenge, and peculiar talent, to be able to fill in the details that allow us to enter into that scene.

Biographical preaching allows us to set various characters within a time and place, so we gain a better understanding of the social customs and political alliances of the ancient world. We can preach about the need to end racial and religious prejudice in our society as a topical or doctrinal issue, or we can preach on Jesus and the Samaritan woman at Jacob's well in John 4. We can talk about the doctrine of grace, or we can preach about the woman who was caught in the act of adultery in John 8:11. We can talk about having faith like a grain of mustard seed, or we can watch while Abraham at the age of seventy-five packs up and leaves Haran with Sarah his wife. Or we can watch him at the age of one hundred when he climbs up Mount Moriah with a knife, the wood, the fire, and his only son, Isaac.

There are monumental figures in the Bible whose lives we would do well to examine not just for purposes of historical review, but because there is so much we can learn from them about what it means to be a Christian in our own time and place. In Philippians 3:4-7, Paul gives us a capsuled version of his own life and spiritual journey, focusing primarily upon his "good-standing" as a leader in the Jewish religious establishment of his day. Then he says, "What things were gain to me, those I counted loss for Christ . . . [I] count them but dung . . . not having mine own righteousness." (Philippians 3:7-9).

I know of no better way to challenge people to love and trust God above anything this world can provide than to focus on this passage. Paul would have us focus less upon our contemporary preoccupations with ethnicity (black, Latino, Asian, Native, and Eastern European). He would urge us to give less emphasis to the spiritual disciplines and religious practices that might give us an inflated sense of piety and, thus, righteousness (tithing, speaking in tongues, mastery of Bible knowledge, and involvement in denominational affairs). All of this he would urge us to consider of no more value than dung when considered in relation to knowing Christ in the pardon of sin and in the hope of heaven.

However, there is a danger in approaching biographical preaching from the perspective that biblical characters offer the examples of godly living that we should seek to emulate. Thus, I want to consider biographical preaching from another, perhaps more useful angle. James Sanders offers an instructive insight on the appropriate way to relate to biblical characters. He says, "Most biblical texts must be read, not by looking in them for models for morality, but by looking in them for mirrors for identity."[14]

If biblical characters are persons whose behaviors we *should* emulate, then they are models for our morality, and we should seek to live up to their spiritual level. If, on the other hand, a biblical character *reflects* the sins and shortcomings with which we ourselves also struggle, then he or she is a mirror of our own spiritual morass. When one considers the biographical stories throughout the Bible, those characters far more often serve as reflections of who we are than they do as models of who we should be attempting to become.

Using this approach to biographical preaching, preachers can shed great light on the human dilemma. Abraham was willing to give his wife to another man just to save his own life. Esau would sell his birthright for immediate gratification. Moses would commit murder in a moment of rage. Gideon would repeatedly put God to the test. A rich young man was more willing to part company with Christ than he was to part with his wealth. Herod was willing to kill the innocent to preserve his power. Pilate declared three times that Jesus was not guilty, but lacked the courage or political will to resist the appeal of the murderous crowd. Biographical preaching opens a great many doors into the human soul. Every preacher should employ this device on a frequent basis.

An even more precise way to approach biographical preaching is to recognize the conflicting impulses, the divided loyalties, the spiritual warfare going on within the biblical characters and, by extension, within ourselves. Judas is remembered only because of his betrayal of the Lord. What has been forgotten is that, like the other disciples, Judas had left everything and everyone dear to him in order to follow Jesus. And for three years, he was as faithful and as faithless as the others. He was capable of great acts of love and loyalty and great acts of failure and moral compromise. However, he is not alone in either of those instances. Biographical preaching forces us to consider the entire life of a biblical character, not a moment or a single day in time. When that is done, we can learn so much more from the character about ourselves, both strengths and weaknesses.

It must be stated that biographical preaching, like all the other forms of preaching, is an art form that needs to be mastered. I remember watching a Public Broadcast System special on the jazz and classical trumpeter Wynton Marsalis. He was teaching a class on playing the Brandenburg Concerto by Bach. He asked a certain student to play a portion of that music as a demonstration for the rest of the class. After listening to the student for a few seconds he stopped him and asked him if he had ever listened to the Brandenburg Concerto being played by an accomplished performer. The young man said that he had not. Marsalis told the class, "If you want to play this kind of music you must first listen to it." It was, apparently, not enough to simply read the notes. You had to know how to interpret and deliver them as well.

The same is true about biographical preaching. It is not enough to just relate the details of the story. You need to know how to set the stage, develop the plot, introduce the characters, and hold the interest of the listeners throughout the process. I would offer a variation on the observation by Wynton Marsalis. If you want to be a good biographical preacher, you need to read or listen to the work of those who have mastered that form of sermon design and delivery.

I would urge people to read the works of Clarence Macartney and Clovis Chappell, among others. Between them there are six classic collections of sermons that highlight the use of biographical preaching.[15] The biblical world is analyzed, the characters are placed within the context of that world, the theological issue is examined, and the implications of that issue for our world are made readily apparent.

(3) Prophetic

One of the absolutely essential needs in every congregation is occasional exposure to preaching that is rooted in the words and witness of the Old Testament prophets. Preachers need to play a role within the life of the congregation that such people as Amos, Jeremiah, and Micah played within the life of the people of Israel. James Ward and Christine Ward begin their important book on this subject of prophetic preaching by writing:

> The natural inclination of the Christian community, like all religious communities, is to adapt its witness of faith to its most immediate human needs. In doing this the community always runs the risk of obscuring the wider dimensions of the gospel, particularly the wider implications of God's demand for righteousness and justice. What is

needed, therefore, is preaching that recovers these wider dimensions and illuminates the ways in which the community obscures them. [16]

Those who preach must appreciate the need to let their sermons play this role in the life of their congregations, their surrounding communities, and their communities of faith.

There is a tendency within congregational life to become overly focused on such pressing matters as the confirmation class, the renovation of the sanctuary, whether or not the church budget will be met, or how to maintain a feeling of intimacy in the face of a rapidly growing membership. What may be lost in the rush to respond to these issues is that congregation's responsibility to respond to an escalating problem of homelessness in the community, or overcrowding in the jails, or the abuse of inhalants by youngsters in the local school district.

Prophetic preaching shifts the focus of the congregation from what is happening to them as a local church to what is happening to us as a society. Prophetic preaching then asks the question, "What is the role or appropriate response of our congregation, association, or denomination to what is happening in the larger society?" Prophetic preaching points out those false gods that people have begun to adopt in lieu of, sometimes alongside of, the true and living God. Most important of all, prophetic preaching never allows the faith community to offer religious rituals, however well done or regularly engaged in, as an alternative to the challenge to be engaged in advancing the cause of justice and righteousness.

The words of the eighth century B.C. prophets, Micah and Amos, come immediately to mind. Both of them condemned Israel because that nation seemed more interested in the acts of animal sacrifice and the observance of religious feast days than they were in the poverty and economic exploitation that impacted the lives of so many people in that society. Both of them attacked Israel because that nation had started to worship the gods of the nations around them and had abandoned its sole confidence in the God of Israel.

As we plan our preaching in the year 2000 and beyond, it is not hard to see how prophetic preaching is needed within our churches and within our society. We worship inside of churches that are immaculately maintained, even though many of our churches are located in neighborhoods that have been reduced to shambles as a result of poverty, drug trafficking, the loss of industry, and the resultant loss of population through flight to the suburbs. In far too many instances, churches say and do nothing about the conditions right outside their doors, or the social policies that caused them. Prophetic preaching is needed if the authentic witness of the church is ever to occur.

The real advantage of preaching from prophetic texts is that we are forced to consider people, issues, and conditions ranging over a period of one thousand years. Prophetic preaching extends from the words of such prophets as Nathan in 2 Samuel 12, whose ministry took place during the reign of King David, to the encounter that John the Baptist had with Herod Antipas in Mark 6.

We are challenged to consider three sets of materials. First, there are the three so-called Major Prophets, deemed as such only because of the length of the books that bear their names. These would be Isaiah, Jeremiah, and Ezekiel. Next would come the twelve Minor Prophets, so-called because their books are much shorter. These would include Hosea, Joel, Amos, Obadiah, Jonah, Micah, Nahum, Habakkuk, Zephaniah, Haggai, Zechariah, and Malachi. Finally, as indicated by an earlier reference to Nathan, would be those other prophetic figures found throughout 2 Samuel and 1 and 2 Kings. The most notable of these would be Elijah and Elisha. Elizabeth Achtemeier's book, *Preaching from the Minor Prophets*, is especially useful in this area.[17]

There is nothing in the Bible that is comparable to the breadth and diversity of the genre that we call prophetic material. Sometimes Israel is at the height of its power and influence, and the message of the prophet is that God is about to bring the nation down. Other times, Israel has been reduced to a laughing-stock among the other nations, but the prophet's task is to remind Israel that God has not forgotten the nation. In both cases, however, the prophet is attempting to focus the people's attention on issues that are broader than how to worship or where to pray. In the face of the shifting circumstances faced by the people of God, the prophets remind Israel of the things that God demands: Do justice, love mercy, walk humbly with God (Micah 6:8).

Warren Stewart, also a former student of James Sanders, writes about the hermeneutic principles that Sanders calls the "constitutive and prophetic" readings of Scripture. Stewart says:

> In biblical times, the constitutive reading of the Torah story, which was based on a supportive interpretation of the Word, gave Israel an identity and a purpose. As the moral as well as the historical context of Israel changed, Israel became in need of a challenging message that would call it back to its original purpose as God's elect. Israel, in such a state, was not in need of a supportive reading of the tradition. The establishment context of Israel called for a prophetic interpretation of the Torah story.[18]

The message of the prophets calls us back to our original purpose as the people of God. It reminds us of how we should have been living all along. It points out to us what we have become as a people. It challenges us to return to the Lord our God.

In his "Letter From Birmingham Jail," written in 1963, Martin Luther King Jr. embodies for us what it looks like to preach from the prophetic texts, and to "be a prophet" in our midst. He wonders how we can build churches that are so beautiful to behold but practice racial segregation and harbor such racial bias, which is so contrary to the teachings of Christ.[19] No doubt, the churches he observed as he traveled throughout the American south in the 1950s and 60s were well-staffed and well-funded, but they were not well focused so far as the great issue of the day was concerned. They needed a prophetic word, which seldom came from within their congregational life. They were focused on a "constitutive" agenda, and what they needed was a "prophetic" message.

Preachers need to make regular use of prophetic texts, and they need to allow the function of the text to become the function of the sermon.[20] The spiritual health and development of the people of God depends upon our paying attention to this literary genre because only when the church is confronted by the passion and urgency of prophetic preaching can we be sure that the wider dimensions of the gospel are not being obscured.[21]

It must be noted, however, that prophetic preaching does not demand the use of a text from one of the prophetic books of the

Old Testament, or any reference to one of the prophets of the classical period. We have all heard sermons based upon a text from a prophetic book that proved to be more "pathetic" than "prophetic." That was usually so because the preacher did not have as his or her focus that which constantly occupied the biblical prophets, namely God's people living in obedience to the will of God, no matter in what condition they found themselves at any given point in time. In the sample sermon at the end of this chapter, I am attempting to have this focus. The sermon is not based upon a text from a prophetic book; rather, it is based upon Psalm 119. However, I hope it is faithful to the intent of prophetic preaching, "speaking truth to power."

Prophetic preaching is when the preacher seeks to bring the will of God to the attention of the people of God, and then, as Elizabeth Achtemeier observes, challenge them "to trust their Lord in all circumstances and to obey him with willing and grateful hearts."[22] Prophetic preaching happens when the preacher has the courage to speak truth to people in power, in the church and in the secular order. We must be especially willing to do this if we are to be faithful to Samuel who confronted Saul, Nathan who confronted David, Amos who condemned Jeroboam, John the Baptist who challenged Herod Antipas, and the many other biblical prophets who were willing to declare the will of God even to those who had power over their lives.

This is consistent with what Walter Brueggemann considers the essence of prophetic preaching. In his book, *The Prophetic Imagination*, he states that the work of the prophet is to be able to project before the people "an alternative future to the one the king wants to urge as the only thinkable one."[23] For Brueggemann, the Old Testament prophets had to contend with something he calls *royal consciousness,* which represents the deeply entrenched forces — political, economic, social, or religious — of Israel.[24] They are the status quo, and they only offer to the people a vision of the future that allows them to remain in power and requires that the masses of people remain marginalized in society. The work of the prophet is to combat that single vision, and show that God can and will bring about a future different from that envisioned by the power elite.

Prophetic preaching requires something more than righteous indignation, however. It requires great humility and the awareness that the sin that is seen in the people who will hear the sermon is equally alive and at work in the preacher who delivers it. We should never preach at the people about their sins. The preferred posture is to preach about the sins that grip us all, and that pull us away from love and loyalty to God.

Before attempting a prophetic sermon, preachers should be informed by the words of a song from my slave ancestors who would say,

It ain't my mother,
It ain't my father,
But it's me, O Lord,
Standing in the need of prayer.

SERMON PREVIEW

The following sermon is an attempt to demonstrate some of the content that constitutes prophetic preaching. It must be stated over and over again that a prophetic sermon is defined by its content, not simply by the fact that it is a sermon based upon a passage of Scripture taken from one of the prophetic books. None of the prophets were preaching from "prophetic materials." Instead, it was their general understanding of God as revealed in the Torah and in their lives that resulted in the content and tone of their preaching.

Part of the prophetic message was calling attention to the way in which religion was being watered down into empty and powerless rituals. Similarly, this sermon is a reaction to something that was being proposed by a member of the United States Congress, which brings us to the next object-lesson of this sermon. The prophets were not afraid to direct their words to the political leadership of their day. We must be willing to speak with similar boldness. I hope to demonstrate all of these techniques in this sermon.

ON YOUR WALL OR IN YOUR HEART?

DEUTERONOMY 6:4-9, PSALM 119:11

It is very likely that there has been more discussion about the Ten Commandments over the last two weeks, than at any time since Moses came down from Mount Sinai holding in his hand the tablets of stone on which those commandments were first inscribed. The reason for the renewed discussion about this ancient moral code is related, not to a sudden rise in religious piety, but to a political maneuver to win passage of a watered down bill dealing with gun control. Congressman Robert Barr of Georgia is a strong supporter of the National Rifle Association and a strong opponent of almost any kind of gun control legislation. After the school shootings at Columbine High School in Littleton, Colorado, and Heritage High School in suburban Atlanta, Georgia, there seemed to be a national urgency to put stronger restrictions in place to control the availability of guns. The only question seemed to be how severe those restrictions were going to be.

Within one month's time, a tough bill had been voted on in the U.S. Senate, and it moved over to the House of Representatives. That is when Bob Barr went to work. As a way of saying that gun control was not the most important action for the Congress to take, he proposed, in a gun control bill, having the Ten Commandments hung on the walls of every school in America. He argued that the problem is not the easy access that people have to all kinds of guns. Instead, the problem is the moral and ethical climate of our nation. Rather than acting to remove guns from the hands of children, Bob Barr proposed that we simply display the Ten Commandments on the walls of their school. Maybe those children would see the Ten Commandments. Maybe they would notice the one that says, "thou shalt not kill." Bob Barr actually said that the shootings in Littleton might not have happened if the Ten Commandments had been posted on the walls of Columbine High School.

That gun control bill was defeated in the House. It was not defeated because people were for or against the Ten Commandments. It was defeated, because the provisions had been so watered down that the bill

This sermon was preached by the author on June 27, 1999, at Antioch Baptist Church in Cleveland, Ohio.

did little or nothing to actually restrict the ease with which persons could purchase guns, especially at gun shows where the problem seems to be the most severe. However, if the bill had passed, and if the provision calling for the posting of the Ten Commandments in schools had been approved, two things would inevitably have happened. First, the law would have been challenged in court and ruled to be unconstitutional. There is little doubt that displaying the teachings of a particular religious tradition in a public school setting supported by taxpayer dollars, where students and staff of other traditions are present, is a gross violation of the First Amendment requirement of the separation of church and state. The government should not be imposing religious values on society, especially in public settings. Those of us who are Jewish or Christian might not have been offended by this practice. But the Constitution seeks primarily to protect the rights of minorities, and thus the concerns raised by Muslims, Buddhists, Hindus, and atheists, all of whom are present in our public schools, would have caused the posting of the Ten Commandments to be disallowed.

However, I believe we as Christians should have been opposed to this practice for another reason entirely. I love the Ten Commandments as a guide for moral living. I struggle each day to make them a part of the foundation of my own life. I have no hesitation in using them as points of reference in my preaching, my pastoral counseling, and as I make decisions in my own life, whether public or private. But I do object to the Ten Commandments as a wall plaque. I object to the notion that deep-rooted social problems can be resolved simply by displaying these words on the wall. I am informed in this view by the Bible itself. Nowhere does the Bible affirm that any value is attached to displaying the Bible, whether on the walls of a school or on a coffee table or shelf in our homes. The Bible is not to be looked at. It is to be studied, adopted, and used as a guide for daily living.

That is the message in Deuteronomy 6. It does say in that passage that the teachings of the law should be posted on the doorposts of the house. However, far from simply being displayed, those teachings should also be talked about when children rise in the morning, talked about when they walk with their family through the day, and further talked about at bedtime. The words that are posted or displayed at the door should be the center of everything that family does both inside and outside the house. Otherwise, the Law has simply been reduced to a plaque. *See the words*, and they will do you good. That is not how our faith or the Bible work.

Would Bob Barr or any of the other sponsors of that ill-fated piece of legislation have suggested that we treat our bodies as they suggest we can treat the soul? Suppose we are given a regiment of prescription medications with clear instructions to "take three times daily." However, instead of consuming them as the doctor instructed, we simply look at them three times a day as they sit on a shelf in our bathroom medicine cabinets. Does it make any sense to believe that medicines designed to effect our physical health will work to our advantage if we simply post the usage instructions on the bathroom walls? And if that sounds pre-posterous, why would it make any more sense where religious faith is concerned?

Consider for a moment the two very different meanings of the word *observed*. One sense of this word means to see. You hear that in the question, "What do you observe when you look around the church today?" In this context, observing something simply means noticing that something is there. Now consider the other meaning of the same word. One of the signs that drivers will undoubtedly see as they travel around says, "Please observe all posted signs." Do you think that simply means notice that the signs are there? Are we free to say to ourselves, "I see a stop sign, but I will not stop"? Does observing a posted sign simply mean seeing it? Of course not. To observe all posted signs means to comply with the information or instructions posted on that sign. To observe a posted sign means to do what it says, or face the conse-quences if one does not do so.

Let's apply that same lesson to the Ten Commandments. I do not think there is any value attached to observing the Ten Commandments if that means simply looking at them as they hang on a wall in a school, a courtroom, or any other public building. It would not disturb me to see them hanging there, but it would not make me believe that society was becoming more moral or ethical. The Ten Commandments must fit into that other sense of the word *observe*. They are not intended to be looked at; they are intended to be obeyed. I am much less interested in Congress succeeding in having them posted on the walls of schools, than I am in having students allow the Ten Commandments to become part of their lives. That is the meaning of Psalm 119:11, "Thy word have I hid in my heart, that I might not sin against thee." The Ten

61

Commandments should be written on our hearts, not simply hung on our walls.

Consider for a moment all the signs you and I see posted in one place or another. Ask yourself if those signs have ever had the effect of changing your behavior. Seeing a copy of the Declaration of Independence does not make a racist or a sexist believe that "all men are created equal." Seeing a copy of the Gettysburg Address does not make me believe that Lincoln freed the slaves because he hated slavery. We see signs that say, "Do Not Litter," but we litter just the same. We see signs that say, "35 mph," but we go at least five miles faster all the time. We see signs that say, "No Smoking," or "No food or drink allowed," but people ignore those warnings. We see signs in the check-out line at the store that say, "10 items or less," but there are always people getting in that line with more than twice that number of items. You may even stand behind them and count out loud as they take each item out of the cart. They saw the sign; it just had no power to change their behavior. Using the Ten Commandments as a sign on a wall in school is not much different. It is very doubtful that the sign will be able to alter anyone's behavior. Hear the words and the warning of Psalm 119:11: "Thy word have I hid in my heart, that I might not sin against thee."

Be careful to notice that the verse does not say, "Thy word have I hid." It says, "Thy word have I hid in my heart." Perhaps our nation has come to where we are not because of the absence of religious slogans on the walls of public buildings, but because of the absence of any clear Christian witness by people who profess a religious faith in any setting outside of their local church. It was not slogans on the wall that eventually ended racial segregation in America. It was people of religious faith, banding together around the slogan of the Southern Christian Leadership Conference, and behind the moral leadership of Martin Luther King Jr., who set out to "redeem the soul of America!" Here and there, one can still see glimpses of such courageous faith in action. But more often than not, all one sees is a tepid and weak suggestion such as hanging a copy of the Ten Commandments on the walls of our schools.

This psalm is a clear warning against reducing religion to a series of superficial acts or sayings. Being a Christian is not about such external things as hanging the commandments on a wall, or hanging a cross around your neck, or placing a Bible in a prominent place in your home. The real issue is whether or not we live by the commandments every day, or seek to be faithful to the man who died on that cross, or read and believe what is written in that Bible. The psalmist says that religion is most real when it flows from the heart. When you love God in your heart, when you pray from your heart, or when you willingly obey the commandments from your heart, then you have become a Christian. When you only notice the Ten Commandments because somebody else hung them on the wall, you are just going through the motions.

Much the same thing applies where prayer in schools is concerned. I do not recall ever having prayer in my schools in Chicago, even before prayer was declared unconstitutional. I can remember being in school in 1954, and in Chicago there was no official time for prayer. There was no moment of silence. There was no voice over the intercom leading us in a moment of meditation. We said the pledge of allegiance to the flag, and the school day got underway. Thus, I have no sentimental recollection about how things were better when there was prayer in some schools.

However, in my judgment, America has not become morally unraveled as a result of the absence of prayer in schools. The real problem is the absence of prayer in the home, and the absence of too many people *from* the home in some church on a regular basis. Prayer in schools is no magic wand. There was prayer in racially segregated schools in this country for one hundred years. Moreover, every meeting of the Ku Klux Klan begins with prayer, so there is nothing mystical about prayer, if it is not done as an act of faith out of a believing heart. We in the faith community must lead the way in cautioning our society against looking for painless solutions to cancerous problems. I say again, what Psalm 119:11 says is true, the word of God belongs in our hearts, not simply on our walls.

Let's consider this passage more carefully. The psalm says, "Thy word have I hid in my heart" THAT I MIGHT NOT SIN AGAINST GOD. Consider that there was a reason why believers were encouraged to let the word of God sink into their hearts. This deep-seated word of God was the only known antidote to the problem of sin. The Bible in general, and the Ten Commandments in particular, serve as a warning device to prevent us from stumbling into sinful conduct. The Bible is very much like the radar devices in so many cars these days. It used to be that people would actually drive slowly, so they would not get a speeding ticket. Then car manufacturers invented the dashboard radar device that alerts drivers when a police car with radar is anywhere nearby. The driver does not know exactly where the police car is sitting, but is warned by the device inside the car, so the driver slows down and drives more carefully.

The Bible works in much the same way in the heart of a believer. It is like a warning system that tries to tell you that you need to slow down and be more careful. If the word of God is hidden in your heart, then you will get a warning when you start doing things that you should not be doing. Call it your conscience if you will, but it is something speaking to you from inside of your spirit, and it is trying to guide you in one way or another. What allows that conscience to work is not external. The conscience is composed of the moral values buried deep in the human heart that stand up and speak out when we begin doing things that we should not be doing. If we listen to our conscience, if we listen to the word of God that is hidden in our hearts, we will not sin. We will turn away from that conduct. We will not speak those words. We will not go to that place with that group. We were on the way. We almost gave in to temptation. And what saved us were not words that we saw written on a wall. What saved us was the word of God that we had hidden in our hearts, so that we would not sin against God. Surely that is what is meant in that powerful twenty-fourth verse in Jude: "Now unto him that is able to keep you from falling . . ."

The Bible is useful to those people who want to know how to avoid sin. The Bible is the answer to the longing soul that wants to know the path that leads to peace with God. The Bible is a repository of accumulated wisdom over the last three millennia, preserved and perpetuated by those who were operating under the influence of the Holy Spirit. It is bread to the hungry, water to the thirsty, hope for the despairing, strength for the weary, and comfort for the sick and dying. The Bible is light for those who wander in darkness, wisdom for those who still wallow in the ignorance of prejudice and hatred, and it is a source of joy for those who discover in its pages that their sins have been forgiven, and they have a home awaiting them in heaven.

All of this, and more, is what the Bible is for those who have hid its words, its parables, its prophecies, and its psalms deep in their hearts. For those who do little more than look at the Bible from time to time, but who do not meditate upon it day and night, it is little more than a plaque hanging upon the wall of a school. The power of the Bible is not unleashed from the outside, in. It is unleashed from the inside, out. "Thy word have I hid in my heart, that I might not sin against thee."

However, the greatest danger in what Congress proposed is not to trivialize the Ten Commandments. That ancient code of faith has faced greater risks than anything this Congress might propose. No, the greater danger is that devout people of faith might be led to believe that we are really addressing what is wrong in our country by posting religious codes on the walls of public buildings, and not be willing to pursue more rigorous solutions. We might feel less urgent about the need for gun control, a review of the death penalty, or programs aimed at the eradication of poverty, if we believe that all that is required is displaying the Ten Commandments. We might not be as outspoken about another war (Kosovo) that cost the nation $10 billion, did not prevent a single Albanian family from being displaced from its home, resulted in bombing dummy targets, and left another cruel dictator in power after the hostilities were over. After all, we do have the Ten Commandments hanging on the walls of our schools. Not only will the suggestion by Congress not resolve the question of gun violence in our schools, but it may do something worse, and that is give us the feeling that something has been accomplished and leave us unwilling to entertain the more complex solutions that are really needed.

Several days after Congress made its suggestion, the editorial board of the *San Francisco Examiner* newspaper issued this satirical response entitled, "Handing down the 10 commandments for Congress." Consider this as good advice for all the people who think it is enough to hang the words on a wall.

1. Thou shalt not trivialize the Ten Commandments by using them for political purposes.
2. Thou shalt not violate the constitutional separation of church and state.
3. Thou shalt not seek to intimidate or embarrass any student whose religious beliefs might be different from those of the majority of students.
4. Thou shalt not seek to establish or promote a state religion, even in ways that seem to some as small and benign.
5. Thou shalt not claim that posting religious creeds such as the Ten Commandments will prevent terrible instances of school violence,

such as the Columbine killings, which involve deep and complex causes.

6. Thou shalt not embrace cosmetic or symbolic solutions to difficult and pressing problems, thereby ignoring real solutions.
7. Thou shalt not equate or confuse putting up posters with changing the moral fabric of the nation for the better.
8. Thou shalt not pretend that God is a supporter of your political party. She may be hedging her bets.
9. Thou shalt not attempt to turn the nation's schools into a real-life version of George Orwell's "Animal Farm," with its totalitarian slogans.
10. Thou shalt not commit acts of gross stupidity in the name of religion, pandering or polls.

There is a song I learned to sing years ago when I was a child in Sunday school. It seems most appropriate in light of the notion that the values and behavior of people can somehow be changed simply by hanging the words in a religious creed on a wall where people are likely to see it as they pass by. The song says:

Into my heart, into my heart,
Come into my heart, Lord Jesus.
Come in today; come in to stay,
Come into my heart, Lord Jesus.

Let that be not only our prayer for our own lives, but our hope for the lives of everyone else, as well. It is much better to have the word of God hidden in your heart, than simply to have it hanging on your wall. It is better to heed the words of Colossians 3:16, and "Let the word of Christ dwell in you richly," than to hope that high school students will pause to read signs hanging in the corridors of their building.

When my son was about four years old, we bought him an inflatable punching bag that stood about three feet tall, had the image of a cartoon character painted on the front, and had several pounds of sand in the bottom serving as a base of support. He would punch that bag and knock it down, but the rounded bottom filled with sand would cause the bag to come right back up again. Over and over, he would punch it and knock it down. And over and over, that bag would come back up again.

I asked him why he thought the bag would go down and then come back up. His response has remained with me over the fifteen years since he spoke these words: "There must be something inside the bag that makes it stand up." Indeed there was something inside that bag that made it stand up, and if we are successful in putting something inside ourselves, like the Word of God, we too will stand up under pressure and in the face of temptation. It is time for the nation in general, and the faith community in particular, to speak up. Should the Ten Commandments be hung on our walls, or hidden in our hearts?

4
The 8 Ls:
Language

The truth contained in the Bible and the accuracy with which we are able to present and interpret that truth as it is contained in any passage of Scripture depends entirely upon our achieving the most accurate translation of the words on which our sermon will be based. This chapter is intended to offer suggestions that will help preachers come to the fullest and most sensitized understanding of the actual words, and their meaning, as contained in the passage that is being analyzed and prepared to serve as the basis of a sermon.

Translating and interpreting the Bible

It must be remembered that the King James Version of the Bible, introduced in the year 1611, and venerated though it is in many places, is not the original version of the Bible. This same point is even more true for the many recent English language versions of the Bible that have been produced over the last fifty years. (The list of such versions would include the New King James Version, the Revised Standard and New Revised Standard Versions, the New International Version, the American Standard Version, Jerusalem Bible and New Jerusalem Bible, the New English Bible, The Living Bible, The Good News Bible, etc.).

The Bible was written in Hebrew and Greek, with some limited use of Aramaic. More importantly, the most recent portions of the Bible were written over eighteen hundred years ago. This statement alone points to two of the biggest challenges in doing exegesis. First, meanings are often lost when a word is translated from one language to another. There may be no equivalent word in English for a certain Hebrew or Greek word. Therefore, translators must search for a word that they believe carries the meaning intended by the original writer. Second, word meanings change over time, or carry more than a single meaning. How does a twenty-first century exegete and expositor know with certainty what is the most accurate and reliable translation of the biblical passage serving as the basis of a sermon? That is the challenge of this chapter.

The issue of *Language* is central to the task of exegesis because the point of the exercise is to determine what a given text is trying to say to the faith community. In order to hear the text accurately one must know, to the highest degree possible, the most accurate rendering of the words in that passage. Who wrote them, and under what circumstances they were initially either written or read, is crucial information. But none of that information is quite as crucial as this step in the process. *"What are the words?"*

Reasons to use the biblical languages

A large part of the debate over the virgin birth of Jesus involves the issue of language. How should the Hebrew word *almah* be translated? Should the passage read, "A virgin shall conceive, and bear a son . . . ", as stated in the King James Version of Isaiah 7:14? Or is the proper rendering, "A young girl shall conceive . . .", as translated by the Revised Standard Version? The theological issues that emerge from that single variance in translation are significant. Such variances occur throughout the Bible because translating an ancient text into both a modern language and a modern era is a complicated process. A responsible preacher is alert to these kinds of translation issues.

In John 21, Jesus and Peter seem to be speaking past each other in a discussion that revolves around whether or not Peter understands what Jesus means by the word *love*. Jesus asks, "Peter, do you love me *(agapas)*?" Peter answers, "Yes, Lord, you know that I love you *(philo)*." The English word *love* is a frail alternative to the many words available to the writers of the Greek New Testament. If the preacher were not to study this passage beyond consulting a single English language translation, it is clear that most of the meaning of the text would be entirely lost. Jesus was inquiring whether or not Peter loved him with that unmerited and self-sacrificing love of God *(agape)*. Peter answered that he loved Jesus with a warm brotherly love *(phileo)*. The preacher needs to see a central question in this chapter: *What are the words?*

In Acts 1:8 Jesus tells his disciples to be "witnesses" for him to the ends of the earth. What might a creative and imaginative preacher do with the knowledge that the Greek word for witness, *martures*, is also the word frequently used, especially throughout the Book of Revelation, for a martyr? In other words, a witness is a person who is willing to remain faithful to his or her testimony for Jesus Christ even to the point of death. We have seen in these two examples that one English word can have three meanings in Greek, and that one Greek word can have two meanings in English. These kinds of subtle uses of language go on all the time in the Bible.

In Amos 8 yet another language device is employed when two words are placed together which, in the Hebrew, sound very much alike but have widely different meanings. God asks the prophet what he sees, and the prophet answers "summer fruit" *(qayits)*. But the Lord says it is not summer fruit but the end *(qets)*. Amos did not simply see the end of one season and the beginning of another. What Amos really saw was the end of the national life for Israel. The subtlety of the language is that the two Hebrew words sound almost identical, but they carry vastly different meanings.

Being able to come as close as possible to the actual words of the text, and to understand the subtle uses to which those words are frequently put, is what the *Language* portion of this exercise is about. It can be said that exegesis is a two-part process, first of identifying what the text says, and then identifying what the text means. However, the first step must be accomplished before the second step can be undertaken. The preacher can go no further until the central question has been answered: *What are the words?*

None of the insights and subtleties mentioned above are difficult to find for those who begin their study of the text by reading it first in the original language of Hebrew or Greek. However, many preachers do not possess that skill, and many who learned the languages in college and seminary can no longer make much use of them because they did not continue to use them on a regular basis.

The old adage about language skills is equally true of Hebrew and Greek, "Use them or lose them."

All is not lost if a preacher cannot use the original languages. There are a variety of scholarly tools, both print and CD ROM, that can provide tremendous assistance to any preacher looking to know as much as possible about a passage that has been translated from one language to another. So far as a CD ROM resource is concerned, I especially recommend something like *i. Preach Bible Reference Library*. This one CD not only contains multiple versions of the Bible, but many other resource tools as well. Several other electronic resources can be equally useful in the exegetical process for those who can employ a computer in their work.

Beginning exegesis with the original languages

The first step in this process, as I learned thirty years ago from Reginald Fuller at Union Theological Seminary in New York City, is to write out the translation of the text in your own words.[1] What one is looking to do is produce a paraphrase of the text in question in one's own words. If you are using the original languages, then write down the translation as you work your way through the passage. This may require the use of a lexicon or theological dictionary, both of which are acceptable tools for this point in the process. Such resources as *The Analytical Hebrew and Chaldee Lexicon* and *The Analytical Greek Lexicon* are useful.[2] I regularly use *Hebrew and English Lexicon of the Old Testament*, by Brown, Driver, and Briggs and *A Greek-English Lexicon of the New Testament and Other Early Christian Literature*, by Bauer, Arndt, and Gingrich.[3]

Reliable theological dictionaries would include the multivolume sets of Kittel's *Theological Dictionary of the Old Testament* and Kittel and Friedrich's *Theological Dictionary of the New Testament*. The multivolume set of *The Exegetical Dictionary of the New Testament* by Balz and Schneider is quite useful. There is also a single volume, *Theological Dictionary of the New Testament*, by Kittel, translated by Geoffrey Bromly.[4] These tools are essential for helping with translation from one of the original languages. And at this point, translation is all the exegete is attempting to do. Issues of word meaning will come a bit later in this chapter.

Exegetical tools for those using only English

If you are working only from the English language, then compare and contrast that passage from the perspective of several different English language translations. *The Layman's Parallel Bible* is especially useful at this point, because it places side by side four different English language translations: KJV, RSV, The Living Bible, and The Modern Language Version.[5] One of the many study Bibles with critical notes placed at both the center and bottom of the page also offers assistance in detecting important translation issues. Both the *Harper's Study Bible* and *The Oxford Annotated Bible* are valuable resources in the RSV and NRSV, and the Schofield Reference Bible is equally helpful as a KJV research tool.[6]

Since the subtleties of language as written in Hebrew or Greek will not be self-evident, the preacher using only English will need to take special note of those words and phrases where the various English translations do not agree. Some of these differences may be of little or no theological importance. But in some cases, the differences in language may mark significant differences of opinion on a matter of importance. Those variances simply need to be noted at this point in the process, but they should never be ignored.

This step is important in today's churches where all the versions of the Bible mentioned above, and many more, are brought and used by various church members during the worship service or Bible class. The preacher or liturgist may announce that the scripture reading is from a certain passage. However, as often as not, because of the differences in translation and interpretation found in the different versions, the congregation may be reading widely different words, uncertain both as to why that is the case, and which words are most accurate. The preacher has no more urgent task than helping people to answer the question, *"What are the words?"* The first step in that process is knowing where the differences in wording occur.

Checking your wording with the experts

Once the preacher has written out in his or her own words a working translation or paraphrase of the text, it is time to compare the words with the renderings offered by biblical scholars in one or more exegetical commentaries. It must be underscored that turning to an exegetical commentary is different than turning to some shortcut to a sermon idea or outline. Such resources as *The Anchor Bible, The Word Biblical Commentary, The Old Testament Library, Interpretation,* or even the old but still critically useful *International Critical Commentary*[7] are all helpful in assisting the preacher in asking the question, *"What are the words?"*

These resources will not attempt to tell you how to shape a sermon, though some of them do offer useful comments about the meaning of a text. Their principal value is helping a preacher discover language and translation issues that he or she might otherwise have overlooked. Even preachers who are fluent in Hebrew and Greek should check their translation with a critical commentary such as the ones listed above. In a world where books and CD ROM materials are being offered at every turn, preachers need to make informed decisions about what to buy. Books that attempt to tell you "what to preach," but do not lead you through the difficult but more important work of helping you establish the most accurate rendering of the words of your passage, are of minimal value.

Creative preaching is not born out of a sermon outline produced by "a panel of experts" who do not know you or the context in which you preach. Creative preaching is the result of a disciplined mind that has resisted the temptation of "what should I say to the congregation?" at least until he or she has resolved "What does this text actually say?" A reputable critical commentary set may be the best investment a preacher can make. Learning how to use those resources to search for the *Language* from which to preach, and not just for a quick sermon idea, may be the most important use to which a critical commentary can be put.

What do these words mean?

Once the words of the text have been determined both by personal translation or comparative analysis, and by checking with the insights of biblical scholars, the preacher must consider the actual meaning of certain words in the passage. Those words fit under certain categories, so knowing which words deserve further study should not be too hard to determine. First, attention should be given to any of the words that reflect a variance between the English language versions that have been consulted. Underline what those significant differences are, and then consult theological dictionaries to see what the words mean, and which of those words you are going to adopt in your preaching.

Most of my life, I have heard the closing lines of the Twenty-third Psalm used with reference to life in the presence of God both here on earth and beyond death. The KJV, RSV, and NIV use the words, "Surely goodness and mercy shall follow me all the days of my life, and I will dwell in the house of the Lord *forever!*" However, the New English Bible ends that phrase this way, ". . . and I shall dwell in the house of the Lord *my whole life long!*" Is the word *forever* synonymous with the term "my whole life long," or are there both some language and some theological meaning issues that need to be resolved before that very familiar passage is preached?

In an equally familiar passage, 1 Corinthians 13, the RSV, NIV, and NEB all say, "If I speak with the tongues of men and of angels and have not *love . . .*" However, the KJV inserts another word and says, ". . . and have not *charity. . .* " Are these words synonymous, or did the word *charity* carry a meaning beyond that which the English word *love* implies? In Philippians 3:8, Paul says, "for whom I have suffered the loss of all things, and do count them but _____." Four different words are used for the Greek word *skubala* that occurs in that text. Those words are "dung" (KJV), "refuse" (RSV), "garbage" (NEB), and "rubbish" (NIV). The last three words may be synonyms, but "dung" seems to have a meaning of its own. There is clearly some language work that needs to be done at this point.

Galatians 5:22 lists the fruits of the Spirit, and among these is *makrothumia*, which is alternately translated, "longsuffering" (KJV) and "patience" (RSV, NEB, and NIV). However, reviewing the meaning of these two words in a theological resource such as *A Theological Word Book of the Bible*, by Alan Richardson[8] will reveal that *longsuffering* and *patience* are two words that have widely different meanings and uses throughout the Bible. The preacher should be aware, therefore, not only of how a word is used in the passage under immediate consideration. The preacher should also be informed by how that same word is used at other places in the Bible, because that one word does not always carry the same meaning. *Longsuffering*, for instance, often deals with God's attitude toward us, while *patience* may focus more on our attitude toward each other.[9] Great preaching is often the result of noticing these differences in the translation and meaning of a single word.

The value of a good dictionary

One of the most important tools for the preacher, even when using an English language translation, is a reliable Bible dictionary that will help in developing the fullest possible understanding of the key words in the passage that are being studied. There is no need to investigate those words, such as *God, sin, grace,* or *forgiveness* that are widely understood in the congregation. That is true, largely because those words have also been incorporated into daily conversation both inside and outside the church. It is a sign of the influence the Bible has had on Western culture that so many words that emerged from that one book have made their way into our standard vocabulary.

However, there are some words that are not necessarily familiar to the person sitting in the pew. In fact, according to a recent article in *The Chronicle of Higher Education*,[10] which focuses on the lack of biblical knowledge exhibited by students enrolled in America's theological seminaries, there may be some words found in the Bible that are not even fully understood by the preacher. The passage under review might include such words as *expiation, propitiation, atonement,* or *incarnation.* In grasping the full meaning of those words a good Bible dictionary would be useful.

Do we really comprehend the meaning of the word *covenant* as an arrangement between two wholly unequal parties, following the model of the suzerainty treaties of the ancient world? Or do we think more in terms of modern contracts between consenting parties? The latter might make more sense in our society, but it would be far from what God was offering Israel at Mount Sinai.

What is a *messiah*, and why is the Greek term *Christ* often used as a synonym? When Jesus says *"Peace* I leave with you, my *peace* I give unto you" (John 14:27), is there anything in our modern language usage that helps us understand the word *shalom* in the Hebrew or *eirene* in the Greek? Even words such as *sin, peace, love, meek,* and *righteousness* carry more meaning in the context of Scripture than might at first seem apparent. Here again, referring to a good Bible dictionary will unlock the full meaning of these words and add depth to how those words are employed in the sermon.

There is no shortage of dictionaries from which to choose. However, *The Interpreter's Dictionary of the Bible*,[11] containing four volumes and a supplement, remains my favorite resource. In terms of a one-volume dictionary, I also recommend *The New Harper's Bible Dictionary*.[12] I say again, that there are several Bible dictionaries and word books from which to pick. A local Christian bookstore will have resources that will aid the preacher in doing a word study in preparation for preaching.

Paying attention to terms and names

In addition to specific words that may appear throughout the Bible, attention also needs to be given to those biblical terms whose full meaning may not be fully grasped by a modern audience. The Bible speaks of *the Spirit of the Lord, the Holy Spirit, the Paraclete*, and *the Spirit of God*. How do these terms compare, and in what ways do they differ?

What is meant by John's comment, "Behold, *the Lamb of God*"? What is meant by other terms such as *bread of life, the Law of Moses, mercy seat, kingdom of God, kingdom of heaven, Alpha and Omega, Judaizers, unleavened bread*, or *only begotten Son*? Grasping the meaning of these, and other, phrases is crucial to understanding numerous passages of Scripture. The aforementioned dictionaries can help in this area as well.

Preachers need to assume that the people sitting in the pew do not know the full meaning of these terms and phrases. Part of the *Language* portion of exegesis is paying attention to any theological term that appears in the text, so that the sermon is informed by what that term means and how it is being used in that passage. In Romans 11:5, Paul speaks about the church of his generation as "a remnant," and compares its experiences to events in the story of Elijah. Elsewhere in Scripture, the church is referred to as "a chosen generation, a royal priesthood, an holy nation, a peculiar people" (1 Peter 2:9). None of these are self-evident terms. Each of them needs to be further explained and placed into the historical and theological context.

In John 1:36, John the Baptist speaks to his disciples concerning

Jesus and says, "Behold the Lamb of God!" In Matthew 21:9, which recounts Jesus' triumphal entry into the city of Jerusalem, the people cry out, "Hosanna to the Son of David." In both Matthew 4 and Luke 4, Jesus spends forty days in the wilderness following his baptism. During that time the devil repeatedly says to him, "If you be the Son of God . . . " The mere fact that people are familiar with these terms does not mean that they fully understand what message each of them is trying to communicate about Jesus. These may be the words, but now the question is, *"What do they mean?"*

There is often great meaning in a name

Much of the poignancy found in the Scriptures is tied to seeing the connection between the proper names of persons or places and the events that surround them. Preachers should make it a habit to see whether or not any part of the meaning of the text is tied to the meaning of any proper noun found therein. Jacob names the place where he had seen the vision of angels ascending and descending a ladder. He called it Bethel, "the house of God." How ironic that in the Book of Ruth, a great famine takes place in a town named Bethlehem, which means "the house of bread." The angel Gabriel tells Joseph, "You shall call him Jesus, for he shall *save his people*" from their sins. Later in that same passage, Gabriel quotes the words of Isaiah 7, which say, "They shall call his name Immanuel, which being interpreted is, *God with us.*"

In the Book of Hosea, the names assigned to the children born to Gomer carry great significance in terms of Israel's unfaithfulness to God. The name Isaac, given to the child born to Abraham and Sarah, is itself a reminder of their first response to the idea that she could bear a child in her old age. Before the name Israel was used to identify a national group or the region of the world in which Jewish people lived, it was the name given to Jacob on the night he wrestled with God in Genesis 32:28.

The given name of the apostle Peter was Simon, but Jesus changed it to Cephas. Both names, Cephas and Peter, carry the same meaning: a stone. However, the two words derive from different origins, Cephas from Aramaic and Peter from Greek. Places such as Tiberias and Caesarea, frequently referenced in the New Testament, are reminders of the status of Palestine as a province in the Roman

Empire. Not every proper name or place will carry significance so far as a deeper understanding of the passage is concerned. However, the preacher needs to keep in mind that every passage ought to be studied with this step in mind. You never know when a name like Moses or a place like Golgotha will be mentioned.

Preaching to the mind of the listeners

Obviously, any preacher who has been through this *Language* process over many years of preaching and preparing to preach will become conversant with these kinds of issues, and much of what is discussed in this chapter and throughout this book can be assumed. However, the entire exercise remains important as a reminder to the preacher that his or her knowing this information is not the point. The ultimate issue is whether or not the people in the congregation understand these terms. It is better to review what some may already know, than to assume that the majority of one's listeners have knowledge that they may not possess.

As an analogy, preachers ought to consider the work of newspaper and magazine writers and editors. It has been suggested that those publications gear their writing style to those who can read at a seventh or eighth grade reading level. Obviously, there are many persons who will read these publications whose reading level, vocabulary, and mastery of complex sentences is vastly superior to that of an eighth grader. Nevertheless, the paper or magazine is written with that level of knowledge in mind.

This is not an insult to the reading skills of the general public. Rather, it is a concession to the fact that the vast majority of the words a person needs to function in our society, except for selected technical terms and phrases that may vary according to region or vocation, have been mastered by the eighth grade. Preachers should approach their sermons with a similar assumption. We should not assume a broad understanding of even the most elementary aspects of biblical knowledge or theological language. As my friend, Otis Moss Jr., often says when he is listening to someone preach, our task in every sermon is to *"make it plain!"*

SERMON PREVIEW

The sermon at the end of this chapter will serve two purposes. First, it will demonstrate how one passage of Scripture (Matthew 1:20-25) is informed by another passage (Isaiah 7:14). Secondly, it will also demonstrate that preachers must deal with the central, though sometimes difficult and controversial passages of Scripture that offer insights into our comprehension of the nature and ministry of Jesus. This sermon also observes how our understanding of a passage of Scripture can depend entirely upon our translation and understanding of a single word in the passage.

THE BIRTH THAT BAFFLES THE MIND: THE PROPHETS FORETOLD HIS BIRTH

ISAIAH 7:14

One of the classics of American literature is *The Education of Henry Adams*. This book is about the early life of the young man who was the son of President John Quincy Adams and the grandson of President John Adams. He entered Harvard University in 1855, and his father gave him one single challenge. It was his responsibility to learn everything that was known. That did not mean learn everything that one could about a particular area of study. Henry Adams was challenged by his father to learn *everything that was known!*

Even in 1855, that would have been a formidable challenge. How much more of a challenge it would be today. Over the last two decades, human knowledge has exploded to the point that what is break-through research today, is old news by next week. You could attend school every day of your life, and you still could not begin to grasp everything that is now known in a single field, or within a single culture. How much less can anyone today expect to learn everything that is known.

When Howard Thurman was a college student in the 1920s, he read every book in the Morehouse College library. Could you imagine any one person reading every book in the college libraries of today? I remember visiting my own college campus several years ago, and browsing through the library. I ran across a book by Paul Tillich, one of the greatest theologians of the twentieth century. In the back of the book was the slip that indicated the list of persons who had checked that book out of the library. My name appeared as an entry in April of 1969. That book had not been checked out again in the intervening twenty years. There is so much information that is coming at us every day. It is absolutely impossible for one person to learn everything that is known by today's standards of human knowledge.

However, let us suppose that whether in 1855 or 1998, one person could somehow get a grasp of all human knowledge. There would still remain some things that the mind cannot comprehend, science cannot

---

This sermon was preached by the author on December 6, 1998, at Antioch Baptist Church in Cleveland, Ohio.

resolve, and research cannot discover. The Bible is full of such things. Has it ever occurred to you that the Bible is full of claims that are absolutely mind-boggling? Perhaps we have been listening to and reading the Bible for so long, that we no longer hear what it really says.

Consider these few examples of things the Bible says that I very much doubt that the human mind can understand. The Bible says that God made the earth and the farthest expanses of the universe in six days. Humans cannot reach the planets in this solar system that are closest to us, and we cannot even see the planets in the most remote portions of the universe. And yet we say with a casual tone in our voices that God made all of this in six days. The Bible says that God split open the Red Sea so the people of Israel could escape the onrushing chariots of the Egyptian army, passing through the parted waves as on dry land. The Bible says that God caused the sun to stand still for twenty-four hours so Joshua could finish fighting a battle.

There are several ways by which we can respond to such assertions. We can, as many people do, dismiss these claims as mythology, or hyperbole, or poetic license. We can insist that these claims should not be taken literally, but should be read through the lens of critical thinking, and, as a result of that, they should be viewed as less than factual. There is, of course, another possibility that modern men and women may not want to entertain. It is possible that there simply are some things that are not known or knowable, so far as our minds are concerned.

These mind-boggling claims continue in the New Testament. The Bible says that Jesus walked on the water, fed five thousand with two fish and five loaves of bread, and healed the sick and gave sight to the blind by the mere laying on of his hands. Most mind-boggling of all, the Bible says that Jesus was born of a virgin at the beginning of his life and was raised from the dead at the end of his life. It does not matter if you and I, like Henry Adams, set out to learn everything that is known. Here are two claims that we will never be able to fully comprehend. These things lie outside the realm of information and dwell in the region of mystery and miracle.

I have discovered that the best discussions about the Bible and religion do not take place anywhere in the church. They take place in barbershops and beauty parlors, where armchair philosophers decide, based upon their own finite knowledge, what are those things which God is capable of performing. These discussions take place with taxi drivers, who, because they know their way around the city, also presume to know their way around the mysteries of the universe. How many times have I heard people in such places assuring me that the claims of the Bible are not true? "I just don't see it," they tell me. "You will never be able to convince me of that," they declare. "There is no way in the world that can be true," they insist. Yet, with their words echoing in our ears, we must find a way to respond to two of the incredible claims of the Bible. One is that Jesus was raised from the dead. The other is that Jesus was born of a virgin.

In 1 Corinthians 15, Paul makes a case for why the belief in Christ's resurrection is central to Christian faith. Paul says that if Christ has not been raised from the dead, then you and I are still in our sins. Worse yet, if God did not raise Christ from the dead, then there is no possibility that we can be raised after we die. Our eternal life with God hinges upon our acceptance of the resurrection of Jesus.

Something equally important is involved in our belief that Jesus was born of a mother who was, at the time she gave birth, still a virgin. Let the wonder, the mystery, the incomprehensibility of this baffling claim settle in upon your minds today. According to Matthew 1:18-25, when Jesus was born, God was bringing to fulfillment an Old Testament prophecy found in Isaiah 7 that said, "A virgin shall conceive and bear a child." This is a birth that has baffled our minds.

Many of us cannot get any further than the seeming inconsistency between the King James Version and the Revised Standard Version. The KJV says, "A virgin shall conceive and bear a child." The RSV says, "A young woman shall conceive . . . ." The RSV is an accurate translation of the Hebrew word, *alma*. For those unable to accept the possibility of a miracle, this "young woman" translation is a way out. Under this scenario, Mary did not have to be a virgin, only a youthful girl, married or unmarried. The possibility of two human parents now enters in, and God is no longer necessary. Problem solved. Case closed. Science triumphs over faith once more!

However, the claim of virgin birth is not, should not, be easily dismissed. There is more at stake than whether or not a Hebrew word has been properly translated. Our whole sense of the ability of God to perform works that we simply cannot understand is also at stake. Today, I want to offer several reasons why you and I ought to build our hopes upon this baffling claim that our minds could never comprehend. First,

I want to suggest that the virgin birth points us toward the mystery that surrounds God. Second, I want to suggest that the virgin birth points us to the absolute majesty of God. Finally, I want us to see that the virgin birth is a central part of the mission of God. You and I may never fully understand the virgin birth, but our entire faith structure is balanced upon our willingness to believe that such an event did occur, and that it occurred for a reason that effects your life and mine.

Consider this first point, that the virgin birth points to the mystery that surrounds God. There are some things about God that we not only do not know, but that we cannot know. God's ways are not our ways, says Isaiah 55, and his thoughts are not our thoughts. This is what God was explaining to Job in the thirty-eighth chapter of that book. Job kept complaining to God about his situation. He kept asking God to explain to him why certain things were happening. Job could not live without knowing the answers to every question. He could not live in that state expressed so powerfully by the late black poet Margaret Walker. In her classic poem, *For My People*, she said that once there was a time when black people "did not know the people who, or the places where, or the reasons why." That was a state in which Job seemed unprepared to live. So he demanded that God explain God's self.

Rather than answer Job's questions, God asks Job to prove that he is qualified to have a question and answer session with the maker of heaven and earth. God begins by asking Job, "Who is this that darkeneth counsel by words without understanding?" That is a short-hand way of telling Job that he was asking questions the answers to which his mind could not comprehend. Job was in over his head and out of his league. "Where were you, Job, when I laid out the foundations of the earth? Where were you, Job, when I put water in the clouds? Where do I keep snow in the summer? Answer if you know!"

For one long chapter of forty-one verses, God reveals to Job that there are some things about God that humanity will never be able to understand. God tells Job, "I bet you can't tell the lightning bolts when to flash across the sky. I bet you can't command the sun to shine, or rain to fall, or the lion to roar." God tells Job that only God who was present on the day of creation knows these things, and Job was not there. As a result, Job, and you and I, must accept the mysteries of God.

The virgin birth is one of these mysteries. I do not know how it happened. I do not know how a girl who has never been with a man can suddenly conceive and bear a child. But I am prepared to accept by faith what my mind cannot understand by facts. I can live with the words of Paul in 1 Timothy 3 where he says; "Deacons should be able to hold the mystery of the faith with a clear conscience." I should be able to tell people that there are some things about God I absolutely do not understand, and not be ashamed or embarrassed in saying so.

However, just because I do not understand it does not mean that God cannot accomplish it. There is not only the mystery of God attached to the virgin birth; there is also the majesty and matchless power of God. There is nothing that God cannot do, even when he has nothing to work with in the way of materials or ingredients. In our Wednesday night Bible class we are studying Genesis. Presently we are dealing with the incredible promise that God made to Sarah and Abraham that she would conceive a child in a barren womb, and give birth to a child at ninety years of age. Upon hearing that announcement, the Bible says that both Abraham and Sarah laughed at such an idea. Their lack of belief caused God to ask this question, "Is anything too hard for God?" What can God not do? In fact, Sarah did give birth to a son named Isaac. That name in Hebrew means, "she laughed." Every time Sarah and Abraham called the name of their son, they were reminded of the promise and power of God, and the fact that they did not believe it could be done. "Is anything too hard for God?"

Look at the virgin birth, and then look at the problems and needs of your life, and see that nothing you face is too hard for God. As long as you are alive in this world, nothing is too hard for God. Are you sick? God has healing power. Are you alone? God can be a friend who sticks closer than any brother. Are you unhappy in your spirit? God can comfort your soul and set joy bells ringing in your heart. Nothing in this life is too hard for God. God can feed the hungry. God can dry the tear-stained eyes of those who mourn. God can rescue the lost and return the wandering prodigals back to their fathers' houses. I ask again: "Is anything too hard for God?"

Moreover, even when you die there is nothing too hard for God. The Bible tells us that God is sovereign over life and death. God can watch over us while we live on earth and unlock the gates of hell and the doors of death to rescue us even after life in this world is over. "One glad morning, when this life is o'er, I'll fly away. To a home on God's celestial shore, I'll fly away." Jesus did raise Lazarus from the dead. God did raise Jesus from the dead. One day, at the command of Jesus, we who have confessed faith in that name will also be raised from the dead. Can you not envision the scene as found in 1 Thessalonians 4?

> *For the Lord himself shall descend from heaven with a shout*
> *with the voice of the archangel, and with the trump of God:*
> *and the dead in Christ shall rise first.*
>
> *Then we which are alive and remain shall be caught up . . . to meet*
> *the Lord in the air: and so shall we ever be with the Lord.*

I do not know how it will happen. I only know that because of God's miracle-working power, there is nothing that is too hard for God.

That is what the virgin birth declares, that nothing is too hard for God. And what I like about it is that God can do anything even when there is nothing to start out with. With nothing in God's hands, God made the heavens and the earth. With nothing in God's hands, God fed Israel in the desert for forty years. With nothing in God's hand, God clothes the lilies of the field and feeds the birds of the air. The majesty and power of God are made obvious by the fact that God can start with nothing and make something.

Many of you may know that Louise Battle is a great cake maker. She makes cakes for all occasions, and she gives cakes away all the time. No sooner have I eaten her last cake, than she is bringing another bag full of more cakes. Suppose I were to ask her to make a cake without using any ingredients? Suppose I was to ask her to make the biggest, best cake she ever made, but to do it without milk or butter or sugar or flour? As good as Mrs. Battle is at baking cakes, she has to start out with something in her hands.

Not so with God. God can do the best work, often while beginning empty-handed. In the virgin birth, God did not need a man. God did not need Joseph. God did not need any human assistance. When God went to work to accomplish our salvation, God did not ask for our help. The virgin birth of Jesus is another instance of the power and majesty of God who can start with nothing and make something wonderful and grand.

Finally, the virgin birth points us to the mission of God. The Bible teaches that you and I are born into a cycle of sin. We are inclined toward disobedience and disbelief. We are prone to wander away from God. By nature we are selfish and cynical. It is for that reason that Jesus tells Nicodemus that "you must be born again." We need to be saved from the penalty of sin, which is death. We need someone who can take that penalty upon himself. We need someone who is not guilty, who can stand before God and plead our case. In the language of the Old Testament, we need an unblemished lamb that is worthy to take away our sins.

Who is worthy for such a task? Romans 3:23 tells us that "all have sinned, and come short of the glory of God." Who is worthy to stand before God? Psalm 51 says, "I was shapen in iniquity; and in sin did my mother conceive me." If all of us are guilty of sin, who can stand outside the problem and save us from sin? The virgin birth answers that question. By being born without a human father, but being conceived by the Holy Spirit, Jesus was born outside the inheritance of sin. Hebrews 4:15 says that Jesus was like us in all ways except one: he was without sin. He was qualified. He was worthy. He was the unstained and unblemished lamb of God who could take away the sins of the world.

That was God's mission, to send someone who would shed his blood and wipe our sins away. That was God's mission, to restore us to a right relationship even though we had sinned. That was God's mission, to provide someone who could do for us what we could not do for ourselves. And so, says Revelation 5:12, "Worthy is the Lamb that was slain to receive power, and riches, and wisdom, and strength, and honour, and glory, and blessing."

The virgin birth cannot be explained or understood; it can only be received by faith. But it is a necessary part of our faith because it opens the door to a wider and deeper understanding of the nature of God. It points to the mystery that surrounds God. It points to the majesty and power possessed by God. It points to the salvation and redemption mission that caused Jesus to come into the world. "A virgin shall conceive and bear a child." The issue is neither the virgin nor the child, but the God about whom it is fair to ask, "Is anything too hard for God?"

5
The 8 Ls:
Location

The next step in the process of biblical analysis is the study of the location in which the text is set. The biblical story does not unfold within a single physical location. The events recorded in the Bible take place not only in Palestine, but also in North Africa, Asia Minor, Southern Europe, the Fertile Crescent, and the entire Mediterranean region. The stories found in the Bible take place in locations that need to be considered if the full meaning and message of the text is to be grasped. This chapter will help the preacher understand the importance of determining both the physical and social location within which the text under review is set.

Where is the biblical story set?
The Bible takes the reader to the tops of mountains where Elijah contends with the priests of Baal and where three disciples observe the Transfiguration of Jesus. We are taken to remote desert regions where Jesus is tempted by Satan and where the wife of Lot is turned into a pillar of stone. We go out onto windswept seas where Jonah is running away from an assignment in Nineveh, and where the disciples find themselves about to sink in a storm on the Sea of Galilee. We travel along twisting roadways between Jericho and Jerusalem where a beaten man is eventually rescued by a Good Samaritan, and between Tekoa and Bethel where Amos has been sent with "the word of the Lord."

The Bible takes the reader into a dark garden called Gethsemane, and into an even darker prison in Philippi, and in both places prayers can be heard. The Bible takes us among the sheep with David, into the pigpen with the prodigal son. It takes us along the streets of Gaza with Samson, to the Persian court with Esther, and by the banks of the River Chebar in Babylon with the exiled people of Israel. We also journey through Samaria with the followers of Jesus, to Crete with a preacher named Titus, and to Rome where Paul plants a church and loses his life. The Bible cannot be fully understood without playing close attention to issues of location.

A brief review of any well-known Bible story will reveal how important it is to pay attention to this issue of physical location. It would be important to have some idea of where Ur of the Chaldees is located if we are to appreciate how far the family of Abram had to travel on their way to Canaan. If God called Jonah to a preaching ministry in Nineveh, then what can the reader assume when Jonah boards a ship in Joppa and sails off to Tarshish? Every Christmas we are reminded that Mary and Joseph made the journey from Nazareth to Bethlehem. Considering the fact that Mary's baby was due at any time, just how far did they have to travel and over what kinds of roads? In the Book of Revelation, John says that he was on the Isle of Patmos. It is important to know that unlike the Greek Isles with which we are familiar today, during that period in history Patmos was a penal colony, much like Devil's Island or Alcatraz. Very often the power of a biblical text is unleashed when the physical setting in which the text occurs is described.

Social location

However, the preacher is not simply in search of the physical location of a given biblical text. It is just as important to understand the social location as well. This is what is meant by the term *Sitz em Leben*, or the social, political, and cultural context in which the people and events are set. Bear in mind that just as the Bible did not occur in a single physical location, it also did not unfold within a single social location. The Bible takes its readers on a two-thousand-year journey that stretches from the call of Abraham around 1800 B.C. to the emergence of a thriving Christian community by A.D. 100. It is almost impossible to comprehend how many social, political, and cultural changes occurred during that period of time.

Israel: From the nomadic era through the conquest
Parts of the Bible describe the people of Israel when they are a wandering band of Bedouins traveling down into Egypt from Canaan to avoid a great famine. The story then shifts social location, and that same group of people spends the next 430 years living as slaves in Egypt. Another shift occurs when Moses leads them out of Egypt and brings them to Mount Sinai where they become the covenant people of God. Following a forty-year trek through the wilderness, they enter into the land of Canaan and gradually become settled there as a tribal confederation.

The preacher needs to consider whether or not any issues of social location may inform the meaning and message of the text being considered. The physical and social shifts related to this part of the history of Israel are both rich and intriguing. Here one finds the story of Joseph, through whom God works to keep the promise that Israel will be a great nation, just when it seems that once again there is no way the nation can survive. Israel enjoys a kind of "favored nation status" during the lifetime of Joseph and the Pharaoh who invests authority in Joseph.

However, there soon comes to the throne of Egypt "A king that knew not Joseph," and suddenly Israel's fortunes are reversed. They go from being welcomed guests in Egypt, to being perceived as a dangerous internal threat. They are viewed as unwanted outsiders, reduced to the status of permanent slaves, and they remain in that status for 430 years. That long period of slavery is followed by the wondrous display of divine power manifested in the Exodus.

One hears the echoes of this shift in physical and social location in the dramatic images found in Deuteronomy 26:5-9,

> A wandering Aramean was my father; and he went down into Egypt and sojourned there, few in number; and there he became a nation, great, mighty, and populous. And the Egyptians treated us harshly, and afflicted us, and laid upon us hard bondage. Then we cried to the LORD the God of our fathers, and the LORD heard our voice, and saw our affliction, our toil, and our oppression; and the LORD brought us out of Egypt with a mighty hand and an outstretched arm, with great terror, with signs and wonders; and he brought us into this place and gave us this land, a land flowing with milk and honey. (RSV)

As the preacher prepares to deal with any aspect of this epic saga, he or she needs to be immersed in the drama and triumph of this story. Where is Israel in terms of the journey along which God is leading them? It is a long way from wandering through Canaan during the lifetime of Jacob to being established in that same land some five hundred years later during the lifetime of Joshua.

From confederation to the United Kingdom

Issues of physical and social location continue during the next two-hundred-year period when Israel evolves from being a loose confederation of twelve tribes to becoming one of the major economic and political powers in its region. Leaders emerge within the nation. First are judges like Deborah, Jepthah, Gideon, Samson, and Samuel. Then come great kings like Saul, David, and Solomon. The nomadic life is exchanged for that of a notable nation-state with a government to manage, foreign affairs to be negotiated, and the political intrigues of a royal court to shock and delight the reader at every turn.

How far has Israel traveled in this short period, not just in terms of miles, but in terms of its social, political, and cultural evolution as well? No longer content to live within the framework of a tribal confederation, Israel urges Samuel to appoint someone to become its king so Israel can be "like the other nations." Of course, that was a complete failure to understand Israel's role. God did not want Israel to be like the other nations. God wanted Israel to be "a light to the other nations." This poignant shift in national self-understanding is captured in 1 Samuel 8:4-7, which says:

> Then all the elders of Israel gathered together and came to Samuel at Ramah, and said to him, "Behold, you are old and your sons do not walk in your ways; now appoint for us a king to govern us like all the nations." But the thing displeased Samuel when they said, "Give us a king to govern us." And Samuel prayed to the LORD. And the LORD said to Samuel, "Hearken to the voice of the people in all that they say to you; for they have not rejected you, but they have rejected me from being king over them." (RSV)

From then on, Israel's national life was dramatically transformed, beginning with the many ways that monarchs would exploit them, as God told Samuel to warn them in 1 Samuel 8:8-18.

From the end of the United Kingdom until 586 B.C.

The reigns of Saul, David, and Solomon became the golden era in Jewish history. The nation would never again enjoy the power and prestige it knew during the time of their rule over a united Israel. The once great nation split following the death of Solomon. Rehoboam, the son of Solomon, and Jeroboam, one of Solomon's most trusted servants, became rulers over separate portions of Israel. The division of Israel is foretold to Jeroboam by the prophet Ahijah in 1 Kings 11:29-39. Jeroboam reigns over the territory occupied by ten of the twelve tribes of Israel, and his territory retains the name of Israel. Rehoboam is left with the people and territory of only two tribes, Benjamin and the tribe by whose name the smaller nation would later be known, Judah.

Following the division of the kingdom, Israel and Judah fall into the most tumultuous periods imaginable. As chronicled in 1 and 2 Kings and in 1 and 2 Chronicles, the nations go through a series of monarchs largely noted for their idolatrous practices, or for their attempts to reform the idolatrous behavior of their predecessors. National life becomes more important to Israel than obedience to the covenant they still claimed to have with God. Finally, the national life of Israel is ended when the Assyrian Empire conquers the nation in 722 B.C.

The southern kingdom of Judah lasts a little longer, but seems not to have learned much, either about God or itself. So in 586 B.C., Judah suffers a fate similar to Israel's. The Babylonian Empire not only conquers Judah, but also sends the nation into exile. The people of Israel, who were regularly reminded through their religious rituals of a time when they were homeless nomads, have become homeless once again. Their nation is conquered, their monarch taken in chains into custody; their temple is burned, their priesthood dissolved, their entire world turned upside down. Much of the Old Testament is colored by these facts, and the preacher needs to be sensitive to these issues.

CHAPTER FIVE

Israel and the empires of the Ancient Near East

As has already been implied, the history of Israel and the early church is played within the larger context of the rise and fall of a series of empires that directly impact upon the lives of the people of God. Already mentioned have been the Egyptians, Assyrians, and Babylonians. They were followed by the Persians, the Greeks, and finally the Romans. Not only do portions of the Bible take place in those locations, but the relationship of Israel or the church to these empires colors almost every aspect of the Scriptures. It is crucial that the preacher engage in this step of the process and pay attention to the physical and social location in which the text occurs.

The Persians end the forced exile and allow the Jews to return home and rebuild their once glorious city. As recorded in Ezra and Nehemiah, many of them do go back. However, after fifty years in exile, two generations of Jews have been born for whom Jerusalem is no longer home. They are members of a group that comes to be called "The Diaspora," Jews who remained outside of Israel, scattered in locations throughout the ever widening circle of empires. For them, to be a Jew no longer means living in a certain physical location. Instead, all one has to do is live by a certain code of religious conduct. The Temple of Solomon is destroyed, never to regain its glory, but the synagogue system is born.

The Greeks follow the Persians, and with them come the pressures of Hellenism. Hellenism, set in motion by Alexander the Great, sought to unite the various nations, tribes, and peoples within the empire by a common culture, including a common language and a common religion. The pressure to accept polytheism, and to abandon their single-minded loyalty to the one God they called Yahweh, had been the constant temptation for Israel. That was the essence of the warning given to them by Joshua before they crossed over the Jordan and entered into their Promised Land (Joshua 24:14-15). So, as the Book of Daniel indicates, by the time the Greek Empire was divided and Israel fell under the control of the Seleucids, Hellenism was being imposed under penalty of death.

For the next five hundred years, Israel struggles with wanting to be returned to its former glory under David and Solomon, while being solidly under the control of powerful colonizing empires with occupying armies. Here again, the preacher needs to be aware

92

of these changes in the physical and social location of the text in question. Many of the books included in the Minor Prophets are shaded by these realities. Some in Israel seethe over the presence of a foreign ruler, and resistance and rebellion is never far from their hearts. Others quickly learn to accept their new status, and accommodation soon leads to assimilation for them. Still others decide to wait for the coming of that one who will establish the Messianic kingdom. It is into this mix of attitudes and expectations that the Christian faith emerges and must be understood.

Location issues in the New Testament
Like the Old Testament, the New Testament also records events that took place within a variety of physical and social locations. Jesus was born in Bethlehem in the days of Herod the King. That is a physical and social location observation. Jesus was crucified in Jerusalem by order of Pontius Pilate, Roman governor of Judea. That, too, is a physical and social location statement. Paul was a Roman citizen from Tarsus who also studied with the famous Rabbi Gamaliel. Followers of Jesus were first called Christians in the city of Antioch of Syria. Paul had to struggle with people he called Judaizers who believed that Gentile converts to Christianity also had to conform to the requirements of the Law of Moses. In other words, they had to become Jewish in order to become Christian. These too are issues of social and physical location to which the preacher needs to be sensitive.

Scriptural analogies of location
1. The Exodus
Let us consider three significant biblical stories and demonstrate what they yield in terms of the issues of physical and social location. Consider first the Exodus, the defining event in the life of the people of Israel. First consider the distance that the Hebrews had to travel from Egypt to Mount Sinai, and then from Mount Sinai to the mountains of Moab where they caught their first sight of the Promised Land. That was an extraordinary long journey for so large a mass of people.

When you consider how hostile and desolate that region was for them, the Exodus story and the crossing of the wilderness takes on

93

added meaning. How hot was it by day as the people pressed their way across the desert? How difficult must it have been to travel by foot over terrain that was punctuated by steep mountains and jagged rocks? Attention to this kind of detail can make the biblical story come alive.

However, the story is not simply about distances traveled. It is also about obstacles overcome and hardships endured. It is about the Amorites and Amalekites who attempted to destroy Israel during that journey. It is about the constant anxiety over a source of food and water adequate for the number of people whose needs had to be met. The story is about leadership squabbles, and about people who wanted to stone Moses to death because the journey was far harder, and lasted far longer, than they had at first imagined. The preacher has not entered fully into the physical and social location of the Exodus story until he or she can make it easy for the listeners to understand why it was that Israel murmured against God and against Moses.

The Exodus is not a book in the Bible, or a story about an uncomplicated journey from Egypt to Canaan. It is a tangle of issues involving physical and social location. It is traveling to a land that you were told had been "promised" to you by the God of your ancestors. Upon arrival, you discover that the land is occupied by people who live inside of fortified cities whose size makes you seem like grasshoppers in comparison to them. It is about the struggle to forget about 430 years of life in a polytheistic and idolatrous country like Egypt, and take on the spiritual discipline of monotheism. It is about becoming the covenant people of God, and then learning that failure to live up to your part of the covenant can have costly, even deadly consequences.

At the same time, the Exodus is the story of God who does the most remarkable things in the most unlikely places. At one point in the journey God dries up the Red Sea so Israel can pass through and escape the onslaught of the chariots of Pharaoh. At another point in the journey, God causes water to pour forth out of a rock in the middle of the desert so Israel can escape the thirst that had nearly sapped their strength. God sends to the people manna and quail sufficient for each day as they travel through the wilderness. God calls Moses to lead Israel out of Egypt, but then refuses to let Moses enter into the Promised Land. Issues of physical and social location are central to an understanding of the Exodus, and of the rest of the Old Testament as well.

2. The Nativity Story

The story of the birth of Jesus is rich in issues of physical and social location. As was mentioned earlier in this chapter, there is the sheer rigor of an eighty-five mile journey, on a donkey, over rough terrain, while being "great with child." However, the story is far more complex. The journey is not voluntary but is required by the decree of Caesar Augustus, emperor of Rome. Thus, Israel is an occupied territory, subject to the whims of a distant ruler.

Then consider Mary, who had to deal with the Jewish law that required that a woman betrothed to one man but made pregnant by another was to be stoned. Imagine the scandal, the gossip, and the presumed infidelity that surrounded this event. Who in Nazareth, including Joseph, was initially prepared to believe that the child in her womb was the work of the Spirit of God?

There is much that can be learned from the physical and social location of the birth, not in the palace of King Herod, but in a stable in Bethlehem. The announcement of his birth was made first to the poor shepherds of the field, not to the scribes and Pharisees who, one would think, would have been anxious to hear that the Messiah had been born. But they would doubtless have disapproved of the circumstances surrounding the birth, and would probably have dismissed the whole episode as a foolish tale, if not outright blasphemy.

Finally, the birth of Jesus brings together a strange assembly of onlookers. Who are these three visitors from the East? They bear costly gifts, they are apparently conversant with the principles of astrology, and they have all come to "worship him." The events took place in a remote corner of the world, but they had been set in motion by Rome in the West, and the message ended up being carried by the three men to the nations of the East.

On the other hand, Luke says it was shepherds who came to visit the baby Jesus soon after his birth. These men of the fields were perpetually unclean from the perspective of Jewish religious law, because of their constant proximity to the dead carcasses of their sheep and their inability to leave their flocks and come to Jerusalem to share in the temple rituals. Yet, they made their living raising many of the sheep that would regularly be used as part of the system of animal sacrifice in the temple in nearby Jerusalem that was not more than five miles away. Did they know when they entered into that stable that they were entering into the presence of the Lamb of God who would forever take away the sins of the world?

The exegete needs to help the listener enter into every phase of this story. There are issues of politics, religious law, social class, and presumed infidelity. These things do not even include the weighty and theologically complex issues that touch upon this story, such as the fulfillment of prophecy and the Incarnation.

3. Paul's missionary journeys

Paul engaged in three missionary journeys. The third trip alone took him from Antioch in Syria to Ephesus, Galatia, Macedonia, Philippi, and back to Jerusalem. Not only should the preacher have some idea of where these places are located, but also an enhanced appreciation of what Paul endured in his three attempts to establish the Christian faith in locations throughout the Roman Empire. Those were grueling journeys by land and sea that took several years to complete.

During his three journeys, however, Paul did not simply travel from place to place, received by welcoming crowds in every city. The three missionary journeys of Paul are rich in lessons of physical and social location. He says,

> Five times I received forty stripes less one. Thrice was I beaten with rods, once was I stoned, thrice I suffered shipwrecked, a night and a day have I been in the deep. . . in perils of waters, in perils of robbers, in perils by mine own countrymen, in perils by the heathen, in perils in the city, in perils in the wilderness, in perils in the sea, in perils among false brethren (2 Corinthians 11:24-26).

Implicit in this passage is the fact that Paul traveled through regions rife with religious and ethnic conflict. The conflicts involved Jews and Gentiles, Romans and the subject people of their far-flung empire. More importantly, reviewing Paul's journeys points out the hostilities that Paul's message about Christ stirred up with Jews, Romans, and the Gentiles in almost every town he entered.

Consider scenes during Paul's journeys that are absolutely alive with issues of physical and social location. There is the Jerusalem Council where the requirements for the conversion of Gentiles was resolved, or so Paul thought. There is the midnight prayer service led by Paul and Silas in a Philippian prison after they had been beaten and chained to a wall. There is the near riot that ensued when Paul revealed the fraud that grew up around the goddess Diana in the city of Ephesus, and the scorn that Paul received when he attempted to challenge the religious practices he observed in Athens. For sheer drama, nothing can compare to the trials through which Paul passed before Felix, Festus, and King Agrippa.

Preachers need to help the listeners enter into these experiences with Paul. This is where Paul went. This is what Paul experienced. Early on in the study of any text, questions of physical and social location need to be considered. This step can quite often unlock rich possibilities for better understanding and for more effective preaching of the text. Not every text will yield as much in this regard, but every text should be studied with the issues of physical and social location in mind.

Modern analogies of location
As a way of illustrating the importance of studying the words of the Bible with an awareness of the location in which those words are found, consider the following familiar phrases spoken in more recent times.

1. Patrick Henry on the brink of the Revolutionary War
In 1775, Patrick Henry said, "Give me liberty or give me death." Taken by themselves, those words ring of a certain courage and conviction, but in the face of what? It is not until Patrick Henry's words are placed in the context of the revolutionary spirit that had gripped the then British colony of Virginia that the full power of his comments can be grasped. We need to hear him within his physical and social location.

2. Winston Churchill during World War II

In 1940, Winston Churchill said, "Never before in the annals of human history have so many owed so much to so few." For those who know the context of those words, they are a glorious tribute to the brave pilots of the British Royal Air Force who defended their country against the dreaded German Luftwaffe in the now famous Battle of Britain. Any attempt to explain the words apart from the context would result, perhaps, in some imaginative statement. But it would be far from the point that Churchill was trying to make.

3. Martin Luther King Jr. during the Civil Rights Movement

In 1963, Martin Luther King Jr. said, "I have a dream that one day my four little children will live in a nation where they will not be judged by the color of their skin, but by the content of their character." What brings those words to life is hearing them in the context of the great March on Washington and the energy of the Civil Rights Movement that was attempting to reverse three hundred years of racial prejudice and two hundred years of slavery in America. Dr. King is best understood only when his physical and social locations are considered.

These same principles that have been applied to statements with which many people are quite familiar, need to guide us in our understanding of a biblical text. They occur within a certain social, political, and cultural setting. Sometimes the fullest possible meaning of a text cannot be reached until these kinds of issues have been considered. Not every biblical text will yield as much at this point as some will, but no text is ready to be preached until this step has been taken.

Other aspects of social location

Social location is not only about political relations. It would involve issues of prejudice that marked and marred human relationships in the ancient world. In the Book of Esther, Haman hated the Jews and sought to have them completely destroyed. In the Gospel of John, a Samaritan woman reminds Jesus that Jews and Samaritans have nothing to do with each other. On the other hand, it is especially poignant to observe that when Jesus taught about what it means to be a neighbor, he talks about "The Good Samaritan," who does what neither a Jewish priest or Levite would do (Luke 10:29-37).

In Matthew 15, Jesus tells a Canaanite woman who comes to him seeking healing for her daughter that "It is not right to take the children's bread and give it to the dogs." In Numbers 12, Miriam and Aaron criticize Moses because he marries an Ethiopian woman. And in Luke 4, Jesus is very nearly killed by a mob because he implied that the love of God extended beyond Israel, and included both Syrians and Phoenicians.

Social location would involve issues of class and gender. It would ask the preacher to be sensitive to the presence of slaves, the treatment of women, the exploitation or callous neglect of the poor, and the despair and hopelessness that gripped such groups of people as lepers and the physically and mentally disabled. What exactly was Paul intending to say by his comments in 1 Corinthians 14:34 and 1 Timothy 2:12 about the role of women in the church? Social location is about Jesus who calls as two of his disciples, a Zealot named Simon and a tax collector named Matthew. That must have been the original "odd couple." Here was a man who was a sworn enemy of Rome now being asked to live and work with someone who had gathered the taxes that supported the occupying Roman army. Nevertheless, they were brought together by Jesus despite their intense ideological differences. I dealt with this very issue of social location involving the disciples of Jesus in a sermon entitled, "And He Called Them His Disciples," preached in Miller Chapel at Princeton Seminary, and printed in the February 1984 issue of *The Princeton Seminary Bulletin*.[1]

Social location is also about Paul, who was both a well-trained member of the Jewish elite but also the providential possessor of something that occasionally proved to be of even greater value to him: Roman citizenship. It is also about Jesus of Nazareth, and the question from Nathaniel, "Can any good thing come out of Nazareth?" I am especially sensitive to the repeated references in the New Testament to people from the African continent. There is Simon of Cyrene who carries the cross of Jesus to Calvary in Luke 23:26. There is an Ethiopian eunuch mentioned in Acts 8:26 and following, to whom Philip opens the meaning of the prophecy of Isaiah. At the end of this chapter I have included several sermons, one of which deals with Simeon the Niger and Lucius of Cyrene who are mentioned in Acts 13:1.

Preaching and the five senses

The best way for the preacher to bring the biblical text alive is to read it with all five senses at full alert. At this point in the process, the Bible is not meant just to be understood. It is now meant to be experienced. What is there in the text in question that can be heard, seen, tasted, felt, or smelled? This is how we experience our world most directly and most dramatically. We do not simply seek to *understand* everything intellectually. Some things can only be explained through the employment of the senses.

That is why Jesus tells so many parables. It was possible for him to explain the doctrines about which he was speaking through the use of rationale argument, but it was far easier to present that same material through the use of stories that allowed him to appeal to the senses. That is why so many of the very best preachers have worked hard to become excellent storytellers. That device helps explain the sometimes subtle issues being examined in this chapter.

What are the sounds that the disciples hear as the storm on the Sea of Galilee sweeps over them or as a crowd of five thousand experiences the miracle of loaves and fish? What can be tasted, such as the taste of the manna and quail in the wilderness of Sinai, or the best wine that has been kept until the end of the wedding feast in Cana? What scents can be imagined, perhaps in the pigpen with the Prodigal Son or the perfumed women with whom he had associated only a few days earlier?

What was it like to experience the Transfiguration of Jesus in Matthew 17? There was the brilliant light that flowed from Jesus, the presence of Moses and Elijah, the dark cloud that came down over the mountain, and the voice of God that spoke out of that cloud. When that full experience is set forth, it is little wonder that Peter said, "Lord, let's build three booths." Peter wanted to stay on what had become for him, "holy ground"; much as the burning bush had been for Moses. There is an old spiritual song that says,

I went to the valley, and I didn't go to stay,
But my soul got happy and I stayed all day!

That was the experience of Peter, and the preacher's task is to help the listener enter into that physical and social location. Only then can the full meaning of the text be grasped.

What were the range of emotions that flooded the heart and mind of Abraham as he went up Mount Moriah to obey God and sacrifice Isaac, and then came back down with Isaac at his side and a ram lying dead in Isaac's place? The preacher must help the listeners enter into both the physical setting and into the fullest possible understanding of the emotional issues that are being felt by the biblical characters. Attention to such details as these gives a depth and substance to preaching that is otherwise inaccessible both to the preacher and those who hear our sermons.

Tools for understanding the location

So far as understanding the physical location of the text is concerned, the exegete's best friend is the *Oxford Bible Atlas*.[2] It contains an invaluable collection of maps, along with commentaries and topographical charts that allow the preacher to clearly grasp the terrain of the biblical world and many of the political and cultural issues that prevailed throughout the biblical world at various points in time.

In addition to a good atlas, any of the major study Bibles will also provide the preacher with geographical and topographical helps. The most reliable of these study Bibles would be *The Harper Study Bible, The New International Version Study Bible, Schofield Reference Bible*, and the *Oxford Annotated Bible*. It would be difficult to fully comprehend how little ground Jesus actually covered, and how far Paul actually traveled without making use of an atlas. The enormity of the Roman Empire and the vastness of the Jewish Diaspora cannot be comprehended until they are considered with a map in one hand and the Bible in the other.

The land of the Bible is not just about geography (nations and distance), it is also about topography (mountains, rivers, valleys, and deserts). When leading a Bible study I often find it necessary to direct people's attention to the map of the biblical world. In order to help them find a location, like Ephesus, I instruct them on how to find the Mediterranean Sea or the Aegean Sea. I remind them that Israel is a strange mixture of terrain for such a small country.

101

It has majestic mountains and great stretches of plains. It has rich farmland and pasture, and not far away is the stifling heat of a blistering desert. The preacher should not only become thoroughly familiar with any geographical or topographical issues in the text. He or she should also take the time, away from sermon preparation, to learn as much as possible about the lands of the Bible. This will make the preacher a better Bible reader because the world in which the text is set will come alive before the preacher's eyes.

Another set of resources will prove to be helpful so far as the issues of social location are concerned. For Old Testament study, I turn to *Understanding the Old Testament* by Bernhard Anderson[3] and *The History of Israel* by John Bright.[4] For the New Testament, I continue to use *Understanding the New Testament* by Howard Kee, Franklin Young, and Karlfried Froehlich.[5] There is also great value in *Introduction to the New Testament*, by Willi Marxsen.[6] I strongly recommend *The Oxford History of the Biblical World*, edited by Michael D. Coogan.[7] For insight into the day-to-day lives of people in the time frames encompassed by the Bible, I recommend *Harper's Encyclopedia of Bible Life*[8] and *The Eerdman's Family Encyclopedia of the Bible*, edited by Pat Alexander.[9]

The Great Commission according to Acts 1:8

There is no passage of Scripture more demanding of a physical and social location analysis than the words spoken by Jesus to his disciples before his ascension in Acts 1:8. The Lord indicates the missionary nature of the church, and establishes a worldwide field through which the church is meant to travel. He speaks about four locations. First he challenges them to be his witnesses in the very city wherein he had only recently been crucified. He meant for them to bring the message of the Gospel to the center of Jewish life and culture. He then sends them throughout all Judea where a common language and theological vocabulary could be assumed as a basis for speaking about Jesus as Messiah.

The task becomes more challenging when he sends them to Samaria, the place he himself had avoided on more than one occasion. In fact, they might have remembered that earlier he had told them to "enter no village of the Samaritans" (Matthew 10:5). Now they are being sent to that ethnic and religious group that they had been indoctrinated since childhood to hate and despise. What must they have thought and felt when they heard those words.

Things get worse, however, when Jesus challenges his disciples to reach out to the whole Gentile world, including Greeks and Romans presumably, whose oppression of the Jews still burns in the psyche of their national pride. This was not just an unimaginable physical challenge, to reach the whole world for Christ. This was a major shift in religious focus for these men, most of whom were Jews who formerly had defined themselves by, even prided themselves on, not being a Gentile. Now they were being sent out to evangelize those people and nations. This is the essence of what is meant by the issues of physical and social location.

SERMON PREVIEW

I conclude this chapter with a sermon designed to illustrate how to be sensitive to the issues of location. It will deal with the Roman centurion who stands at the foot of the cross in Luke 23. The presence of that man is an example of both physical and social location. This sermon is also meant to illustrate the point that vast numbers of biblical texts are better understood when attention is paid to the issues of physical and social location. The questions of "who" and "where" are of great value when attempting to fully understand the meaning of a biblical text.

A REPORT FROM A ROMAN

LUKE 23:32-47

There are three men whose comments tower above all else that was said or done on that day at Calvary when our Lord, Jesus, was crucified. There is no more magnificent moment in all of biblical literature, perhaps in all of human history, than when Jesus shouts out from the cross, *"Father, forgive them; for they know not what they do."* Where is the grace and mercy of God more perfectly on display than when Jesus seeks pardon and forgiveness for those who are in the midst of putting him to death?

When it comes to high drama, what can beat the scene when one of the men hanging on the cross next to Jesus cries out, *"Lord, when you come into your kingdom, remember me."* In the words of this dying man are two of the great hopes of the Christian faith. The first is that, like this criminal, it does not matter how low we have fallen in life. You never fall so low that God cannot, or will not, reach down and lift you up again when you turn to God through faith in Christ. Certainly that was documented yesterday in the *Plain Dealer*, when it reported on a husband and wife who went from being drug users and dealers, to copastors of one of the fastest growing congregations in this city. You never fall too far from the reach of God.

The second lesson from this dying man is that it is never too late to come to Christ. I do not want to use the life of this man to suggest that we should spend all of our lives doing whatever we please, and then at the end, while lying on a sick bed, or waiting for our execution at the hands of the state, we suddenly give our lives over to Christ. I remember how many people who went to jail in the Watergate incident over twenty years ago, suddenly became very devout Christians. If they had accepted Christ earlier, the Watergate affair would never have occurred.

I would warn all of us against the example of St. Augustine, one of the early church fathers from the fourth century. He lived a rather wild and reckless life during his early years. Someone told him that he should turn to Christ and be saved from his sins. Augustine's response was, "Yes, but not now." Do not wait until you are in prison before you turn to Christ.

This sermon was preached by the author on September 6, 1998, at Antioch Baptist Church in Cleveland, Ohio, as part of the sermon series, "Conversations at Calvary."

But I do not doubt that you can be reached and saved in prison or anywhere else. It is never too late to come to Christ.

There is, however, one more moment that is just as powerful and just as poignant as the two moments when we (1) know that God will lift us and (2) when we know that it is never too late to come to Christ. That moment comes when the Roman centurion who was in charge of the detail of Roman soldiers that presided over the execution looks up at Jesus and glorifies God, and says, *"Truly this was a righteous man."*

Matthew and Mark report on the words of this centurion somewhat differently. They state that the centurion said, *"Truly this man was the Son of God."* Do not let the difference in the wording concern you too much. Matthew and Mark were written with a Jewish audience in mind. Their mission was to tell the story in such a way that Jews would come to the conclusion that Jesus was the long-awaited Messiah. When they report that the Roman centurion declared Jesus to be the Son of God, they were suggesting that even the hated Gentiles acknowledged what the Jews refused to accept: Jesus is the Messiah.

Luke, on the other hand, was written with a Gentile audience in mind. Luke was trying to explain who Jesus was to people who did not have a background in Judaism, and for whom terms such as Messiah would be of no importance. Luke knew that the larger world would not be converted to Christ if the only people who acknowledged him were other Jews. Luke needed a witness who would have credibility when the story about Jesus was repeated in places like Athens, Corinth, Ephesus, Antioch, and Rome. Who would have cared in places like that, if some dying criminal declared that Jesus was his Lord? Who would have listened in the Gentile world if the only people who had a positive thing to say about Jesus were his disciples, most of whom lived within twenty miles of where Jesus lived in Nazareth. Luke knew that somebody else had to speak that "good word" about Jesus, if the gospel was going to reach into the Gentile world. Thus for Luke, the issue is not the variation in what the centurion says. For Luke, the issue is that while standing at the foot of the cross, while presiding over the execution of a man that Rome had put to death, the Roman officer in charge of the execution declares for all to hear that *". . . this is a righteous man."* This centurion, a word which refers to one soldier who was in command of one hundred other soldiers, was praising God and paying honor to Christ by saying that he was *". . . a righteous man."* That phrase would carry great significance throughout the farflung Roman Empire.

It is this same logic that applies to why the early church needed the skills and talents of both Peter and Paul to be established. It is safe to say that if Peter had attempted to establish the church alone, it would have taken much longer. It might not have occurred at all. Peter was the right man to carry the gospel to men and women like himself, hardworking and plainspoken. But he would not have appealed to the rabbis and Pharisees. That required someone like Paul. Peter would not have been successful challenging the followers of other religions in Asia Minor and Southern Europe. That took someone like Paul.

Let this be the first lesson we draw from the words of the centurion. In God's attempt to win the whole world back to himself, God needs and uses the gifts and talents and positions of everybody. The world will not be saved by the efforts of those of us who are preachers. The world will not be saved if we are relying upon a process that involves those outside of Christ deciding to come inside the church and hear a sermon. The fact is, they are not coming. We as Christians will have to find ways to go out after them. We need Christians who work not inside the church, but inside of schools, and factories, and airports, and hair salons, and barber shops. The world will not be saved solely by the eloquence or earnestness of all the preachers who have ever lived. The world will be saved by the combination of gifts and talents that God has placed inside of every one of us. That means lay and clergy, male and female, black-white-Asian-Latino-Indian. Each one of us, in the places where we find ourselves each day, serve God best when we do what that centurion did: declare while we are on duty that Jesus is a righteous man.

This is the principle that informs most missionary efforts around the world. The day is long gone when people from one country and culture and skin color go forth to evangelize people of another country and culture and skin color. It is recognized that what missionaries from the United States can do best is train persons from within that country and culture to evangelize among their own people. Time and time again, I run into students at the seminary who have come from countries such as Rumania, Korea, Kenya, Taiwan, India, and various nations in the Caribbean and in Latin America. What a privilege it is, first of all, to be able to work with those students and equip them for ministry in places where I will never physically go. But what a wonder it is to see them get their degrees, and pack up their books, and go back to their native lands and announce that Jesus Christ is Lord. Think of it. In places where people practice everything from Buddhism, to Confucianism, to Islam, to Voo Doo, God finds and fixes just the right people from those cultures to go back into those cultures and preach the gospel of Jesus Christ.

That is the first thing I want you to notice about this Roman centurion. God needed his voice to be heard because there were people who would listen to him who would not listen to Peter, James, or John. And God needs every one of us in Antioch to let our voices be heard in praises to God and in honor of Christ. There are people who will listen to you, who will not listen to me.

Notice something else about this Roman centurion. He was willing to go against what all the other Romans involved in the death of Christ were doing. As Luke tells the story, this centurion was the only Roman in Jerusalem who speaks a kind or favorable word about Jesus. Even though he had to stand alone, he was still willing to stand up for Jesus.

Let's start with the Roman governor, Pontius Pilate. He was the one man in Jerusalem who had the power to prevent the crucifixion from ever happening. He could have kept Jesus from going to that cross. Do you see him wavering as he stands in judgment over our Lord? In his heart he believes Jesus to be innocent. On three occasions he states that he "finds no fault" in Jesus. By the way, I always find it interesting that while Peter denied Jesus three times, it was Pilate who three times defended him. But in the end, he exchanged his conscience and his own convictions in order to appease the people (Mark 15:15). It is Pilate who delivers Jesus to be crucified, even though he knew that Jesus was innocent. But he would not stand up.

It was Roman soldiers who flogged Jesus and put that crown of thorns upon his head. It was Roman soldiers who mocked him, put a soldier's purple cloak upon his shoulders, and laughingly called him a king. It was Roman soldiers who shaped the cross upon which Christ was crucified, and it was those same Roman soldiers who nailed him to that cross. It was Roman soldiers who gambled for his garment while he suffered on that cross, no doubt his groans of pain audible to their ears. Roman soldiers did it all. Yet, here is the centurion in charge of all of those Roman soldiers, who took his orders directly from Pontius Pilate, who stands up at Calvary and says that Jesus is a righteous man. With the other Romans standing around, he says what he believes to be true. He was not concerned that what he said might get back to Pilate. He was not worried about losing popularity with his countrymen who did not share his view of the man who had just died on that cross. Here is a most unlikely man, standing in a most unlikely place, saying a most unlikely thing: *"Truly, this was a righteous man."*

I think all of us would be much better Christians if we were not so worried about what others would think of us if we dared to speak about or act out our faith in public places. Let me remind you that there will be no stars in your crown in heaven just because you talk about Jesus while you are here in the church. Talking about Jesus while you are in the church is like Mark McGwire hitting a home run in batting practice. It may look good, but it does not count. What counts for Mark McGwire is whether he can hit that same home run when someone from the other team is pitching, trying his best to strike him out. What counts for us as Christians is what we are willing to say about Jesus when we leave the safe confines of our own churches and return into the larger world where men and women are regularly cursing the God we love.

You have often heard me refer to the man who used to stand outside of the department stores on Public Square sharing his faith with those who passed by. He would preach for a while and blow on his saxophone for a while. In rain, snow, or blazing heat, that man would be out on that corner telling others about Christ. I can still hear him. *"Young lady, do you know Jesus? Young man, have you been saved?"* One day he even saw me coming and called out to me asking if I knew Christ as Lord. I told him that I thought so, answering in a jovial manner because I knew the truth about my relationship with Christ. But he did not like my answer. *"You think so? Can't you be sure?"* Suddenly I found myself getting upset at this street-corner preacher challenging my relationship with Christ. I told that man with all the dignity I could muster that I was the pastor of Antioch Baptist Church. Without skipping a beat, he said, *"Very good, but do you know Jesus as your Savior?"*

What about you and me today? When will we ever have as much boldness and daring as that centurion at Calvary or that street preacher on Public Square? Or will we keep all of our best witness, our best testimonies, and our best confessions locked up inside this church? Praise God for men and women like the centurion who stand up and speak about what they believe even when no one stands up with them. We all should seek such faith.

Finally, while Luke reports the words of this centurion differently than do Matthew or Mark, let us be clear about what it is that this centurion is saying in Luke 23. When read in English, it sounds as if the centurion is saying nothing more than that Jesus was a good man. What comes to your mind when you hear these words, *"Truly this was a righteous man"?* Standing behind the English word is the Greek word *dikaos,* which means both "innocent" and "without sin." This Roman is declaring what Hebrews also declares, that Jesus is like you and me in all ways except one. He alone is without sin (Hebrews 4:15). While Jesus is hanging from the cross, accused of crimes against Rome, a Roman centurion announces that Jesus is without sin. All the charges were false. The trials should have never have been held. His hands and feet should never have been pierced with nails. His brow should never have been scarred by the sharp, brittle tips of thorns. *"This is a righteous man . . . innocent man . . . sinless man."*

In a sense, what the centurion says in Luke is not all that different from what he says in Matthew and Mark. They both suggest something about the nature and character of Christ. You and I, who stand in need of a savior, must be sure of who it is who is worthy to fill that role. Who is able to atone for our sins? We need a righteous and sinless man. Who is worthy to be the Lamb of God who takes away the sins of the world? We need a righteous man. Who is himself without sin, so that he can take all of our sins upon himself? We need that righteous man of Calvary. We need that Jesus who was crucified. We need that precious Son of God. We need that fairest of ten thousand, that bright and morning star.

Jesus is not just a good man, he is righteous . . . without sin. Jesus is not just a profound teacher of religion, he is righteous . . . without sin. Jesus is not just the founder of another religious tradition, he is righteous . . . without sin. One of the greatest hymn writers of all time was Fanny Crosby. Among the songs she wrote are, "Blessed Assurance," "Close to Thee," and "Draw Me Nearer." On her tombstone are written these words: "She did what she could!" What more could be said about any of us, than that we did what we could with what we had? I suggest that we apply these words to Jesus. He did what he could. He died so that we might live eternally. He did what he could. He shed his blood to wash our sins away. He did what he could. He was raised from the grave, and in so doing opened up for us a passageway out of hell and the grave so that we can find our place at the welcome table in the kingdom of God. He did what he could. He was a righteous man . . . sinless . . . innocent. On Calvary he did what he could, and even that centurion came to understand that what was being done was being done for him. Thank God for these *remarks from a Roman!*

6
The 8 Ls: Leads

This chapter will focus on the exegetical step I call *Leads*. This simply means that preaching is enriched when the preacher pays close attention to the words and deeds of and all the major characters in a given text. It will be argued that this is a valid principle of interpretation whether the character under review is the protagonist or the antagonist, the good-guy or the bad-guy, the hero or the villain.

Learning to preach from various perspectives

Many people have heard the parable of the prodigal son preached from the perspective of the younger son, the elder brother, and the father. The notion that each of them offers an important perspective from which that story can be more fully understood is beyond dispute. This chapter contends that the principle of multiple perspectives in a single passage can be extended to the entire Bible.

Why would the birth story of Jesus be told, and no one attempt to understand why Herod, a despotic monarch of the ancient world, would react as he did? Can we not learn something about the story of the Exodus by telling it from the perspective of the Pharaoh who had to bend his will to the will and power of the God of his own slaves? Who was Pontius Pilate, and how do we understand him as a political leader in the midst of the furor that surrounded the arrest, trial, and eventual crucifixion of Jesus? In other words, the truth of the passage can be reached not only by identifying with those persons who are considered to be on God's side, but also by viewing those same texts through the eyes of those who stood over against the will of God.

This chapter will also remind the exegete that many passages have roles that Hollywood or Broadway might refer to as "supporting actors and actresses." They are not the central characters in the story, but without them the story would lose much of its meaning. Anna and Simeon are not major players in the birth of Jesus, but their presence in the story is instructive. The women who grieved for Jesus as he carried his cross to Calvary through the streets of Jerusalem would fit into a similar category. So too would all of the names of people who were mentioned as sharing with Paul in his missionary journeys and his imprisonment: Silas, Barnabas, Luke, Timothy, and John Mark. Harry Emerson Fosdick preached a masterful sermon on Demas, one of Paul's on-again-off-again disciples.[1] There is much benefit to this kind of attention to detail. Thus, part of the study of any given biblical text is an analysis of the major and minor characters.

Preaching is greatly enhanced when it is remembered that much of the Bible can be read and preached from the perspective of more than one character in the text under review. This chapter deals with the search for *who*. Who said or did what? Who went where to meet with whom? Who is the person under review: a Pharisee, a harlot, a foreign ruler, or a disciple of Jesus? What do I need to know about that person or group of persons in order for the full meaning of their presence in the text to be appreciated?

Who is speaking to us from the text, a child, a parent, a sibling, or a spouse? Is it a friend or an adversary? Is it a prophet like Nathan confronting a king like David? Is it a prophet of the king, like Hananiah, confronting a prophet of the King, like Jeremiah? Who is the person whose actions are the center of attention: Zaccheus, Nicodemus, Bartimeus, Lazarus, or Barabbas? In preparation for preaching from a text, the preacher needs to consider all the characters included in the passage. More than that, the preacher needs to remember that the sermon can be preached from the perspective of virtually anyone who is present in that story. That is what my series on Luke 23:32-49, used throughout this book, is attempting to demonstrate. The sermon at the end of this chapter is another attempt to make the same point.

Another approach to developing a sermon series

Here, again, is the point first made in Chapter One in the discussion about *Limits.* The preacher does not have to limit himself or herself to just one character, and neglect to address the others. By taking a close look at every character present in the story the preacher has another opportunity to think about a series of sermons that move from one character and one perspective to another. This point bears repeating: namely, that developing a sermon series at one or more points during the year is a prudent approach to preaching. Rather than being viewed as a lazy approach to the work of the pulpit, it actually allows the preacher to maximize all of the results turned up by serious and deliberate biblical analysis. Beyond that, it establishes a sense of anticipation and expectation within the congregation as they look forward to the next sermon in the series as the weeks unfold. I say again, the series on Luke 23:32-49 went for ten weeks. The interest level for the congregation was as high at the end as it was at the beginning. And the need to do additional exegetical study and to envision both the structure and content of each of those sermons kept the preacher well focused for the entire time as well.

The parable of the good Samaritan

As an example of this practice of paying close attention to every character in a text and considering how the shape and insight of the text shifts when viewed from the perspective of each of those characters, consider the parable of the good Samaritan. In the process of doing a thorough exegesis of the passage one can consider from how many different perspectives that one parable can be told. To be faithful to the intent of the parable, which is to ask and answer the question, *"Who is my neighbor?"* one can see how the actions of various persons in that story shed light on the question raised with Jesus, and on the answer he provided. There are at least three leads, three characters, and three perspectives from which the issue of being a neighbor can be addressed.

1. The priest and the Levite
a. The heart versus the letter of the Law?
Jesus obviously is reacting with some degree of cynicism to the presumed piety and the apparent self-righteousness of the lawyer who asks the question, "Who is my neighbor?" Given the fact that the hostility between Jews and Samaritans was intense, it must have

been hard for this man to hear that a Samaritan would stop and help a beaten Jewish man after both a priest and a Levite had passed him by. How is it possible that a Samaritan would do for a Jewish man in need what two of the beaten man's own countrymen would not do? That observation becomes even more ironic when it is noted that the two men in question were religious leaders.

The preacher needs to discover how the role of the priest and the Levite had evolved by the time of Jesus. What were their duties, and might any physical contact with a man who might be dead in any way prohibit them from the performance of those duties? There is much in the Levitical Code that speaks about the ways a priest can become defiled, and thus render himself unable to perform his functions in the Temple. The man might have been dead, and so, their passing him by might have been based upon that fact alone, and their need to maintain ritual purity.

Was Jesus offering a subtle lesson in the difference between the spirit and the letter of the Law? Without a doubt, the priest and the Levite could quote all of the Old Testament laws dealing with mercy and compassion. But on that road between Jericho and Jerusalem, with the bandits perhaps still in the area, it was better to pass by on the other side. Jesus does not say that they were on their way to perform some ritualistic role. He does not say that the priest or the Levite had some urgent business that needed their immediate attention. All he says is, if you want to know who your neighbor is, look at who acted in a neighborly fashion to the beaten man. It was not the person you would have thought. A priest and a Levite certainly knew what their responsibilities were under the Law, but failed to perform them. It was a hated and despised Samaritan who demonstrated love and kindness. But surely the priest and the Levite had a good excuse. Or did they?

b. Racism and the lack of compassion on "those people"

Is it possible that the priest and the Levite passed the man by because he was not Jewish? The text does not say that he was. He could have been one of any number of racial or ethnic groups that traveled the road from Jerusalem to Jericho. Perhaps the priest and the Levite would have stopped if he had been one of them. Perhaps if they could have detected something of his identity without having to touch him, they would have known that he was a member of the household of Israel, and then they would have done what the Law required. But if he was just another (you fill in the blank), then let him just lie on the road and die!

There are many people in churches across the country and around the world who know what the Bible says, and can quote it at great length. However, they have a remarkable capacity to only allow their religion to influence them when a matter involves someone within their own racial or ethnic group. Their love and sense of accountability and responsibility do not extend beyond those boundaries of race or ethnicity.

My wife, Peggy, was born and raised in Elberton, Georgia. She always dreamed about getting married in The First Baptist Church of Elberton, Georgia. That is a classic Southern Baptist Church, with a towering steeple, great white columns, and a sweeping staircase leading from the church down to the street below. She had seen many bridal parties going in and out of that church over the years, and she wanted to be married there when her time came.

There was only one problem. My wife was African-American, and The First Baptist Church of Elberton, Georgia, did not allow black people to enter the church, except perhaps in some custodial role. She could not get married there because the church conformed to the social practice of racial segregation that gripped almost all of the southern United States. The language of Paul in Romans 12, that the church should "be not conformed to this world," did not seem to apply to most places where Christianity was practiced in the American South.

At the end of Chapter Three, I include a sermon entitled, "On Your Wall or In Your Heart?" based upon Psalm 119:11. While I have never been inside that church in Elberton, Georgia, to be sure, I would not be surprised if somewhere on one of the walls of the sanctuary or in the pastor's study there is some plaque quoting the words of Jesus or the Ten Commandments. I am sure the church has religion hanging on the wall. But whether it has ever penetrated their hearts is another matter.

I am intrigued as I drive through the South to notice yet another manifestation of "on the wall" religion. Almost everywhere one drives one sees Christian academies attached to local congregations.

115

I was at first amazed to notice how many of those schools were chartered and opened between 1958-1970. Then it dawned on me that most of those schools were opened as a way of providing white "Christian" families a way to avoid dealing with desegregation in the public schools as ordered by the 1954 *Brown v. the Board of Education* decision by the United States Supreme Court. Religion has certainly been tainted by the perverse influence of racism in this country. Might it have also been a factor in the parable of Jesus? Is that why the priest and Levite passed by on the other side?

Were the priest and Levite on their way to a larger event that made stopping to help that man a lower priority? Had they done their religious service for the day, and were now heading home for a well-deserved rest? Or did they just not care about the man? After awhile we see so much of that kind of thing, it no longer moves us. They might have been as numb to that experience as people in the twenty-first century have become when they hear about shootings and killings night after night on the evening news or when they read about violence in the headlines of the morning paper.

This kind of indifference to the heart of our religion is also at home in the black church. I remember hearing Dr. Martin Luther King Sr. (Daddy King), commenting on this passage in the context of his own experience one Sunday on his way to church in Atlanta. He said that he passed by a man who seemed in distress on the street. He decided to stop and help the man, but things got involved, he lost track of time, and by the time he finally arrived at church the service was nearly over. The deacons asked him, "Why did you miss church today?" He answered them, "I didn't miss church; the Lord and I had service with a man on the streets this morning."

c. Class distinctions?

Was their any class distinction at work in this story? After all, priests and Levites were a privileged group. They lived a fairly secure lifestyle. They may not have been any more interested in that man if he was in good health, but of a lower social class. Priests and Levites occupied hereditary offices. They came from the best families. They worked within the context of the central institution in ancient Jewish society. They might have seen that beaten man as just another day in the life of "the rabble of Palestine."

The preacher can find any number of ways to view the story of the Good Samaritan through the eyes of the priest and Levite who saw the beaten man but "passed by on the other side." Every church is full of people like that. There may also be far too many preachers like that, who see the wounded and battered people of the world, and for one reason or another just pass by on the other side. I speak to this issue in my book, *Preaching to the Black Middle Class.* There I contend that far too many black people who have reached middle class economic status respond in precisely this way to the impoverished black people who remain in an economic underclass despite the booming economy that has lifted so many people out of poverty in the last decade.

In that book, I state that I have come to understand the story of Dives and Lazarus in Luke 16 in two different ways. For most of my life, I heard that story preached as an indictment on a complacent white society that walked past and stepped over the oppressed and impoverished black minority. More recently, with the rise of a substantial black middle class, I read the story of Dives and Lazarus from another, more incriminating perspective. The rich man, Dives, is the prosperous and overly complacent black middle class, preoccupied with the pursuit of BMW automobiles and Rolex watches. The poor man, Lazarus, is the deeply impoverished black underclass, left behind and largely untouched by the Civil Rights Movement of the 1960s and the stock market boom of the 1990s. Trying to get this modern Dives to care about and show compassion for this modern-day Lazarus is no less difficult than it was in the days of Jesus.

However, the issue of class division is by no means limited to the black middle class or the white Southern church. Here in Cleveland, the vast majority of white Protestant, Catholic, and Jewish congregations have fled the city and moved to more spacious locations in the suburbs. Their decision to move may also be perceived as their desiring a safer location. Is this not another version of seeing the beaten man on the road, but choosing to pass by on the other side?

Who is my neighbor? The answer seems to be either who belongs to my congregation, to my social class, or whoever can afford to live in my section of the community. That is probably not the answer Jesus was looking for when he told this story. One thing is sure:

priests and Levites are still passing needy people by crossing over to the other side of the road!

2. The innkeeper
a. Hotel or hospital?

There is great potential for preaching this story by viewing it from the perspective of the innkeeper. In fact, I would argue that the innkeeper is the least studied of any of the possible perspectives, but may offer the greatest point of application so far as the ministry of a local church is concerned. The story of the good Samaritan, told from the perspective of the innkeeper, is a great way to challenge a congregation on the issue of what it means to be a good neighbor.

Consider that the beaten man was brought to the inn by the good Samaritan. Consider further that the innkeeper was only given two denarii (less than one dollar), and was asked to take care of a beaten man who needed everything from food to a place to rest and recover for a period of several days. The innkeeper was told by the Samaritan that whatever the expense for the care given to the man, beyond the two denarii already given, would be paid when the Samaritan returned that way again.

There are several thoughts that could have passed through the mind of the innkeeper that would be consistent with the overarching issue of "Who is my neighbor?" First is the issue of prejudice and hostility that defined Jewish and Samaritan relations. Could the innkeeper trust the Samaritan to keep his word and come back to pay the balance of the bill? The second issue could be just how long it would be until the Samaritan returned, and whether the innkeeper could afford to offer services and then wait for full payment. A third possibility is whether the innkeeper even wanted to take on such a responsibility. After all, he was running a hotel, not a hospital. His line of work was bed and breakfast, not bandages and blood. Was it not an act of neighborliness for the innkeeper to accept the beaten man, especially under the circumstances?

b. The local church as an innkeeper

The preacher can be especially helpful to any local church by simply drawing an analogy between the role of the innkeeper in this passage, and the role that most local churches are called upon to play on an almost constant basis. It is not a far leap in the meaning of the text, to go from the inn and the innkeeper to the church (pastor and congregation). Will we or will we not open our doors and our hearts to the beaten people of our society who are being constantly referred to us by people who often do not want to get involved themselves?

Someone is homeless! Send her to the church. Someone is hungry or unemployed, and needs something to eat! Send him to the church. Someone is addicted, intoxicated, abusive, or deranged. More than once over the course of my ministry, all of these people with all of these problems have presented themselves at the door of the church where I served, and I do not think I am alone in this experience. Even more frequently, when a solution to these problems is being sought after, I have heard people who belong to no congregation raise the question, "Why don't all of these churches get together and do something about this problem?"

c. What can you do with two denarii?

As often as not, churches do respond to the problems that present themselves at our doors. But then there is the problem of the two denarii. That is usually all we have to work with, the two denarii left by the congregation on the previous Sunday, the two denarii given by a foundation or other funding source who have convinced themselves that they cannot support a church, but expect the church to find a way to respond to the pressing problems all around.

Here in the Greater Cleveland area, churches house homeless families, tutor children who are lagging in their academic performance, provide testing and counseling in the area of HIV/AIDS, sponsor units of Alcoholics Anonymous, serve hot meals to impoverished people, offer free medical tests and treatments to the medically uninsured, and give emergency relief to people and families whose money has run out before the month has ended. They do all of this without huge grants either from any government sources, private foundations, or endowment funds left to the church. They do this with two denari; and the faith that next week the congregation will replenish the funds that have been exhausted.

What is happening here in Greater Cleveland is happening, I am sure, all across this country. Why do churches do such things? Why

119

should churches do such things? They do all of this, because, like the innkeeper, they want to show themselves to be a good neighbor. They do it, because they want to act out their faith. They do it, perhaps because a preacher has used the parable of the good Samaritan as an analogy for how a local church should respond to the people and problems that are brought to their door.

3. The Samaritan
a. Can any good thing come out of Samaria?

Why does Jesus refer to this Samaritan as *good*? Does the adjective refer to the kindness he displayed toward the beaten man on the road, or does it refer to the fact that during those days no Samaritan was ever considered to be *good*? In fact, the average Jew during the time of Jesus would have considered the phrase, *good Samaritan,* as an oxymoron.

Does the accent fall on what the man did or on who the man was? I suspect it is a combination of both issues, but what Jewish audience would ever have expected such an act of love and sympathy from such a man? Hearkening back to the comments of Nathaniel in John 1 when he asks, "Can any good thing come out of Nazareth?" The audience to which Jesus was speaking might well have asked, "Can any kind thing ever come from a Samaritan?"

b. Origins of the hostility between Jews and Samaritans

It would not be a shock if that Samaritan knew exactly how Jews at that time in history felt towards Samaritans. It would also not be surprising if he felt the same way towards them. After all, this was a hostile relationship that stretched back over hundreds of years. Jews and Samaritans, while all offspring of the twelve tribes of Israel, were divided by some deeply entrenched theological differences. The Samaritans of Jesus' day were the racially mixed descendants of those persons who were moved into the district of Samaria (2 Kings 17:29) after the deportation of thousands of Israelites by the Assyrians in 722 B.C., and those Jews who were never deported (Ezra 4:2). Their mixed race heritage made them unacceptable to those Jews who lived in Judea.

The Samaritans claimed to be the true Israel. They acknowledged only the Torah, the five books of Moses, as being authoritative. Hence, they rejected the authority of the history, prophets, and other writings of our Old Testament. They rejected the temple in Jerusalem as the center of religious life, and Jerusalem itself as their capital city. The Samaritans insisted that their capital was in Shechem, inside the territory of Samaria, and their temple was situated on Mount Gerizim.

As Leonard J. Greenspoon writes, "In effect, supporters of the Samaritan claim to be the true Israel were drawing from the same traditional sources as the Judeans, but with vastly different interpretations and consequences."[2] Greenspoon continues, and attempts to speak about this conflict from the Judean perspective. He says,

> From the Judean or Jewish perspective, two things were clear: God had chosen Jerusalem to be the site of his Temple, and, despite their claims, the inhabitants of Samaria were a culturally and religiously mixed people, not the homogeneous monotheistic community they claimed. A Judean text, 2 Kings 17: 24-44, provided crucial support for this position.[3]

He continues to lay out the historical basis of the conflict. He adds:

> When exiled Judeans or Jews returned from Babylon to rebuild their city, they brusquely rejected offers of help from the Samaritans, whose words of friendship they regarded with utmost suspicion. Nehemiah viewed with horror intermarriage between the son of a priestly family from Jerusalem and the daughter of a leading Samaritan family (Nehemiah 13: 28-29).[4]

It is probably safe to say that the typical Samaritan had been conditioned to think no more warmly toward Jews than Jews had been conditioned to think about Samaritans.

Now consider the parable of Jesus from the perspective of the Samaritan. Why should he stop and help that beaten man? The Samaritan would have been forgiven for saying to himself, "That man would not stop to help me, why should I stop to see about him?" Five hundred years of prejudice, feuding, contempt, and

CHAPTER SIX

conflict over the most central theological issues governed every encounter between Jews and Gentiles. The relations were so strained, that the Samaritan woman whom Jesus encountered in John 4:9, was shocked that he would even speak to her, not only because she was a woman, but because she was a Samaritan. She said, "How is it that you, a Jew, ask me to give you a drink, who is a woman of Samaria? For Jews have no dealings with Samaritans."

c. A Samaritan who did not conform to this world

Despite all the things that divided the Samaritan and the beaten man, their common humanity seems to have become the point of connection. Somebody was willing to step outside of the hundreds of years of enmity, and extend a hand of sympathy and support to a member of the despised group commonly referred to as "You people!" Obviously, telling a story about a *good* Samaritan stretches the idea of "who is my neighbor?" as far it could possibly go for the audience being addressed by Jesus. The preacher who wants to preach from this text needs to get inside of these hostilities and realize what a moving scene it is that Jesus sets forth when "one of them" shows kindness to "one of us."

In Romans 12:2 Paul challenges the followers of Christ with the words, "Be not conformed to this world: but be ye transformed by the renewing of your mind, that ye may prove what is that good, and acceptable, and perfect, will of God." Whatever other examples there may be of what it looks like to "be not conformed to this world," the actions of this Samaritan must certainly serve as a stellar example. If only African Americans who continue to view every aspect of their existence through the lens of hostility towards all white people because of slavery, could consider this passage. If only the white churches and synagogues that are fleeing the urban centers and relocating in suburbs where racial diversity is not an issue could rethink their white flight through the prism of this passage.

Can there be any more important message or challenge than this perspective in a world so badly divided by issues of race, class, and ethnicity? Preaching the story of the Good Samaritan from the perspective of the Samaritan himself opens a multitude of ways by which the issues of diversity, tolerance, and historic discrimination and prejudice can be addressed. We have all heard sermons that

122

applaud the Samaritan for doing what neither the priest nor Levite was willing to do. Taken a step further, we are challenged to "go and do likewise."

The beaten man

One of my faculty colleagues at Ashland Seminary, Dr. Kenneth Walther, reminds us that the most neglected perspective in this story is that of the beaten man around whom all of the action occurs. My teaching assistant, Pamela Hairston, has written a sermon from this perspective which she entitles, "A View From the Ditch." It must be conceded that viewing the passage from this perspective is far more speculative, and thus is open to far more distortion of the true message that Jesus was intending to communicate, namely, "Who is my neighbor?" However, having issued that caution, it is still possible to wonder aloud what might have been going through the mind of the beaten man as the other characters in the story come and go.

What might he have thought as he saw the religious leaders approaching the place where he lay? More interesting would be what he might have thought as he watched them pass him by on the other side of the road? His view toward the priest and the Levite is not unimportant, because it would probably echo the view that many in our society have toward the church and churchgoers. The modern church is constantly condemned and regularly criticized by people who argue that we too are walking by on the other side.

Those of us who do ministry in the inner city see people literally in the street every day. Homeless, addicted, mentally deranged, and without resources, it must seem strange to them to see us go in and out of church, driving past them in both directions. We typically say nothing to them, and should we have to walk past them on our way to the parking lot, we hope and pray that they say nothing to us. God forbid that they ask us for a dollar, or a match to light a cigarette, or a simple hello that acknowledges their humanity.

Most people who read this parable presume that they are the good Samaritan, always willing to stop and help a stranger. When this text is viewed from the perspective of the "beaten man" near us, that man may cast our compassion and mercy in a very different light. We owe it to ourselves to read the parable from this perspective.

The lawyer who asks the question

The final perspective from which the text can be preached, while keeping a focus on the question of "Who is my neighbor?" is the lawyer who asks that question in the first place. In doing this, we tie the parable back to his initial interest in what is required to inherit eternal life. This man correctly responds when Jesus asks him in Luke 10:26 about what is written in the Law. That is not surprising since knowing the content and various interpretations of the Law was his vocation.

In Luke 10:36, Jesus asks a very different question. Jesus asks him, "Which of these three do you think showed himself to be a neighbor to the man who had fallen among thieves?" The man's answer is very interesting for what he does and does not say. He does not say, "It was the Samaritan." Perhaps he could not bring himself to say or acknowledge something commendable about someone from that hated and despised group. Instead, he says, "It was the one who showed mercy."

Bad enough that Jesus portrays a Samaritan as the embodiment of being a neighbor, he also challenges the lawyer with these final words, "Go and do likewise." That was not what the lawyer wanted. He was not looking for a new assignment. He wanted to be confirmed in the level of religious piety he had already achieved. Surely he had memorized enough Bible verses, practiced enough spiritual disciplines, and tithed enough each week at the temple to be assured of eternal life. The last thing he probably wanted or expected was this challenge to stop quoting the Bible and start acting out its precepts and teachings in the city where he lived.

How content and self-satisfied he must have felt when he quoted the Law in verse 27, because in verse 28 Jesus responded by saying, "You have answered correctly. Do this and you shall live." I wonder how he felt when Jesus told this story in answer to his question and then challenged him to go beyond the form of religion in which he was entrenched and "do likewise"?

Did he take the step that Jesus was calling for? Or was he like the rich young ruler in Matthew 19:16-22, who also wanted to enter eternal life? When Jesus told him to keep the commandments, the young man answered, "All of these I have kept since my youth. What do I still lack?" Jesus challenged him to take another step,

124

and to sell all his possessions and give the proceeds to the poor. Hearing that, the rich man turned and walked away because he was rich.

How did the lawyer in Luke 10 respond when challenged by Jesus to "Go and do likewise"? We will never know the answer to that question. But that question becomes an effective point of transition from ancient Palestine to the present day. Having heard the parable preached from the perspective of the lawyer, the preacher needs to be sure to challenge the listeners to "Go and do likewise." Whether or not they accept the challenge is a good indicator of what that lawyer chose to do as well.

Summary

What I have demonstrated with the story of the Good Samaritan can be replicated with hundreds of passages throughout the Bible. Preaching can come alive when the story is told from a particular point of view. The more frequently people have heard a particular passage serve as the basis of a sermon, the more important it is to find new angles from which to approach those texts. I have certainly heard many sermons based upon the parable of the Good Samaritan. However, this chapter suggests that there are still several ways by which new insight can be brought to the question of "Who is my neighbor?"

SERMON PREVIEW

I end this chapter with a sermon from the Luke 23 passage that offers a perspective from the "the onlookers" on the events at Calvary. I share this sermon as a way of demonstrating that much can be learned when a biblical text is considered from the perspective of every person or group that is mentioned within its established limits. There is the possibility of uncovering some insights that might have been overlooked if one were only to consider the so-called major characters.

A WORD ABOUT THOSE WHO ONLY WATCHED

LUKE 23:32-43

Almost everyone who gathered at Calvary on the day that Jesus was crucified had come there for some significant reason. The Roman soldiers had come to perform the grizzly task of execution. They were the instruments of Roman justice. They nailed Jesus to his cross. They sat at the foot of the cross and made sure that the three crucified men were all dead before they returned to their barracks. Those soldiers had a reason for being at Calvary. They had a job to do.

The Pharisees and other Jewish leaders also had a reason for following Jesus all the way to Calvary. They wanted him dead. They wanted Jesus and his message removed from the scene. They believed that the teachings of Jesus were in conflict with Jewish law as passed down to them from Moses. More importantly, perhaps, they feared that if people began to follow Jesus in even greater numbers, continuing to call him "The King of the Jews," it might make the Romans suspicious and apprehensive. The Romans, not known for their mercy or patience, might just destroy the Jewish people if they felt they could not peacefully control them. For those reasons, and who knows how many more, they came to Calvary to see a man put to death who they saw as a threat to national security.

Many of the women who had followed Jesus all the way from Galilee, and at least one of the disciples of Jesus, John, were standing near the cross. We all know what brought them there. It was surely a mixture of grief that he was being killed, and shock and horror that their dreams of the return of the Messiah seemed to be thwarted. It would have been easy to pick them out of the crowd that stood beneath the cross of Jesus. While so many others were shouting insults at Jesus, this handful of followers were the ones looking up at Jesus through tear stained eyes. Grief and sadness had drawn them to Calvary.

Not all the Jewish leaders had come to celebrate the death of Jesus. At least two of them, Nicodemus and Joseph of Arimathea, were sympathetic to Jesus, may have even become believers in what he was

---

This sermon was preached by the author on July 26, 1998, at Antioch Baptist Church in Cleveland, Ohio, as part of the sermon series, "Conversations at Calvary."

teaching. They risked social and political consequences for carrying their concern for Jesus into that public place. No longer did Nicodemus come at night to speak with Jesus. According to the Gospel of John, Nicodemus helped to carry the body of Jesus to the tomb of Joseph, and brought spices to assist in a proper Jewish burial. Joseph and Nicodemus came to stand at Calvary because love drew them there.

However, there were some other people standing near the cross of Christ, and I cannot understand what they were doing, or why they had come. Luke 23:35 describes them this way: "The people stood by, watching." They had no particular mission at Calvary that day. They did not come out there to enforce the law, whether Roman or Jewish. They did not come out to taunt Jesus or hurl insults in his face. And they did not come to weep for him, or to bury his battered body tenderly and reverently when the crucifixion had done its ugly work. They came to Calvary as onlookers. They came to Calvary to watch. They had no stake in the transaction. It is hard to tell if they were emotionally involved at all. Were they a part of that Palm Sunday crowd, who now had come to see what had happened to Jesus in less than a week's time? Had these people gathered the day before in the courtyard in front of the Judgment Hall of Pontius Pilate and shouted to have Barabbas released and Jesus sent to the cross? Why did they come to Calvary on the day that Jesus died?

Perhaps they are like people in all generations who are drawn to spectacle, no matter what is going on. No matter what the tragedy may be, some people are going to stop and watch. Mind you, I did not say stop and help. I said they will stop and watch. How many people would you want to bet gathered as close as they could to the U.S. Capitol Building last Friday when a gunmen killed two people and wounded a third? When bodies were found lying in the streets of East Cleveland, there were people in the neighborhood who had gathered to watch. None of them, of course, had seen or heard anything, but they had come out to watch. For those of us who drive a lot, how many times has traffic been tied up, sometimes for miles, because an accident has taken place. While traffic can still get by, it has slowed to a crawl because so many people just want to take a look.

One of the most tragic aspects of America's racial history is the practice of lynch mobs. Between 1896 and 1930, more than 3000 black people, men, women, and children, were known to have been hanged from trees. It was not enough that first they had been beaten, that their ears had been cut off, or that the testicles of the male victims had been stuffed into their mouths, sometimes before they were killed. The worst part was that after all of that had been done to human beings, white people would actually come out to watch while black people were lynched. They packed lunches and took pictures of themselves standing next to the dangling bodies. I do not know why anyone would want to turn the torture and death of another human being into a spectator event, but there they stand at the foot of the cross of Christ. They are onlookers at a critical moment in history.

There are certain times and places when it is appropriate just to be an onlooker, to be in the audience, simply to watch what others are doing. The musicians in the Cleveland Orchestra do not expect that you will bring your instrument with you to one of their concerts and play along with them from your seat in the concert hall. That is a time to be an onlooker. When you go for a game at Jacobs field to watch the Cleveland Indians, you can bring along a glove just in case a foul ball comes your way. But it is not likely that the Indians' manager is going to call on anyone from the stands to come in to pinch hit or be a relief pitcher. There are times when all we are expected to be, when all we are allowed to be, is an onlooker. There are times when the 200 members of an orchestra can play while 2000 or more just look on. There are times when the eighteen players at Jacob's Field can play while 45,000 look on.

However, one's relationship to Jesus Christ is no occasion to be an onlooker. This is one of the experiences in life during which a person must not stand idly by while others are involved. The work of the church is no place for a few people to do all the work while all the rest just stand around like onlookers. Are you an active member of Antioch or just an onlooker? Have you decided to get involved in the programs and ministries of this church? Do you find yourself coming out to the church for more than just the Sunday morning service? Are you really a Christian, or are you simply an onlooker who is watching while others struggle to do the work of Christ? Around the cross of Jesus, people gathered for a purpose, whether they were Roman soldiers, Jewish Pharisees, or grieving friends and family. But then there were the onlookers. There were some people who just came out to watch.

I fear that far too many members of Antioch are like the people in

Luke 23:35; they are just observers. They are onlookers. They are content to watch while others do all the work. That is not what being a Christian is all about. Let me ask you to consider whatever organizations you belong to that you are truly passionate about and committed to. It may be a fraternity or sorority. It may be a college alumni group. It may be the Masons or Elks or Eastern Star. For some people it is a bowling league, a bridge club, or a travel group. With that organizational affiliation clearly in mind, ask yourself how much time and money you gladly invest in that activity. Then take the time and money you invest and compare that to the amount of time and money you invest in the life of the church beyond the Sunday morning service. It will quickly become crystal clear where it is that we are deeply involved, and where we are little more than onlookers.

Let me suggest several ways by which you and I can more easily determine whether we are onlookers or active participants in the church of Jesus Christ. First of all, think about our worship here at Antioch. Do you really come to worship and to praise God, or are you just an onlooker? The chief reason that we gather each Sunday morning is to worship and praise God. However, it does seem to me that far too many of us never enter into the spirit of worship. We are here, and the music is being lifted, and the word is being declared, and others around us are sharing in the experience, but some of us are just onlookers. We do not sing when it is time to sing. We do not support what others are doing. We are either reading the bulletin, or talking to our neighbor, or looking and speaking critically about what somebody else is doing as he or she attempts to worship God.

Second, you are an onlookers if you are not helping us to meet our financial goals for the church. If you come to church to receive a blessing, even if you praise God to the highest, you remain an onlooker unless you are willing to be a blessing by sharing in the stewardship needs of this church. We sit on a crucial corner in this city. We can have a significant ministry in this neighborhood and beyond. We are on radio and television six days a week. We house a hunger center, a Head Start program, three AA groups, an HIV/AIDS testing and information center, and we support domestic and foreign mission efforts to the tune of $65,000 each year. We operate other programs that keep this church open and busy seven days a week. It remains the case, however, that twenty percent of the members of this church are still providing eighty percent of the financial support. That means that so far as their stewardship and financial support is concerned, eighty percent of the members of Antioch are little more than onlookers. People come to church, but they do not worship with enthusiasm, and they do not give with generosity. They are still onlookers. They show up, but they let somebody else do all the work both in worship and stewardship.

Finally, unless you are willing to let the teachings of Jesus Christ, which are learned here, become the rules and guidelines by which we will live each day when we leave this sanctuary each Sunday, then coming to church is just a matter of observation. It is a sight-seeing tour. The essence of our faith as Christians is not observation but participation. It is not simply what we do when we gather in worship on Sunday. More important is what we do, how we live, the words we speak, and the attitudes we display as we move through the world each day. Let me challenge all of us to see this transition from sanctuary to street corner as the greatest indicator of our status as onlooker. What a shame it would be if we spent every Sunday listening to stories about Jesus and his followers and how they turned their world upside down. Then, when our time came to act we proved to be little more than onlookers.

Many athletes and others who have sought to live active lives have drawn strength from the words of President Theodore Roosevelt. In his early years, Roosevelt was somewhat weakened by physical ailments, but he overcame them and lived a rugged and active life. In a motivational speech to a group of young people, Roosevelt offered the following words. Let them be our words today, words that will protect us from being little more than onlookers in the church or in the world. He said,

> The credit goes to that man who is actually in the arena,
> Who strives valiantly,
> Who knows the great enthusiasms, the great devotions,
> Who spends himself in a worthy cause.
> Who at best, knows the triumph of high achievement,
> And who, at the worst, if he fails,
> At least fails while daring greatly.
> So that his place shall never be among those weak and timid souls
> Who know neither victory nor defeat.

Not everybody who came to Calvary came with a purpose or a point of view. Some just came to watch. They were onlookers at one of the greatest events in human history. Is it any different for you and me today? Are we actively involved as Christians, in our worship, in our stewardship; and in our service? If not, we are no better than those who, with nothing else to do that day, showed up and looked on at the crucifixion of the Son of God.

7
The 8 Ls:
Links

This chapter is meant to encourage the preacher to think intentionally about other biblical passages that may have informed or influenced the passage now under review, or to be sensitive to other passages that may simply come to mind during the exegetical process. A sermon will typically be based upon one or two primary texts. If a lectionary is employed, a third and even a fourth text may be considered.

However, once the primary texts have been determined it is important to engage in the step called *Links*. In this step, the preacher is first looking to see if and how the primary texts can be further illumined by referring to other passages of Scripture that may quickly come to mind. The preacher also wants to consider those texts that may have been brought to his or her attention while doing the research attached to any of the previous steps in this process.

Connecting New Testament texts
to Old Testament origins

The most common form of linking will occur in those numerous instances when some New Testament passage is either a direct quote from or an indirect reference to some Old Testament passage. Any sermon based upon a New Testament text that references a character or event in the Old Testament should involve some review of the appropriate Old Testament passages where those references are initially found. This would include such common Old Testament material as Passover, Pentecost, the Exodus, circumcision, the role of the lamb in making sacrifices to God, or the meaning of the Sabbath day, among many others. All of those issues are frequently referred to throughout the New Testament.

It would include any reference to major characters that first appear in the Old Testament, but are referenced in the New Testament as well. Such characters as Abraham, Moses, Jonah, Elijah, Rahab, Solomon, David, and the Queen of Sheba would be on that list. So, too, would such Old Testament prophets as Isaiah, Jeremiah, Micah, Zechariah, Malachi, and Elisha. Whenever these names appear, whether in the Gospels or the Epistles, the preacher should take the time to understand these persons in their own historical context, and perhaps gain a better understanding as to why they are being referred to in the New Testament passage.

Continuity and discontinuity

The *Links* step is especially important where Old Testament terms and doctrines are concerned. The preacher will want to be careful that he or she is not suggesting any religious practice or personal moral conduct that may have been relevant for Old Testament Israel, but is no longer binding upon the Christian community. *Links* is the point to inquire about the principle of continuity versus discontinuity. By these terms I refer to the principles by which it can quickly be determined which parts of the Old Testament remain binding and authoritative for Christians.

Some words and concepts of great theological significance may begin in the Old Testament, but they carry over into the New Testament with equal weight and authority.

At the same time, some practices and concepts are simply abandoned "because of Christ." Continuity would involve such concepts as the people of God, sin and forgiveness, Scripture as the revelation of the will and word of God, an impending day of judgment, and an emphasis on justice and compassion toward the poor.

Discontinuity would involve such practices as circumcision and other forms of legalism, and any and all suggestions that one must be an offspring of the seed of Abraham to be an authentic member of the faith community. It would also include any notion that sins can be atoned for through any form of ritual sacrifice, or that discipleship is defined by the observance of special days and special diet. Preaching should link verses in such a way that this interplay between continuity and discontinuity is easily visible. Much of this is at the heart of the ministry of Paul as he and the elders of the church in Jerusalem debate what ought to be required from Gentiles who convert to Christianity without ever having been practicing members of the Jewish religion (Acts 15).

Linking serves a useful purpose when it shows how terms and concepts that begin in the Old Testament are preserved in form, but not in function in the New Testament. Israel practiced water baptism, as evidenced by the ministry of John the Baptist. But that baptism served a different purpose than it would after the establishment of the Christian community. Similarly, the ordinance/sacrament of Communion grew out of some of the elements of the Passover meal. However, in the upper room Jesus breathed an entirely new meaning into the bread and cup. Of course, long before there was a Day of Pentecost (Acts 2), when the Holy Spirit manifested itself in the life of the church, there was the Jewish festival of Pentecost (Exodus 34:22 and Deuteronomy 16:10), which fell fifty days after Passover and marked the beginning of the fruit harvest.

It is because there are so many references in the New Testament to people and events that first appear in the Old Testament, that the *Links* step is important. It is even more important, because the meaning of certain terms, or the authority they had in the Old Testament, may not transfer into New Testament theology. Men and women still need atonement for their sins. That concept is a matter of continuity. However, that atonement has been accomplished once and for all through the blood of Christ, not through the annual offering of the blood of bulls, lambs, and pigeons. That is a matter of discontinuity.

Links and the teachings of Jesus

The practice of looking for *Links* is especially true when dealing with the words of Jesus. Consider the following instances when words spoken by Jesus fit into this pattern. In Matthew 4:1-10, it is reported that Jesus is tempted three times by Satan. Three times Jesus responds by quoting from various portions of the Book of Deuteronomy. "Man shall not live by bread alone" (cf.8:3), "You shall not tempt the Lord your God" (cf.6:16), and "You shall worship the Lord your God and him only shall you serve" (6:13). This is one of many reminders that Jesus had so thoroughly internalized the Old Testament (his Bible), that he could easily draw from its content in times of need.

Jesus refers to the Law of Moses in Matthew 5

In Matthew 5, in the context of the Sermon on the Mount, Jesus repeatedly says, "You have heard that it was said . . . but now I say unto you." Here, he is not merely quoting the passages from the Old Testament. Instead, he is referring to them in the process of making a point about his own earthly ministry. In Matthew 5:21 he is referring to the sixth commandment found in Exodus 20:13. In Matthew 5:27 he is referring to the seventh commandment found in Exodus 20:14. In Matthew 5:33 he refers to making vows and using the name of the Lord while doing so. In that instance, he quotes from passages found in Leviticus 19:12, Numbers 30:2, and Deuteronomy 23:21. In Matthew 5:38 he speaks about the law of retaliation and quotes Exodus 21:24, Leviticus 24:20, and Deuteronomy 19:21. Finally, in Matthew 5:43, he speaks about loving one's neighbor but hating one's enemy. In so doing, he quotes from Leviticus 19:18 and Deuteronomy 23:6. Clearly, Jesus is stating that his message is not an attempt to abolish the Law of Moses, but to make the regulations even more stringent.

Other links that illumine the words of Jesus

The *Links* process suggests that the preacher study the passage from which Jesus is quoting as a prelude to preaching on the materials in the Sermon on the Mount, or which Jesus quotes in his response to Satan in Matthew 4. This pattern of Jesus either directly quoting or indirectly referring to an Old Testament passage occurs throughout the Gospels. What can be learned about Jesus' visit to the synagogue in Nazareth in Luke 4:16-19 by studying the passage in Isaiah 61:1-3 from which he reads that day? Jesus spoke these words from the cross: "My God, my God, why hast thou forsaken me?" How does our understanding of those words in that context change if we recognize that they might not have been a cry of desperation, as I have heard too many Good Friday sermons suggest? Suppose Jesus was quoting those same words found in Psalm 22? Then he was assuring himself in the midst of that awful experience that he was still in the presence of God.

In Luke 11:29-30, Jesus makes an explicit reference to the story of Jonah and the people of Nineveh. In Luke 13:35 he links his ministry to the language of Psalm 118:26, "Blessed is he that cometh in the name of the Lord." In teaching on the rules that govern divorce in Matthew 19, Jesus quotes first from Genesis 2:24, and then offers a commentary on the passage in Deuteronomy 24:1 that speaks to that same issue. In John 6:49 Jesus refers to the story of manna in the wilderness found in Exodus 16:4-12. In Mark 2:23-28, Jesus speaks at length about the story of David eating bread meant only for the priests found in 1 Samuel 21:1-6. Over the course of his ministry, Jesus quotes from or refers to materials found in the Law, the Prophets, the Psalms, and various Old Testament narratives. In order to be sure that the preacher has the fullest possible understanding of those words from Jesus, it would be important to refer to those passages from which he is quoting and notice the context in which those words are set.

The Old Testament and the birth of Jesus

It is clear that the New Testament writers want us to understand the birth of Jesus in light of various Old Testament prophecies. They see the birth of Jesus occurring in the city of Bethlehem (Luke 2:1-7) as fulfillment of the messianic prophecy found in Micah 5:2. The fact that he was born of a virgin, according to Luke 1:34-35 and Matthew 1:23, is seen as fulfillment of the prophecy in Isaiah 7:14. The slaughter of the babies of Bethlehem by the order of King Herod described in Matthew 2:16 is seen as the fulfillment of a prophecy in Jeremiah 31:15. The thought that Joseph might put away his betrothed wife, Mary, instead of putting her to shame (Matthew 1:19), is based upon the law found in Deuteronomy 24:1. The decision for Jesus to be taken into Egypt until after the death of King Herod is seen as fulfillment of, or at least a reenactment of Hosea 11:1. Finally, the birth of Jesus, the Son of God, is often viewed in light of the prophecy of Isaiah 9:6, which says, "Unto us a child is born, unto us a son is given."

The Old Testament and the Passion Story of Jesus

Many times, however, the actions of Jesus are best understood in light of some Old Testament prophecy or legal principle. This is especially true for the many Old Testament references that surround the passion story. The triumphal entry into Jerusalem cannot be understood as a messianic event unless it is viewed in the light of the words found in Zechariah 9:9. When Jesus drives out the money changers from the temple, he quotes Isaiah 56:7, which says, "My house shall be called a house of prayer." Any reference to the Last Supper must be set in the context of Jesus transforming the elements of the Passover meal, best detailed in Deuteronomy 16:5-8.

Jesus warns his disciples that all of them will abandon him before that night is over, and he does so by quoting Zechariah 13:7: "I will strike the shepherd, and the sheep of the flock will be scattered." During his trial before Caiaphas, the high priest, Jesus associates himself with what is viewed as a messianic prophecy found in Daniel 7:13. It should be noted that the money given to Judas, thirty pieces of silver, is the amount referenced in Zechariah 11:12-13. It has been mentioned earlier in this chapter that the crucifixion scene itself is better understood if read in light of Psalm 22.

When Jesus refuses to answer his accusers during his trials, as recorded by the various Gospel versions, he calls to mind the language of Isaiah 53:7: "He was oppressed, and he was afflicted, yet he opened not his mouth." And the fact that he is crucified alongside two malefactors (thieves-insurrectionists-killers) reminds one of Isaiah 53:12: "because he hath poured out his soul unto death: and he was numbered with the transgressors; and he bare the sin of many."

It is especially intriguing that when Jesus dies on the cross the veil of the temple is torn in two (Matthew 27:51). This reference carries profound implications for both the design and purpose of the temple veil as described in Exodus 26:31. It also speaks to those priestly functions that took place behind the veil of the temple, functions that are no longer necessary in light of the atoning work of Christ on the cross (Leviticus 16:1-14). The Jews who had sought to have Christ executed were also in a rush to have his body removed from the cross before the beginning of the Sabbath (John 19:31). That, too, involves a link to an Old Testament passage (Deuteronomy 21:23), which speaks about not leaving overnight the body of a person who had been executed by being hanged on a tree.

When the preacher engages in this *Links* step, the main objective is to consider whether any passage under review is a quote from, a reference to, or is otherwise informed by any other passage of Scripture. If that has been determined to be the case, the preacher is obligated, at least during the exegetical process, to read and consider that other passage. Whether or not any of the fruit of that additional research ends up in the sermon depends upon how much light it sheds upon the meaning of the primary text(s).

Whether or not any of the findings appear in the sermon, the discipline of this *Links* step should take place in the study.

The heroes of the faith in Hebrews 11

No book of the New Testament requires as much attention to the step of linking as the Book of Hebrews. Most of Hebrews 11 is a recalling of the heroic men and women mentioned in the Old Testament who have become examples to members of the Christian community of the first century A.D., of what it means to "keep the faith." Clearly, one cannot preach about any of those persons mentioned in Hebrews without studying them in the Old Testament context in which their story is told or their heroics are recorded.

By the same token, the rest of the Book of Hebrews is an attempt to explain who Jesus is by comparing and contrasting him to various aspects of Jewish ritual religious life, such as the High Priest, the various Old Testament covenants (Abrahamic-Mosaic-Davidic), and the practice of making sacrifices as an atonement for sin. Once again, the preacher needs to engage in the *Links* step in order to better understand what Hebrews is trying to communicate.

The Acts of the Apostles and the epistles of Paul

It is not uncommon for links to exist between some event described in the Acts of the Apostles and something that Paul mentions in one of his many epistles to various churches and persons. An obvious example would be the Jerusalem conference in Acts 15 and Paul's comments about his ministry to the uncircumcised in Galatians 2:1-10. Paul speaks candidly about his persecution of the Christian community in Galatians 1:12-13, and those events are described in Acts 8:3, in 9:1, and again in 22:19.

Paul reports both in Acts 14:5-6 and 2 Timothy 3:11 the persecutions he suffered in the city of Iconium, and the fact that he went on preaching the next day in the nearby city of Derbe. His vision to preach in Macedonia is described both in Acts 16:10 and 2 Corinthians 2:13. Priscilla and Acquila, Paul's "fellow workers," are mentioned both in Acts 18:2 and in Romans 16:3-4. Paul refers to his status as a Pharisee and a lifelong follower of the Law of Moses in both Acts 26:4-5 and in Philippians 3:5-6. And in both instances, he acknowledges that he has abandoned that identity in favor of his new life in Christ. One of Paul's three experiences of being shipwrecked and adrift at sea is mentioned both in 2 Corinthians 11:25-26 and Acts 27:27-38. This pattern of association between the Acts of the Apostles and the epistles of Paul occurs over and over again. In fact, looking for these links is a good way of following Paul through his missionary journeys.

Links and the Synoptic Gospels
Just as the preacher needs to be on the lookout for any links when the words and actions of Jesus are involved, so too should this step be engaged in when preaching from the Synoptic Gospels (Matthew-Mark-Luke). The objective here is not to search for any Old Testament connections or origins to the passage in question. Instead, one is looking for any variances in the form or language of stories and characters that appear more than once in the New Testament itself. This is especially important when preaching from the Synoptics.

Very frequently the same parable is told in one or more of the Gospels. Just as frequently, the same event is described. However, there can be wide differences from one Gospel rendering to another. There are scholarly tools that can be quite helpful at this point. None more so than *Gospel Parallels,* edited by Burton H. Throckmorton Jr.[1] Consider just a few of the instances when preaching from a synoptic passage requires some attention to linking. The teachings of Jesus called the Beatitudes, delivered in the context of the Sermon on the Mount in Matthew 5:1-12, occur again and with several variations and additions in Luke 6:17-26.

139

The Lord's Prayer, which appears in Matthew 6:9-13 in the context of the Sermon on the Mount, also appears in Luke 11:1-4. However, the context is different, as is the wording of the prayer.

The parables of the sower and of the mustard seed appear twice, in Matthew 13:24-32 and Mark 4:26-32, and there are differences in the two renderings. The healing of a woman with an issue of blood and the raising of the daughter of Jairus are stories that appear in all three Synoptic Gospels: Matthew 9:18-26, Mark 5:21-43, and Luke 8:40-56. All three Synoptic Gospels acknowledge that Jesus demonstrated his power to restore sight to the blind when he visited the city of Jericho. However, the three versions vary in some of the details. Matthew 20:29-34 says that Jesus healed two blind men, neither of whose names were mentioned. Mark 10:46-52 states that Jesus healed a man named Bartimeus. While in Luke 18:35-43, one blind man is healed but his name is not mentioned.

It is interesting to note that anyone attempting to preach about Palm Sunday had better avoid the Lukan version of that story. Both Matthew 21:6-10 and Mark 11:11 state that people in the crowd laid their garments and branches on the ground as Jesus passed by. However, Luke only refers to garments, not to any branches being cut and laid down. The Luke version also does not mention the use of the word "Hosanna" or refer to Jesus as the Son of David.

In Matthew 18:12-14, Jesus talks about a man who rejoices over one of his one hundred sheep that has been lost and later found. That same story reappears in Luke 15, where the lost coin and the lost son are added to the restoration of the lost. In Matthew 18:15, Peter asks if he should be willing to forgive someone as many as seven times. That same issue appears in Luke 17:3-4, except in that version Peter does not appear, and Jesus offers that instruction without being prompted by one of his disciples.

This pattern of the same stories appearing in Matthew, Mark, and Luke is so common, that the preacher wants to be sure to look for that from the outset. When the preacher notices these differences, be they subtle or substantial, some attempt ought to be made, through the use of the various research tools mentioned in earlier chapters, to account for these variations. It may be a matter not only of different authorship, but of markedly different intended audiences as well. The preacher would probably not want to attempt an explanation of the Synoptic problem in a sermon. However, here is an instance where research for the sermon can lead into a subsequent Bible study or teaching opportunity on a question that would be of great interest to the average churchgoer.

Old Testament phrases in the New Testament

Most people are familiar with the words, "the grass withers and the flower fades, but the word of our Lord shall stand forever," which can be found in Isaiah 40:6. Yet the same words also appear in 1 Peter 1:24-25. The equally familiar words, "Beat your swords into plowshares and your spears into pruning hooks," are found in both Isaiah 2:4 and Micah 4:3. However, in Joel 3:10, those images are reversed and that passage reads, "Beat your plowshares into swords, and your pruning hooks into spears." And speaking of Joel, the events that occurred on the Day of Pentecost in Acts 2 are interpreted by Peter as being the fulfillment of words spoken in Joel 2:28-29.

Here again, the object of this demonstration is to show how many times the review of one verse of Scripture forces the preacher to consider additional biblical passages. This is absolutely essential if the meaning of the primary text for the sermon is to be fully understood. That is what is entailed in the *Links* step of the process.

SERMON PREVIEW

The sermon at the end of this chapter takes the reader back to the series based upon Luke 23:32-43, so the concept of making use of a sermon series is further underscored. However, this sermon also makes use of a number of additional biblical passages that shed light on issues being discussed in the primary text. Thus, the issue of *Links* is also being further illustrated.

THE NONCONFORMING CHRIST
LUKE 23:32-43

As Jesus hung from his cross on Calvary, he was three times subjected to the same statement, *"Save yourself."* That statement was uttered by the Romans who took delight in putting to death as a common criminal someone whom they believed had passed himself off as "King of the Jews." It spoke to the power and unrivaled strength of Rome that they could laugh at this man who had been called a king. The same words had been spoken by one of the criminals who was being crucified next to Jesus on that day. His call to Christ was not in faith, as if he believed that Christ could save himself from that terrible death. It also was not in scorn, mocking Christ for claiming to be something that he really wasn't. His was a cry of desperation. Crucifixion was the most excruciatingly painful form of death yet invented, and that man was desperate to be spared the agony. Thus he cried out, *"Save yourself, and us."*

Notice that the third group that called upon Jesus to *"Save yourself"* were the Jewish leaders. The Bible not only reports their words, but also speaks of the attitude, the spirit, and the contemptuous tone in which those words were spoken. Luke 23: 35 says, ". . . the leaders *derided* him." That word does not carry the full weight of the Greek word *empaizein*, which actually means they *sneered* at Jesus. It was not just the words they spoke, but the tone of their voices, and the look on their faces, and perhaps even the smug delight in their eyes as they looked upon Jesus nailed to that cross. In fact, the Greek language would suggest not simply that the leaders were sneering at Jesus, but that they *kept sneering*, as if their taunts and insults were being hurled at Jesus during the whole six hours that our Lord was hanging on the cross. What had Jesus said or done that caused these Jewish leaders to hold him in such hate-filled contempt? Why did they *keep sneering* at Jesus?

This was not the first time that Jewish leaders *sneered* at Jesus, according to Luke. When Jesus finishes telling the story of The Unjust Steward, Luke 16:14 says that "the Pharisees who were covetous, heard all these things and derided *(sneered)* at him." Let this be clearly understood. So

---

This sermon was preached by the author on August 2, 1998, at Antioch Baptist Church in Cleveland, Ohio, as part of the sermon series, "Conversations at Calvary."

far as Luke's Gospel is concerned, the Jewish leaders had been trying to get rid of Jesus for a long time. In Luke 4 they were angry with Jesus, because he declared that the love of God was not limited just to the Jews, but extended to a Syrian named Namaan in the days of Elisha, and to a Phoenician woman in the days of Elijah. In Luke 5 they were angry with Jesus because he presumed to be able to forgive sins (5:21). In Luke 6 they were angry because Jesus and his disciples picked corn, or appeared to work, on the Sabbath (6:2). In Luke 7 they criticized Jesus for allowing a woman called a sinner, probably a prostitute, to anoint his feet with ointment she had kept in an alabaster box (7:39). In chapters 11 and 12, Jesus repeatedly warned the people to "beware of the Pharisees, the lawyers, and the scribes." These three groups were all part of the leadership of Israel at that time. Jesus told the parables of the lost sheep, lost coin, and lost son, because the Pharisees had criticized him for associating with sinners (15:2). When Jesus made his triumphal entry into Jerusalem on what we call Palm Sunday, the Pharisees demanded that Jesus tell the people to stop shouting his praises. That is when Jesus says, *"If these do not praise me, then the rocks will cry out"* (19:39-40).

Luke 22:2 says explicitly *"the chief priests and the scribes sought how they might kill him."* It was this group that gave money to Judas, who would later betray Jesus in the Garden of Gethsemane. It was this group that would have Jesus arrested. And it was before the high priest, Caiaphas, the leader of this group, that Jesus endured the first of several trials on the night before he was killed. When neither Pilate nor Herod found Jesus guilty of any crime deserving death, it was this group of Jewish religious leaders who kept clamoring for the Lord's death. And when Pilate allowed the crowd to select whether Jesus or Barabbas would be released, it was the leaders who influenced the people to call for the release of Barabbas and the crucifixion of Jesus. They had wanted Jesus out of the way for three years, and now they were standing at the foot of his cross, *sneering at him,* their mission now complete.

Who were these *"leaders,"* and why did they want Jesus to be killed? The New Testament speaks of at least five groups of people who constituted the leadership of the nation of Israel. There was the high priest who presided over the temple in Jerusalem and who was the ultimate authority on all matters religious and political. The high priest's position had been passed from father to son by blood succession before the Romans conquered Israel. After that, Rome appointed the high priest to make sure he was a person who would not stir up any trouble for them. There was a group called the Sanhedrin. This was like our U.S. Supreme Court and the Congress wrapped up into one. These seventy men met with the High Priest to interpret the secular and religious laws for the nation. There were Pharisees and Sadducees; in some respects they were rival political parties in Palestine, and they also held somewhat differing theological views. There were lawyers, or scribes, who were the teachers of the Mosaic Law and the ancient equivalent of teachers of religion in a college or seminary setting. Finally, there were the elders. These were people who, because of their advanced age and the wisdom they had accumulated over the years, were given special honor and were allowed the best seats in the synagogues. Take all of these offices, duties, and groups and add them together and those were the leaders or rulers who were *sneering* at Jesus that day.

Now comes the question of why they wanted Jesus dead. The answer, plainly stated, is that Jesus would not conform to their understanding of what it meant to be a truly religious person. These leaders wanted Jesus dead because he was undermining their authority among the people regarding what constituted truth in religion. Jesus taught and believed things that were unacceptable to the religious leaders of his day. As a result, they would not rest until Jesus had been removed from the scene.

It is always interesting to watch what happens when someone departs from the established opinion of his or her day, and it is not as unusual as we might think. Much the same thing is going on right now, and we are failing to make the connection. Last week, Associate Supreme Court Justice Clarence Thomas gave a speech at the National Bar Association, the annual gathering of the black lawyers in America. Many of the members of that group wanted to have Thomas' invitation to speak to that group revoked. They did not even want to hear what he had to say. When he finally gave his speech, he lashed out at the people who had been criticizing and condemning him for failing to understand the law and civil rights issues in the same way that they saw those issues. He said that he was entitled to hold an opinion different from Jesse Jackson or the NAACP or even Thurgood Marshall, whose seat on the court Thomas filled in 1991.

Clarence Thomas has been attacked for failing to support the view of most black civil rights groups on the question of affirmative action. He does not agree that affirmative action is an appropriate tool at this point in the struggle for civil rights, even though he was a beneficiary of affirmative action when he was admitted into Yale Law School in the 1970s. However, despite almost a decade of constant criticism, I must confess a certain admiration for the courage that Thomas displayed last week. He literally walked into the lions' den, reinforced by nothing but his own personal convictions that he was on the right side of the issue.

Take all of the scorn and verbal attacks and insults that black people have heaped on Clarence Thomas for most of this decade, all because he did not go along with the majority opinion on how to achieve civil rights for black Americans, and you begin to understand how Jesus was viewed by the Jewish leaders in our text in Luke 23:35. This does not mean that I think Clarence Thomas is to be compared to Jesus in any other way. I happen to share the view that Thomas is a hypocrite, denying to others a program of assistance that opened the door to the position he holds today. I also believe that racial considerations still block opportunities for blacks and other minorities, and programs like affirmative action continue to play a useful role. But having said all of that, the issue remains the same. It is a dangerous thing to break ranks with the majority on an issue of importance. This treatment of Clarence Thomas is a case of intellectual intolerance, based upon the truthfulness of no one's ideas but one's own. And whether black people in America like it or not, Thomas and other black conservatives will continue to be a force in the shaping of American public opinion. I do not agree with their positions, but I wonder if I have their courage to stand up in the face of a hostile majority in defense of the ideas in which I believe.

However, intellectual intolerance is not the worst form of intolerance. Religious intolerance is far worse in its consequences, and that is what filled those leaders who were *sneering* at Jesus. There is no vengeance like that of a religious group that is out to defend its faith, whether against those who they feel are twisting its teachings, or against those who hold a different religion altogether. Two months ago, we heard about nuclear testing being done by Pakistan and India, neighboring countries that are sworn enemies. Why do these two nations hate one another so intently? Before 1948, when the British still controlled India, that region was all one country. When the British left and India declared its independence in 1948, not only did India separate from the British, but also Pakistan was born out of India, largely because of religious differences. India is primarily Hindu, and Pakistan is almost totally Muslim. Now these

145

two nations are threatening each other with nuclear annihilation, all because they have religious conflicts. This is religious intolerance.

In the African nation of Sudan, an awful war is going on, and the principal weapon is food. The Muslims who control the northern part of Sudan are withholding food and supplies from the Christians who live in the southern part of that country. Hundreds of thousands of people in the South have died, and their only crime is being Christian. The Christians in the South could be spared the suffering if they would only convert and join the religion of the Muslim majority. But they keep the faith they have in Christ, and they take the suffering that comes as a result of that decision. The whole world looked with horror at Northern Ireland earlier this month when three young Catholic boys were killed in their homes by a bomb thrown into a room where they were sleeping, by men who did not want Catholics in their Protestant neighborhood.

How many of you know people, perhaps in your own family, with whom you cannot enjoy a peaceful relationship because of some religious conflict? Jehovah's Witnesses will not step inside any church but their own Kingdom Halls, nor acknowledge the validity of any religion but their own. Many Pentecostals discount the value of any religion that does not celebrate speaking in tongues. Some Baptists will deny a place in heaven to anyone who has not been baptized by immersion. Catholics will not receive Communion from a Protestant minister.

Denominations are breaking up because of apparently irresolvable conflicts. Shall we ordain women into the ministry? Is homosexuality based in genetics and a matter of who a person is, or is homosexuality a behavioral decision rooted only in how one chooses to live? Is there any inconsistency in being pro-life where birth is concerned but pro-death where capital punishment is concerned? If it is wrong to take a human life in the womb, why is it right to take a human life in the electric chair or gas chamber? These are issues that divide Christians across this country, and there are compelling arguments on both sides of these questions.

Religious intolerance begins the moment that you and I conclude that only our views on a subject are right, and the only thing other people can do is agree with us or end up in hell. On the other hand, while we may choose to be tolerant, and to respect other people's right to hold a certain view, we must have the personal courage to stand up for the things we believe in, no matter who is willing to stand up with us. That is the kind of person Jesus was, and that, I suggest, is also what got him killed. He was a nonconforming Christ.

Let me suggest to you today, that one of the best things you and I can do as a mark of our relationship and discipleship with Christ, is to find our own ways to become nonconformists in the face of the things that this world would like for us to accept. During the eighteenth century, George Washington and Thomas Jefferson were nonconformists when it came to accepting British colonial rule. However, they continued to conform on the question of slavery. It required men and women like Frederick Douglass and Harriet Tubman to bring an end to slavery simply by being nonconformists on that issue. A few weeks ago, people gathered in New York State to celebrate the one-hundred-fiftieth anniversary of the Women's Suffrage Movement. Women like Susan B. Anthony and Elizabeth Cady Stanton lived during an era when women could not vote in this country. But they became nonconformists, and because of that, more than 50 percent of our national population became politically empowered. You and I would still be riding in the back of the bus and going to separate public facilities if people like Rosa Parks, Fannie Lou Hamer, Martin King, and John Lewis had not been willing to be nonconformists in the 1950s and 1960s. Apartheid would still be the order of the day in South Africa had not people like Nelson Mandela and Steven Biko become nonconformists who refused to accept things as they were, and determined to take a stand no matter what others chose to do. The world has been shaped and history has been made by those men and women who, in the face of criticism and condemnation, took a stand contrary to the majority view at that time. They were nonconformists, and the world is a better place because of them.

As Christians, you and I live under a mandate for nonconformity with the world. Paul says in Romans 12, *"Be not conformed to this world, but be ye transformed by the renewing of your mind, that you may prove what is that good, and acceptable, and perfect, will of God."* In a world obsessed with sex and sexual scandals that have all but consumed the public political dialogue, we are challenged to not conform. In a society driven by the need for stimulation that leads to addictions to drugs and alcohol, we are challenged to be nonconformists. In a society that is still too conscious of issues of race, class, age, and gender, we as Christians are challenged to be nonconformists. It is risky to break

147

ranks with the views held by the majority, but this is the example Christ has set for us.

Where would you and I be today if Jesus had not been willing to break ranks with the religious views of his day? If he had conformed and done what the scribes and Pharisees wanted him to do, you and I would still be trapped inside the inescapable problem of sin. If he had conformed and said what Pilate and Herod wanted him to say, you and I would have no power greater than the political powers of this world to which we can turn and upon which we could cast our hopes. If he had conformed to his own impulses of self-preservation as they arose within him in the Garden of Gethsemane when he asked God to *"let this cup pass from me . . . "* we would not have the hope of abundant life now, or the hope of eternal life beyond the grave. How different this world would be, and the lives of we who call ourselves Christians, if Christ had just been willing to conform.

Today we shout *HALLELUJAH,* because Jesus was a nonconformist. He did not accept things that others believed. He did not turn back because others would not walk with him. He took his stand on what it meant to be a child of God, and it cost him his life. He was a victim of religious intolerance. However, death was not the end of that story. Philippians 2 says that because he did not conform and gladly went to that cross, *"God has given him a name that is above every name."* Today we celebrate the name of Jesus. Today we trust in the name of Jesus. Today we find salvation in the name of Jesus. Today we pray in the name of Jesus. Today we sing the praises of the name of Jesus. Today we declare to the world that there is power in the name of Jesus. Thank God for Jesus, our non-conforming Christ. On the day that he died, his enemies *kept sneering* at him. Today, they are all dead, but he is alive forevermore. All hail the power of Jesus' name, let angels prostrate fall. Bring forth the royal diadem and crown him Lord of all.

8
The 8 Ls:
Lessons

The first six steps in this process have involved the kind of careful scholarly research that assists the preacher in determining, as thoroughly as possible, what the text under review actually *SAYS!* This has been accomplished by engaging in the establishment of the limits of the passage, the determination of the literary type, the establishment of the physical and social location, the discovery of the leads, and the additional insight that comes from investigating and analyzing the links. However, with all six of these steps being done, there is one thing more that must be done before the preacher makes any attempt at writing a sermon. It must be determined what the text *MEANS!* Not until we know both what the text *SAYS* and *MEANS* are we ready to think about writing a sermon. That is the objective of this chapter.

Anyone who reads Matthew 5:48 will know that Jesus *SAYS* "Be ye therefore perfect, even as your father which is in heaven is perfect." Having read the words, one is left with the deeper and more profound issue of what does Jesus *MEAN* when he speaks these words. Anyone can read the words in Ezekiel 37 where God *SAYS* to the prophet, "Can these bones live?" Once again, knowing what the text *SAYS* is not quite enough. One pores over every word of that passage and wonders what God *MEANS* by that phrase.

What did Thomas Jefferson mean?

There are numerous and quite familiar examples outside of the Bible of this difference between what is said and what is meant by certain texts. In the Declaration of Independence these words can be found, *"All men are created equal."* Every high school freshman in the country knows what is said in that most famous of all American political phrases. What has divided us as a nation over the intervening 224 years is what that phrase actually meant to those who wrote it and heard it in 1776. Did it mean "all" men or just white men? Did it initially mean all white men, or just free white men? Did it include any women in 1776? What was being implied about the status of African Americans and all the Native Americans scattered throughout the British colonies at that time?

We have always agreed on what the text says. What we have taken hundreds of years, a Civil War, and a Civil Rights Movement to resolve is what those words mean. And the first meaning that must be sought is not the meaning we impose upon that phrase, but the meaning we think Jefferson, Franklin, Adams, and the others intended. Understanding what is said does not always result in understanding what is meant.

Interpreting the United States Constitution

Another way to consider the need to interpret a biblical text is to consider all that goes into the struggle to interpret the Constitution of the United States. Like the Bible, the U.S. Constitution is a document to which millions of people turn in a search for direction and guidance. The determination of what actions, laws, and statements are and are not "constitutional" occupies a good deal of the time of an entire branch of our government. The challenge is not in determining what the U.S. Constitution *SAYS*; the challenge comes in trying to reach some understanding of what it *MEANS*.

The process begins by reading the actual words as written and ratified by the founders of the nation in 1787. Constitutional scholars devote entire careers to the attempt to understand the social, political, economic, and foreign policy concerns that guided the Constitution framers' thinking as they hammered out this document. Until one understands the U.S. Constitution at that level, one probably does not understand it at all.

However, the search for meaning never ends with a reading of the words in their own time and place. In the relatively short period of time that the Constitution has been in force, a great many things have changed in America. In order to apply that text to our contemporary society, the work of constitutional interpretation must occur. One does not jump from the late eighteenth century to the early twenty-first century. One needs to study how the constitutional issue under review has been interpreted over the entire intervening period of time.

There are court precedents, beginning soon after 1787, that have to be considered at the district, appellate, and U.S. Supreme Court levels. Some of those findings will support the position that a given perspective is seeking to uphold. Other findings will seem to rule against them. What do you do in those instances when the precedents send conflicting messages? Then there is the composition of the present judiciary, along the lines of liberal and conservative and male and female, that reads the words of the Constitution, reviews the precedents, and then seeks to render a ruling that is directed to an issue presently under review. Needless to say, the whole process is one of interpretation of the text, from beginning to end.

How could it be any other way? The questions with which Americans struggle in the twenty-first century were impossible for the founders to imagine, much less to provide guidance on the Constitution. Is abortion a legal or an illegal procedure? Should retail sales over the Internet be subject to sales tax? Should the burning of the American flag be a protected form of free speech? Was the 1954 U.S. Supreme Court ruling *Brown v. the Board of Education* that ordered an end to "separate but equal in public education," a violation of states' rights under the Tenth Amendment of that same Constitution? It is not enough to simply read the United States Constitution in the face of these complex issues. A process of deliberate interpretation must take place.

Martin Luther King Jr. and the Promised Land

On the night before he was murdered, Martin Luther King Jr. spoke to an overflow house inside Mason Temple Church of God in Christ. That crowd had gathered despite a fierce thunderstorm that had settled over Memphis, Tennessee. How many times since 1968 have clips of that speech been heard on television, on radio, or recited as part of one of the thousands of King Day programs that occur annually across the country? At the end of that speech, almost as if he was already looking death in the face, King said, *"I may not get there with you, but I want you to know tonight that we as a*

151

people will get to the Promised Land." That is what he said, but what, exactly, did he mean?

Was he talking about a Promised Land in the Old Testament sense of the word, like a land where black people could begin to build a nation of their own? Was this a nationalist vision uttered by someone who had given up on integration as a possibility? Or was his use of the words "Promised Land" just a metaphor for the integrated society and the attainment of equal justice under the law to which he had devoted the previous thirteen years of his life? We all know what Dr. King said, but what exactly did he mean?

The money or the motto?

Inscribed on every piece of U.S. currency, coin and paper, are the words, *"In God We Trust."* Not only that, but the words are also etched into the marble walls of the United States House of Representatives, visible to the entire world when the president of the United States delivers the annual State of the Union Address. Every American knows what is being said, in terms of the literal meaning of the words. But are we as sure about what was meant when that phrase was agreed upon?

Does it imply that we as a nation put our trust in God above all other resources available to us? Does it mean that we trust God more than the money on which those words appear? Or is that language little more than another instance of what Robert Bellah speaks about in terms of a "civil religion?" Is it like saying that we are "one nation under God," to use that language of the Pledge of Allegiance? Clearly, with regard to the phrase "In God We Trust," and in each of the other instances mentioned above, it is not enough to know what the text SAYS. We need to press a little further and look a little deeper to see if we can ascertain what these phrases MEANT to those who first spoke or wrote them, and to those who first read or heard them.

The work of hermeneutics

This same principle discussed in the examples just listed can, and must, be applied to the study of biblical texts. The preacher and exegete must work diligently to uncover what the text actually says (steps 1-6). But having done that, the work is not yet complete.

152

Next comes the task of reaching back across thousands of years of history and bridging the gaps in culture and language in order to discover what the text meant to those who wrote or spoke the words, and to those who heard or read them.

It is around the search for the meaning of a biblical text that the discipline called hermeneutics has arisen. The assumption of hermeneutics is that the Bible was not written with a twenty-first century American audience in mind, much less my middle class, African American, American Baptist congregation in Cleveland, Ohio. Rather, there were issues occurring at the time of the writing of those texts that the biblical writers were attempting to address. Before the preacher seeks to say in a sermon what the text means to us today (homiletics), he or she needs to determine what the text meant to its original audience in Jerusalem, Babylon, Corinth, or Rome (hermeneutics). The preacher needs to understand the lesson that the text was attempting to communicate to those persons for whom the material was initially and primarily intended.

It is one of the great wonders of the Bible that a book that was written for various audiences of readers, the most recent of them being nearly two thousand years ago, can still speak with such power and authority to people in the twenty-first century. There is no other book of similar age that has been preserved and passed on through as many generations and across as many cultural and historical divides as the Bible. It is a powerful thing to realize that each successive generation finds within the pages of that book words that it is willing to receive as the very word of God. At any point in the intervening two thousand years, one of those generations could have decided that the Bible was no longer revelatory or authoritative. Had that happened, the Bible would doubtless have been relegated to the antiquities section of the library, along with other writings from that same era that did not survive beyond the medieval era. But unlike the writings of Catullus or Homer, Josephus or Philo, the Bible continues to speak with authority to people in successive generations all over the world.

However, just as the Bible has had meaning, sometimes widely differing meaning to generations through these two thousand years, the texts in the Bible also carried an intended meaning for those who first encountered those words. We dare not rush to suggest what the Bible may mean to people alive in our own time and place before we take the time to discover what the Bible was attempting to say to its original readers. And again, the issue is not what the Bible SAYS, but what the people who heard the words understood them to MEAN.

How to search for the meanng in the Bible

One of the best ways to study the Bible is to understand it as a collection of books written in response to one of a series of traumatic events in the life of Israel or the early church. Those traumatic events in the Old Testament would have included the covenant between God and Abraham, the Exodus from Egypt and the conquest of the Promised Land, the challenge to follow monotheism in a polytheistic culture, and the need to explain the exiles of 722 and 586 B.C. In the New Testament, traumatic events would have included the reaction to the claim that Jesus was the Messiah, that his passion was now an alternative to the rituals of second temple Judaism, and that those Gentiles who converted to Christianity did not have to be circumcised as a precondition.

How does the covenant between God and Abraham serve as a model for God's faithfulness even in the face of disobedience, dishonesty, or seemingly impossible circumstances? It takes thirteen chapters for the saga about Joseph to be told, but only one verse for the theological message to be established: "You meant it for evil, but God meant it for good" (Genesis 50:20). God is sovereign and can work through the worst of circumstances to accomplish the divine will and purpose in history. The gospel song by Thomas A. Dorsey states this message even more graphically, "The Lord will make a way somehow."

From the time of the Exodus from Egypt to the possession of the land of Canaan, until the fall of first the Northern and then the Southern Kingdom, the question is, "What does it mean to be the people of God? What does it mean to have no other gods before Yahweh?" This issue may be raised in any number of ways, from the story of the golden calf during the sojourn at Mt. Sinai, to the charge given by Joshua to the assembled tribes of Israel in Joshua 24. It continues through the reign of King Solomon who sets up shrines to the gods of his foreign wives in 1 Kings 11, to the encounter in 1 Kings 18 between Elijah and the priests of Baal. If one preaches from these texts but does not recognize the theological theme that binds the material together, one might be able to make some delightful observations on one issue or another, but the main point will have been missed. The preacher must not only notice what the text *SAYS*, but must pay even closer attention to what the text *MEANS!*

Much of the Old Testament is an attempt to explain how and why Israel was uprooted from the Promised Land and sent into exile (Diaspora) in 722 B.C. and again in 586 B.C. Similarly, much of that material deals with how the people of Israel should seek to keep faith with their God whether sitting by the banks of the River Chebar (Psalm 137), working as royal courtiers (Daniel 3 and 6, and Esther), or upon their return from exile to their homes in Israel (Ezra-Nehemiah). The reason these stories were preserved by Israel is because they offered meaning to people who were trying to make sense of these earth-shaking events in their national life.

Much of the New Testament revolves around the arguments given for why Jesus is to be accepted as the long-awaited Messiah of Israel. By what authority does he heal or forgive sins? What significance should be attached to his resurrection, so far as his divinity and his authority are concerned? By what right does he call himself the Son of Man? What is meant when the Gospel of Mark begins with the words, "The beginning of the gospel of Jesus Christ, the Son of God" (Mark 1:1)? What is John saying, different from Mark, when he writes in John 20:31, "These are written, that ye might believe that Jesus is the Christ, the Son of God; and that believing ye might have life through his name"? What should we make of Peter calling him "The Christ, the Son of the living God" (Matthew 16:16)? Other insights may be drawn from any of these stories, but what is being debated is the identity and authority of Jesus of Nazareth.

Another overarching issue in the New Testament is the encounter between the gospel of Jesus and the Gentile nations who have no previous experience in the lifestyle or the language of Judaism. Who can become a Christian, and under what conditions? That is the question for an Ethiopian eunuch in Acts 8:27, a Roman jailer in Philippi, described in Acts 16:33, and a slave named Onesimus in the Book of Philemon. In each of these instances, the question at hand is not simply what the text or passage or verse says, but what it means, and how it sheds light on one of the overarching issues that rests at the heart of the New Testament. Before a passage is considered in terms of what it might mean to a modern Christian audience listening to a sermon, it needs to be determined what the meaning of the text was to the first people who heard the gospel preached or who listened while an epistle was being read.

The shifting meaning of a text through history

At the most technical level, hermeneutics would also urge the preacher to consider what the texts have meant and how they have been interpreted at various times and in various locations over the two-thousand-year history of Christian biblical interpretation. What did Augustine or Tertullian do with this passage? How does some medieval preacher like Savanarola or Chrysostom understand this passage? What can I learn from the way Luther or Calvin interpreted this text during the Reformation, or Wesley or Whitfield during the Great Awakening? How was this passage handled by the proslavery and abolitionist preachers of the American antebellum era?

Within a more recent time frame, the preacher might wonder how the passage was preached during the Civil Rights Movement, or the Vietnam War era, or in light of the political scandals from Watergate and the impeachment of Richard Nixon, to Monica Lewinsky and the impeachment of Bill Clinton. How have I heard other preachers handle this passage? What can be learned by studying the work of those of a different age or racial or denominational group than my own, or by considering the biblical analysis of the liberation-feminist-womanist theologians of the latter part of the twentieth century? In short, before I attempt to say what the text means to me and what it says to my congregation, I need to listen to what that text has said to others in both the near and distant past.

Studying the history of a text
1. Books
This information is not as hard to ascertain as might be imagined.

There are some marvelous resources that can help preachers follow the use of biblical texts through the years. So far as becoming acquainted with the history of text usage over the years, I heartily recommend those sermon series that collect the work of such notable preachers as John Calvin, Martin Luther, Alexander Maclaren, Joseph Parker, Charles Spurgeon, G. Campbell Morgan, George Truett, Gardner Taylor, and others.[1] There is great value in regularly reviewing *20 Centuries of Great Preaching*, edited by Clyde Fant and William Pinson.[2] There are collections of sermons without number, both around common themes and on unrelated topics. *Biblical Sermons*, edited by Haddon Robinson, and *The Preaching Tradition*, edited by Dewitte Holland, are both useful in this process of seeing how various texts have been interpreted over the years.[3]

2. Journals and periodicals

There are very useful periodicals that help preachers see how others in the profession have approached the same text that they may now be considering. Among these are *The African American Pulpit, Pulpit Digest, Preaching,* and *The Living Pulpit.* A disciplined review of these journals, not looking to replicate the sermon, but certainly seeking to learn how texts have been interpreted by others, is a useful exercise for any preacher.

Preaching can be tremendously helped through the ministry of the journal *Interpretation.* It helps the preacher think in precisely the way that is being argued in this chapter. It forces him or her to think theologically and to look for the theological themes that are the heart and soul of the Scriptures. The preacher can also be especially helped by *The Living Pulpit,* which, unlike the other above named journals, deals with a single doctrine or theological theme per issue. A review of the back issues of that journal alone would go a long way toward aiding a preacher to think theologically. Just as important is the fact that each of those back issues allows the preacher to see how other preachers and theologians have approached the very text that they may be planning to use in an upcoming sermon.

I know that Karl Barth once observed that a good preacher ought to have the Bible in one hand and a newspaper in the other. Frankly, I hope that the hand that holds the Bible will also make some room for the other technical and scholarly resources discussed in this chapter and throughout this book. The books of biblical theology arc many, and they vary according to the liberal or conservative leanings of the preacher who is looking for tools to use. At this point, my intent is not to point preachers to my particular favorite biblical theologian, but to point them toward the discipline of identifying and referring to some biblical theologian who helps them get beyond what the text *SAYS*, and aids them in discovering what the text *MEANS*.

3. A word about biblical commentaries

One needs to approach the use of entire sets of commentaries with caution. It is not uncommon for some volumes in the set to have more value, and to reflect more careful scholarship than other volumes in that same set. Furthermore, various commentary sets serve different purposes. Some focus primarily on textual questions, and therefore are more helpful in terms of what the text *SAYS!* Others are really designed to provide the preacher with sermon ideas, and so they spend little, if any, time examining the theological meaning of the text. With this word of caution, and recognizing how many books there are from which to choose, I continue to find *The Anchor Bible* and *Word Biblical Commentary* to be useful in this area. The former reflects a so-called liberal view of Scripture, and the latter reflects a conservative view of Scripture.

The best design for a biblical commentary is the *New Interpreter's Bible*. Following the design of its 1956 predecessor, *The Interpreter's Bible*, this new series offers both an NIV and NRSV translation of the text. Following that is a brief theological analysis of the passages being examined, typically by a noted theologian or biblical scholar. Finally, it offers a brief commentary on the passage by one of the leading preachers or professors of preaching. This design is ideal for use by a pastor who will find in a single volume several resources and usually the insights of more than a single contributor that aid in the exegetical process.

There is also a new commentary series called *Interpretation*, which is not to be confused with the quarterly journal mentioned earlier in this chapter. Those wishing to do exegesis for preaching might want to be aware of the following three resources as well.

They are *The Westminster Bible Companion Series, The Abingdon New Testament Commentary Series,* and *Interpreting Biblical Texts,* also by Abingdon. While becoming somewhat dated, *The Old Testament Library Series* by Westminster still offers much both in what the text *SAYS* and what the text *MEANS.* All of these resources can be helpful to the preacher who wants to take the time to search for the lessons that the text has to offer.

Developing the discipline of thinking theologically

I will concede that there is a temptation for preachers to skip this step altogether. They may be content to rush off and write a sermon once they have some idea of how that text speaks directly to them in their own time and place. This may be due to the fact that they do not leave themselves the time for the kind of sermon preparation being suggested here. It may simply be that they do not know how to search for the meaning of the text. The central thing to remember when studying the Bible is that one is studying a theological document. No matter how many other uses some people may attempt to make of these texts, the Bible must be read theologically. The preacher, therefore, must come to think of himself or herself as a theologian resident within the congregation. This status means, among other things, that the preacher must bring a disciplined approach to the study of Scripture. The preacher should not attempt to teach the congregation everything he or she has learned, whether in the intensive study of seminary, or through years of independent study. However, the preacher should attempt to call upon all of that information and experience in an attempt to assist people in understanding the fullest possible meaning of the biblical text. The text must be read and interpreted theologically.

The Bible is not a history book, and thus one should not use the Bible to fix dates and times of the events recorded. We do not know, nor do we need to know, in what year Abram left Ur of the Chaldees, or Israel came out its slavery in Egypt, or Jesus was born in Bethlehem. The point of these texts is not when the event happened. The point is the *meaning* that has been attached to those events. Abraham is not revered because he left Ur in a particular year. Abraham is revered because he left Ur on a journey of blind faith, and became the model of the faith and trust that all of

159

us should seek to have in our relationship with God.

Without intending any disrespect to the endless and perpetual search for "the historical Jesus," the things recorded in the Bible are more about faith than fact. It does not mean that the things recorded did not actually happen. It does not mean that we are dealing with myths and fables. It simply means that what is important about those events is not "that they happened," but how those who experienced the events sought to understand them. That must be remembered at all times as one reads and seeks to preach the Bible. Failure to do so will inevitably result in the endless arguments and quarrels that so delight those who are sure that the world was created six thousand years ago, based upon their calculations of the dates, generations, and events mentioned in the Bible.

There is no historical evidence to verify any of the miracles of the Bible. No one can prove that Israel crossed the Red Sea, or the Reed Sea, as if on dry ground. There is certainly no evidence of a substantial portion of the Egyptian army being reported as drowned in their pursuit of recently released Hebrew slaves. However, one can preach about the Exodus even though one cannot verify that it ever happened. There is meaning in the passage. For Israel, it meant that the God they served was greater than the power of Pharaoh, the most powerful man on earth. It meant that the God who worked to set them free from slavery was the same God who had earlier worked to create the heavens and the earth. It meant that if God created the various elements of nature, God could certainly manipulate them to achieve the liberation of God's people. That is hermeneutics.

It is also hermeneutics when James Cone, writing three thousand years later and looking back on a different experience of slavery, observes that the Exodus experience is a reminder for African American slaves in the eighteenth and nineteenth centuries that God does not will their bondage. Instead, God actively identifies with the oppressed, and that is why the slaves chose to sing,

> *Go down, Moses,*
> *Way down in Egypt land,*
> *Tell old Pharaoh,*
> *To let my people go.*[4]

Every biblical text that purports to describe some historical event requires this search for theological meaning. The issue is not simply what the text says, but what the text means.

The Bible should also not be read as a scientific treatise on the origins of the universe. The ongoing feud between the advocates of creationism and evolution both miss the point, and both by an equally wide margin. Nothing better illustrates how the creation vs. evolution debate misses the central theological issue than the May 22, 2000, issue of *Christianity Today.*[5] The Bible is not attempting to answer or respond to the questions raised by either group. The question for the Bible is not a matter of "Did God create the universe?" Neither is it a question of "How long did it take God to create the universe?" The real issue is the power and the sovereignty of God over everything that God has made, and the authority and prerogative that God has to impose the divine commandments upon that which God has made. It is obedience, not acknowledgment, that God most desires!

When I was growing up in Chicago I would sometimes forget that I was living in an apartment where someone else paid the rent and provided the food. Every now and then my mother would say to me, "As long as you live in my house you must live by my rules." That was a discussion about nothing more or less than ownership and authority. It was because she had provided for my living environment that she assumed and maintained the right to determine the rules under which I would live there. Every landlord who leases an apartment to a tenant does precisely the same thing.

This is the meaning that we need to attach to the story of creation; it is about ownership and authority. What difference would it make, theologically, if God made the world in six days, or if the world and especially its life forms evolved over a period of six million years, if the people who live in that world do not honor God and obey God's commandments? The church does not honor God when it insists on its answers to questions that neither God nor the Bible is raising.

The preacher must not be content to simply repeat, over and over again, what the Bible says. At the heart of preaching is giving insight into what theological insight is being communicated. This is the search for meaning. This is the work of hermeneutics. No passage

161

should be preached until there is certainty of what the text *SAYS* and *MEANS!* It is this search for the meaning the text had for its original audience, in its own time and place, that is the objective of the seventh step in this exegetical process. The preacher needs to know what lesson the text had for its first readers. Only then can the work of hermeneutics give way to the work of homiletics.

The best books in biblical theology

In order to provide the very best in the way of resources for the preacher who wants to think about the Bible theologically, let me close this chapter with a few recommendations. These do not come simply from my own preferences, but after consultation with faculty colleagues at Ashland Theological Seminary. Preachers would do well to consider the work of Brevard Childs in *Biblical Theology of the Old and New Testament*. High marks are also given to *Theology of the Old Testament* by Walter Brueggemann. In the area of New Testament theology the consensus choices are three: *New Testament Theology* by G.B. Caird, *New Testament Theology* by Gerhard Hasel, and *Theology of the New Testament* (2 volumes) by Leonard Geppelt.

To this list of texts can be added a book that attempts to bridge hermeneutics and homiletics, *Preaching Christ from the Old Testament: A Contemporary Hermeneutical Method*, by Sidney Greidanus. After spending enough time with these giants in the field of biblical theology, thinking theologically about the Scriptures will become second-nature.

SERMON PREVIEW

I end this chapter with a sermon taken from the Luke 23 passage, this time focusing on the impenitent man who died next to Jesus on Calvary. In this sermon, I attempt to lay out several theological issues that may have informed Jesus as he heard, but never responded to, that dying man. What is observed in this sermon is equally instructive as we seek to call out to the Lord in our own lives today. Once again, the technique of "listening to and learning from" a conversation between two biblical characters is employed.

THE UNREPENTANT MAN ON THE CROSS
LUKE 23:32-45

There is a part of language use called the subjunctive mood that allows us to talk about things that have not yet been achieved, but which might become true or factual at some point in the future when certain conditions have been met. The usual indicator of this subjunctive mood is the presence of the word *IF* at the beginning of the sentence or phrase in question. The best biblical examination of the subjunctive mood is found in Psalm 90 where it says, *"The days of our years are three score years and ten; and if by reason of strength they be fourscore years, yet is their strength labour and sorrow; for it is soon cut off, and we fly away."* Notice that living for four-score years is not a certainty. It is a condition that might happen if one has the strength. It is subjunctive. It is marked by the word *IF*.

There is a popular poem by Rudyard Kipling that is entitled, "If." Perhaps you have heard a few lines of this poem before.

> If you can keep your head when all about you are losing theirs
>> And blaming it on you . . . ;
> If you can dream—and not make dreams your master;
>> If you can think and not make thoughts your aim . . . ;
> If you can talk with crowds and keep your virtue,
>> Or walk with kings—nor lose the common touch . . . ;
> If you can fill the unforgiving minute with sixty seconds
>> Worth of distance run—
> Yours is the Earth and everything that's in it,
>> And—which is more—you'll be a Man, my son!

Notice that while the promise or hope offered by this poem is everything that earth can afford, it is all still conditional. It is in the subjunctive mood. It only happens *if* you can do all the things suggested. Nothing is guaranteed. Certain conditions must first be met. Whenever someone uses the word *if*, you know there is something more that must be said or done before the matter can be resolved.

That is what is at stake in the conversation on Calvary that involves the

This sermon was preached by the author on July 19, 1998, at Antioch Baptist Church in Cleveland, Ohio, as part of the sermon series, "Conversations at Calvary." It was first published in the May/April 1999 issue of the journal *Preaching*.

163

three men who are hanging on crosses next to each other. Jesus is on the center cross. On one side of Jesus is a man who has somehow come to recognize that he is dying in the presence of the Son of God, and this man asks Jesus to remember him when the Lord comes into his kingdom. This man has no doubt, no uncertainty, and no reluctance. He turns to Jesus and calls him *Lord!* Notice, however, that this is not the case for the man hanging on the other side of Jesus. He makes no confession of faith. He asks nothing with the conviction that Jesus is able to meet his request. He approaches Jesus in the subjunctive mood, *"If you be the Christ, save yourself and us."*

This scene on Calvary points to the fundamental challenge that faces persons as they make up their minds about a relationship with Jesus. Some people are persuaded already. They believe it is possible to *"take their burdens to the Lord and leave them there."* They accept what Jesus says in John 15:7, *"Ask whatever you will and it shall be done unto you."* But not everybody is in this group. Some people are still unconvinced. They do not have enough faith even to raise a prayer, much less to believe that prayers can be answered. At worst they are cynical about God, not even believing that God exists. At best, they are subjunctive, giving conditions within which they are challenging God to operate. Perhaps they can be persuaded, IF. . . Perhaps they will believe, IF . . . Perhaps God is real, IF . . . .

That is where this text leads us, to a man who could not pray in the affirmative. He could not simply ask for what he wanted. He was not yet convinced that the man dying by his side was able to do what he wanted to have done. So he casts his request in the weakened condition of the subjunctive mood. *"IF you be the Son of God, save yourself and us."* What a weak and timid way to come before God. How can you pray with power when you are stuck behind the word *IF?* How can you find a sweet relief at the altar of prayer when you can go no further than *IF?* Why bother to pray at all? Prayer has no wings to soar and no power to dig deep, because it is stifled by the uncertainty and indecisiveness of *IF.* There may be no more tragic scene in all of the Bible than this scene on Calvary. There, in the middle, is the Son of God. On one side is a man whose bold appeal to Jesus has just won him a place in paradise. And on the other side is a man who can only curse his own condition and challenge Jesus to prove to him that Jesus is who others have claimed him to be. *IF . . . .*

I find it interesting that Jesus never bothered to answer that dying man. When the penitent man on the other cross turned to Jesus and called him Lord, that man was heard and he was blessed beyond measure. But this man received absolutely no response from Jesus. The old song has told us that Jesus *"never said a mumbling word."* Well, we know that he did say several things during the time of his trial and crucifixion. The song actually wants to suggest that Jesus never complained about his treatment, and he never looked to blame anybody else for what was happening to him. But he did speak on several occasions. We know that he spoke seven words from the cross. We know that he spoke to a group of women as he carried his cross through the streets of the city, and fell beneath that heavy weight. However, while Jesus spoke to some people during his hours of suffering and pain, there were others to whom Jesus did not speak a single word. This man was one of those people.

Why do you suppose Jesus did not answer that man? I think, first of all, that Jesus did not have to say or do anything more to prove to that man, or anybody else, that he was the Son of God. For three years, while traveling throughout Palestine, Jesus had repeatedly proven who he was. *IF?* Let the use of that word strike you with all of the shock and dismay that it must have had for Jesus. What does a man have to do to prove that he is the Son of God? When Jesus performed his first miracle and turned water into wine, his mother may have requested it because there was no more wine. Jesus did that miracle, because for the first time he was revealing who he was. When he healed the sick, gave sight to the blind, made the cripples to walk, and even raised the dead back to life, he was proving who he was. When he commanded a howling wind to cease its terrible roar simply by saying, "Peace, be still," he was demonstrating beyond doubt that he was the Son of God. When he spoke in parables and preached with power, so much so that the people had to declare, "Never a man spoke like this man," Jesus was revealing who he was. I suspect that Jesus concluded that he had already done enough to show the world who he actually was.

Are you convinced today that Jesus is the Son of God? Do you reach out to him like the malefactor who went home with Jesus to paradise, or are you still hounded by doubts and uncertainties? Are you still waiting for Jesus to prove himself to you? What have you said to Jesus in the subjunctive mood? Perhaps you said, "If you are real then heal my body? Is that your condition for believing in God? Some people talk to God like one of my seminary classmates, who told us that he promised God that he would go anywhere God sent him. We were all so impressed by his loyalty and devotion that we almost failed to hear everything that my friend said to the Lord. What he said, in total, was that he would go anywhere the Lord sent him, beginning in New York City where we were living, if it was no farther south than Baltimore and no farther west than Pittsburgh. He was not volunteering to serve, he was establishing the conditions under which he would serve. His was a subjunctive service defined by that same word *IF!*

There needs to come a time in our lives when we stop asking God to prove himself to us, and stop giving instructions on how we want God to behave as a precondition for our service and belief. That is how Satan came before Jesus in the wilderness in Matthew 4. *"If you be the Son of God, turn these stones into bread."* Jesus does not need to prove himself to us. The marks of his majesty and divinity are all around us. What person who once was sick and knows for a certainty that God heard your prayers and raised you from that sick bed, will stand here today and declare that Jesus Christ is Lord? What foul sinner who was snatched from sinking sand and established on a solid rock of faith so that your life today is vastly different than it used to be, will share your conviction that Jesus is the Son of God? Who is able to listen to the words of this song and declare that it speaks the sentiments of your own heart?

> *O how well do I remember, how I doubted day by day;*
> *For I did not know for certain that my sins were washed away;*
> *When the Spirit tried to tell me, I would not the truth receive*
> *I endeavored to be happy, and to make myself believe.*
> *But it's real, it's real, O I know it's real;*
> *Praise God, the doubts are settled, For I know, I know it's real.*

Jesus did not answer that dying man, because he had already said and done enough that should have settled that man's doubts. What about you and me? Do you know in your heart that Jesus is real, or are you still waiting, throwing up ifs, and standing in the subjunctive mood until Jesus proves himself to you?

The second reason why I think Jesus gave that man no answer is, because unlike the other dying man who did confess his own sins and acknowledge his wrongdoing, this man wanted to be saved from his suffering without acknowledging his sins. That is not the kind of thing that sends Jesus into action. With Christ things work in the exact opposite order. It is not a matter of his living up to our standards and expectations, but our responding in the way that he expects. I love that verse in 1 John 1:9 that says, *"If you confess your sins, he is faithful and just to forgive your sins and to cleanse you from all unrighteousness."* Notice, however, that in this verse the first step belongs to us. If we confess our sins then God will act. Now we are not establishing the conditions for a future relationship; it is God who is setting the terms.

This is the way God worked with Israel in the Old Testament as well. Where in the Book of Exodus does Israel say to God, "If you get us out of Egypt, then we will serve you and be your people?" No. It worked the other way around. God called all the people together at the foot of Mount Sinai and said, "If you will hear my voice and keep my commandments then I will be your God and you will be my people." It is not we who must test God to see if God is faithful to God's word. It is always God who tests us to see if we can and will be faithful to our word.

The faithfulness and power of God should never be our concern. God is faithful enough to wake us up each morning to see another day, but it is entirely up to us whether or not we wake up singing: *"I woke up this morning with my mind stayed on Jesus. Hallelujah!"* God is faithful enough to give us the continued activity of our limbs and our mind. It is entirely up to us, however, whether or not we are willing to sing, *"Take my life and let it be consecrated Lord to thee. Take my moments and my days, let them flow in ceaseless praise . . . "* It is not God, but we who must stand beneath the scrutiny of the word IF. It is not God, but we who must be proven to be faithful.

Do not test Jesus; just trust him. Let us not ask Jesus to prove himself faithful to us. Instead, let us seek with all of our hearts to prove ourselves faithful to him. See how these two men represent the right and wrong way to pray to the Lord. One man turned to Jesus out of an attitude of trust, and his reward for that was a home in paradise that he would inherit that same day. The other man sought to put Jesus to the test, to make Jesus prove to that man's satisfaction that Jesus really was the Son of God. That man received nothing at all.

Finally, and perhaps most importantly, this man with his subjunctive relationship to Christ was asking for something that was impossible to accomplish. He said to Jesus, *"Save yourself and us."* He obviously did not understand the theology of the cross. He did not comprehend the issue of substitutionary atonement or vicarious suffering. This man did not know anything about Isaiah 53, where it says that *"He was wounded for our transgressions, he was bruised for our iniquity, the chastisement of our peace was upon him, and by his stripes we are healed."* Do we all understand that Jesus could not do both of the things this man was requesting? Jesus could not save himself and us. In fact, Jesus could only save us by not saving himself. By staying on that cross, Jesus was paying the penalty for all sinners for all time. He was dying the death that we deserved as the consequence for our disobedience toward God. By staying on that cross, he was wiping away the stain of our sins from before the eyes of God.

Understand that Jesus could have come down. The story has no power if there was no possibility of his coming down. But he had more than enough power to come down. If he could raise Lazarus up from the grave, he had enough power to come down from the cross. If he could feed five thousand people with two fish and five loaves of bread, he had enough power to come down from the cross. And God who was watching in heaven also had the power to intervene at any moment and rescue the Son of God from that instrument of torture and death. He could have sent ten thousand angels to wing their way down from their positions in heaven and set him free from that cross. God could have shaken the earth, as he would later do for Paul and Silas to open their prison's doors and loose their chains. The point is that Jesus could have come down from that cross. The gospel is that he would not come down because he was willingly sacrificing his own life so that he could save your life and mine from the penalty of sin.

And by the way, this is why I claim Jesus as my Savior and Lord. I am glad that he fed five thousand souls one day on a mountainside in Galilee, but that did not feed my stomach. I am glad he turned water into wine at a wedding feast in Cana, but my thirst was not quenched. I am glad that he was able to calm an angry storm that swept over the Sea of Galilee, but I was not threatened by those howling winds and crashing waves. But when he died out there on Calvary, he was dying there for me. When he shed his blood on that cross, he was washing away my sins. When he sacrificed his life, it was so I would be able to enjoy abundant life and inherit eternal life when I die.

There are no *Ifs* in my relationship with Christ; there are only affirmations. He is my Rock in a weary land. He is my Shelter in the time of storm. He is my Deliverer from the strong hand of Satan. He is my Key to the gates of glory. He is *"my help in ages past and my hope for years to come, my shelter from the stormy blast and my eternal home."*

9
The 8 Ls:
Life Application

The ultimate challenge of preaching is to take the materials that have been gathered in the exegetical process (steps 1-7), and transform them into a sermon designed to offer some spiritual nurture for a specific congregation. Of course, that congregation lives in a world that is at least two thousand years removed from the setting of the biblical text. How to make that transition from then to now, and from the study of an ancient text to addressing its truths about the lives of a modern congregation, is the focus of this final chapter.

The skill phase and the creative phase in preparing to preach

At this point, the words of Joseph Stowell in his interview in *Biblical Sermons* come to mind. As stated earlier in this book, Stowell breaks the work of the preacher into two parts or processes, the "skill phase" and the "creative phase."[1] One can equate his skill phase with the exegetical work that has been discussed in the preceding chapters of this book. He says that the skill phase is like a person who goes to the grocery store and buys all of the necessary ingredients for some food item. The creative phase occurs when those ingredients are carefully and intentionally mixed together to create the desired food item.

Stowell expands upon his point about the skill and the creative phases in sermon preparation. He says, "My weakest sermons have been ones I preached when I finished the skill phase and did not take time to let it germinate and, as John Stott says, take it into the world of real people."[2] Thus, the creative phase not only involves moving from text analysis to sermon design, but doing so with a specific mean and an intended audience in mind. This is where the rich and broad variety of themes and topics so often heard in today's preaching are rooted. Each preacher brings a variety of talents, perspectives, and intentions to the task of preparing a sermon.

It is possible that two preachers could set out to do the skill phase with the same text, and by the end of step seven they could wind up with much the same information. All they have done up to that point is go shopping, checklist in hand, for the needed ingredients. It is virtually impossible that those same two preachers would create the same sermon from those common ingredients. It is at the level of the "creative phase," sermon design, sermon designation, and sermon delivery that the miracle and majesty of preaching may emerge.

I have heard the Scottish preacher Peter Marshall preach about the Exodus story on a record entitled "Encounter in Egypt." I have heard my own seminary advisor, James Cone, comment, lecture, and preach on that same story innumerable times. Both men were expert in doing the skill phase. However, when I heard the finished product, the two sermons had almost nothing in common except the use of the same text. The creative phase of preaching took them in different directions.

As part of my teaching at Ashland Seminary, I begin by establishing the *8 Ls* methodology for doing biblical exegesis. That is my approach to the "skill phase." However, the eighth step, *Life Application*, involves the use of a model for engaging in the creative phase of preaching. This model is also based upon the use of alliteration, and involves eight words, all of which begin with the letter *E*. The words are,

1. Exegetical
2. Evangelical
3. Environmental
4. Emotional
5. Experiential
6. Epigrammatical
7. Evocative
8. Ethical

It is when these steps are engaged in, or steps similar to these as defined by other preachers and professors, that the uniqueness of each preacher is unlocked so he or she can engage in the creative work of preaching.

1. Exegetical

Everything that is found in the first eight chapters is devoted to this topic. However, I want to include it at the beginning of this listing as a reminder that if preachers want their sermons to be *living water for thirsty souls*, they should take the time to clearly comprehend both what the biblical text *SAYS* and *MEANS*.

2. Evangelical

This word, *evangelical*, desperately needs to be rescued from the clutches of those who employ it as a synonym for a set of issues far more reflective of the Republican Party than the Kingdom of God. When I suggest that preaching should be evangelical, I am not suggesting that preaching must adopt the politically correct position on such issues as a return to school prayer, student-led prayer at school events, tax credits for families who want to enroll their children in private or parochial schools, or overturning *Roe v. Wade*, which would result in making abortions illegal in this country. Not only is the word *evangelical* not being used that way in this chapter, but also it is a gross disservice to Christian history that any group would ever seek to link the idea of being evangelical to conformity with any social agenda.

I am using the word evangelical as an indicator of the New Testament and Reformation roots of the word. Carl Henry, writing in *The New International Dictionary of the Christian Church*, says,

> The term means pertaining to the Gospel (as expounded by the four Gospels) or conforming to the basic doctrines of the Gospel (as enunciated by the New Testament as a whole). By extension it signifies one who is devoted to the Good News or "Evangel" of God's redemptive grace in Jesus Christ.[3]

The Oxford Dictionary of the Christian Church speaks more directly to the Reformation roots of the term when it says, "In a wider sense, the term Evangelical has been applied since the Reformation to the Protestant churches by reason of their claim to base their teaching pre-eminently on the Gospel."[4]

Principally, I use the word *evangelical* to stress the need for a sermon to be biblically based and Christ-centered. Preaching needs to point people to the Good News of the gospel of Jesus Christ. After all of the exegetical work has been accomplished, the preacher must ask himself or herself how all of that will be fashioned into a sermon that will result in an encounter between the congregation and the Christ of Calvary.

At the beginning of this book, I spoke about a deacon in my first parish in Montclair, New Jersey, who asked me every Sunday morning, "Rev, is there any word from the Lord?" The use of the word *evangelical* is designed to push the preacher to shape a sermon that is not a collection of personal opinions, politically correct observations, or quotes and quips from prominent people. Rather, an evangelical sermon is the preacher's very best effort to present a word of hope or help, or a word of comfort or challenge, that is grounded in a thorough analysis of a portion of Scripture. "Reverend, is there any word from the Lord?"

There is a way to discover whether or not one's preaching is evangelical in the sense in which the term is being used here. Does your preaching regularly engage people around the major doctrines and themes of the Bible? Do you speak about the sovereign power of God, the love of Christ as revealed by his death on the cross, or the power and promise of the resurrection? Do you challenge people to understand properly the role that the sacraments and ordinances play in the life of a Christian? Do you speak about Christian discipleship, the outreach and mission of the church, and the regular practice of stewardship as an authentic act of worship and obedience? Do you challenge people to "love one another" across or despite differences in race, culture, language, and gender? Finally, does your sermon ever present people with the challenge of personal salvation through faith in the atoning work of God in Jesus Christ? Or as we so often say in the Baptist church, does your sermon flow into an "invitation to discipleship?" The first challenge in designing and delivering a sermon is to be sure that it is an evangelical message.

3. Environmental

The next challenge of sermon design and delivery is to be sure it is relevant to and informed by the setting in which it is being delivered. Every sermon must be understood as an encounter between the word of God and the people of God meeting together in a particular place, at a particular time, for a particular reason. Preaching does not take place in a vacuum. Instead, preaching happens within social, cultural, theological, and ideological settings. The preacher must work hard to understand how the word of God speaks to the congregation that has gathered at that time and place. What is the environmental setting in which the people of God gather to hear the preaching of the gospel?

a. Paul as an example of knowing one's environment

Preachers should learn one simple lesson from the ministry of Paul. This great apostle had a knack for directing his epistles to the specific needs and circumstances of the church or individual to whom that epistle was addressed. Paul did not write to Philemon those lessons he intended for Timothy. Paul did not write to the church in Philippi about matters that were occurring in Corinth. Paul did not examine in Romans the same doctrinal concerns that one finds in 1 and 2 Thessalonians. Paul wrote, and presumably preached, with an awareness of the environment in which his words were directed, and to which his words were addressed.

b. Examples of environmental differences in today's church

Effective preaching requires that we bring that same level of environmental sensitivity. We need to be aware of the people who constitute the congregation and the pressures and problems that confront them. Is this an inner-city congregation struggling to maintain ministries that relate them to issues of homelessness, poverty, and substance abuse? How to motivate that congregation to engage in a ministry that it has long been avoiding, or to keep the faith even though their efforts over many years have not lessened the problem, is an issue of environmental relevance.

Is this a rural congregation in an agricultural community, like the Salem Mennonite Church in Salem, Ohio, where I recently preached? The issues there are somewhat different. Farm prices, urban sprawl, the benefits and hazards of pesticides, and the challenge of maintaining small, family owned farms in the face of the threat of agribusiness, are among the issues that may lead them to ask the question, "Reverend, is there any word from the Lord?"

The list of possible environmental issues is nearly unlimited. Is this church largely populated with senior citizens? Is it a suburban and largely affluent white congregation where many of the corporate executives in a community are members? Is it a church where preaching is central to the worship experience, or does music or free flowing praise define how worship takes place? Does this church give special focus to motivating men to take a leadership role, or does it seek to move women into roles of leadership that had long been denied to them? Does this church expect the preacher to follow the liturgical calendar in themes, if not in the actual lectionary texts for the day?

A very important environmental question is the length of the sermon and the service. I can recall being invited to preach in the chapel of an Ivy League university and being reminded that the congregation was accustomed to a service that was no longer than forty-five minutes in length, sermon included. I have been known, on more than one occasion, to preach a sermon that was forty-five minutes in length. However, that was in a different environmental setting. I did what I had to do in that university chapel in fifteen minutes, and was invited back annually for the next several years.

By contrast, I often went to preach at my uncle's Church of God in Christ congregation (Pentecostal) in Maywood, Illinois. That environment was quite different from the Ivy League university chapel. That Pentecostal service lasted well over three hours, and in that setting one of my forty-five-minute sermons would not have been considered too long. In fact, that was the average length of my uncle's sermons. Neither service would have been well served if I had been ignorant of or indifferent to their worship environment.

In the forty-five-minute service in the university chapel, the people listened attentively, but they never said a word while the sermon was being preached. In the Pentecostal sermon, the congregation was so vocal and so comfortable with the talking back to the preacher that is so common in black churches, there were points in that sermon when I had to be silent until the people had finished talking. In fact, at one point in one of those services a man sprang to his feet, began running in a circle around the interior of the sanctuary to the accompaniment of the organ, bass guitar, drums, and the rhythmic clapping of the congregation. After several trips around the church he returned to his seat and I continued with my sermon. As the popular 1970s song by Sly and the Family Stone said, *"Different strokes for different folks."*

c. Learning from the shepherds

This issue of environment can be taken to an even deeper and more helpful level of preaching, especially as it relates to those who preach to the same congregation week after week. The more you know about the people in your congregation the more you can direct your preaching to address issues that you know will be helpful for them. One thinks about the role of a shepherd who not only feeds the flock in general, but also takes care to meet the needs of particular sheep: the very young and the very old, the weak ones, and the ones who need some special grass. This is the beauty of the image of the shepherd in Isaiah 40:11, which says, "He shall feed his flock like a shepherd: he shall gather the lambs with his arm, and carry them in his bosom, and shall gently lead those that are with young." One can almost see the shepherd keeping an eye not only on the flock, but also on each individual sheep therein.

d. The pastor as shepherd

Seward Hiltner was the chief proponent of a model of pastoral ministry that he called "the shepherding model."[5] What he implied about the role of the pastor in counseling, sick visitations, and administration, also applies to the work of the pastor as preacher. He or she not only preaches sermons that are relevant to the life of that congregation, but the preacher also has a clear idea of some of the spiritual needs of individual members of the congregation. Who is battling with cancer or HIV/AIDS, depression, or some other physical or mental illness? Who has a child or spouse in prison? Who has just lost a job, and with that, the possible loss of car, home, and lifestyle? How does one plan a sermon, and a year of preaching as well, so that the needs of teens are met, as well as the needs of their parents and grandparents? In John 10:14, Jesus says, "I am the good shepherd; and know my sheep. . . ." We may not be the Good Shepherd, but every pastor can be *a good shepherd* by just paying close attention to the environment in which he or she feeds the sheep and the flock of God.

4. Evocative

Many sermons that I have heard over the last thirty years of my professional life as both a pastor and professor of preaching have failed to achieve their full affect because the preacher never got around to asking for anything from the listeners. The sermon was not designed to *evoke* a response from the congregation or from any persons or groups within the congregation. The preacher told us everything that was on his or her mind. The preacher told us what the biblical text *SAID* and *MEANT.* What the preacher so often did not do was answer the questions I discussed in the Introduction, *"So what"* and *"What next?"*

Every sermon needs to have an objective of what is going to be asked from the congregation as an appropriate response to that message. Every preacher needs to know what the response is or the next steps he or she hopes to evoke from the listeners. Here is where journalism and preaching part company. Both of them deal with the *what,* the substance of some issue. However, preaching also involves the *so what,* and the preacher's job is not complete until some answer has been given to this *so what.*

I have been greatly helped by Robert McCracken's book, *The Making of the Sermon,* in which he states that there are four things a preacher can seek as the appropriate response to the sermon. There are four responses to the *so what* question. He calls them (1) to kindle the mind, (2) to energize the will, (3) to disturb the conscience, (4) to stir the heart.[6] Let the preacher seek to *evoke* any one of these four possible responses, and preaching will take on added urgency and challenge.

a. Kindle the mind

Persuading people to think, especially about something which they tend to approach with a closed mind, is a very difficult thing to do. Sometimes challenging one's listeners just to think about a complex or controversial topic is all a sermon ought to attempt to achieve.

However, setting forth what the issues are, and identifying why the topic requires their most rigorous and reverent reflection, is the responsibility of the preacher.

The issues that can kindle the mind of a person who hears a sermon can range from their view on a doctrinal issue, to some aspect of human sexuality, race relations, the ordination of women, the status of gays and lesbians in the church, international issues of war and peace, or some action or position taken by that church's denominational hierarchy. It takes courage for the preacher to raise some of these issues because they can be so divisive. One of the ways to lessen the risk of division, and to open the door to further dialogue and possible action later on, is simply to examine the matter carefully in the sermon, and invite people to think and reflect on what has been said.

William Sloane Coffin preached the best example of a sermon that I have read or heard that ended with a focus on kindling the mind. He had been part of a delegation from the United States that visited over the Christmas season with the American hostages who were being held in Iran in 1979. That hostage crisis would last for over four hundred days and contribute to the failure of Jimmy Carter to be reelected president of the United States. Rather than attack and lambast the people of Iran for the injustice of the hostage crisis, Coffin reminded his listeners that the United States government had played a direct role in creating the conditions that resulted in the overthrow of the Shah of Iran, the rise of the Ayatollah Khomeini, and the taking of the American hostages. He ended that sermon by saying, "I guess we all have a lot that we need to think about this Christmas."[7]

Let the example of William Sloane Coffin be instructive, not only in his willingness to preach a sermon that would kindle the mind but also in his willingness to take on a subject of such depth and substance. People can be called to think about something before they are asked to do anything. Being called to think is an appropriate call to action. I challenge people who do ministry in the various environments that make up the body of Christ to be willing to engage their congregations around the critical and complex questions and concerns that so vex our society. You do not have to know the answer to the problem. That answer may come if we just have the courage to raise the issue and the wisdom to simply ask people to think about it for a while. The first outcome of preaching can be to kindle the mind.

b. Energize the will

The second possible response that the preacher can attempt to evoke from the listener, according to McCracken, is to energize the will. This is the sermon that seeks to motivate people to take a certain action or engage in a certain activity. The action that is desired may be mentioned in the biblical text itself, or it may reside within the intention of the preacher. Either way, the challenge at hand is to persuade the people who hear the sermon to engage in the action that is being set before them. In speaking about *energizing the will*, McCracken suggests that people need to be encouraged, even urged to act. Perhaps they were first invited just to think about some issue, but now the time has come to move beyond thought and reflection and take some concrete steps. Using every power of persuasion known to him or her, the preacher needs to end some sermons by setting some action steps before the congregation, and then urge them to take those steps.

The steps that are involved can be matters of personal piety and individual discipleship. It can be a challenge to spend more time in prayer or in Bible study. It can be a challenge to practice the principle of 10 percent tithing of one's income in support of the ministries of the church. It can be a challenge to take a more active part in the programs and outreach ministries of the congregation. It may even be something as basic and fundamental as accepting Jesus Christ as Lord and Savior as a direct and immediate response to the sermon that has been preached.

The preacher may need to energize the will of the listeners to respond to matters that exist beyond the life of the congregation, but still relate to the work of the kingdom of God. There are children that need to be mentored, tutored, even adopted. "Who will accept that challenge?" There are hot meals to be served at the local hunger center or fed to people in nursing homes who are frequently unable to feed themselves. "Will anybody answer this call to serve?"

The ability to energize the will is related to the skill of the preacher in employing those biblical texts that point in exactly that direction. Even if the sermon is not based upon these texts, they can be used to drive home this final call to action. In Isaiah 6, God says to the prophet, "Who can I send, and who will go for us?" Then the prophet, his will having been energized by the challenge from God, answers and says, "Here am I; send me." This is the quintessential biblical model for energizing the will.

There are, however, other models. In Matthew 25 in the Great Judgment scene, Jesus says that whether or not we enter into the kingdom of heaven depends, in large measure, on whether or not we respond to the needs of those who are hungry, thirsty, naked, sick, or imprisoned. Finally, James 2:14 says, "But what does it profit, my brethren, if someone says he has faith but does not have works?" James 2:17 then concludes that, "Faith, if it does not have works, is dead."

There are other appeals that people use to motivate others into taking an action. Athletic coaches appeal to pride and glory; combat commanders appeal to patriotism and the tyranny that needs to be driven from the land. Sales persons appeal to how affordable their product is, and how much time and effort can be saved if only one buys what they are selling. Investment bankers assure us that there is money to be made if only we take the risk. Political candidates paint a picture of how much better off the nation will be if people vote them into office. In virtually every area of life, we have all had some direct experience with this need to energize the will.

Preaching is no different. Many people may not know what is the right thing for them to do, and knowing it still may not motivate them to volunteer to do it. The preacher must, on some occasions, end the sermon with an appeal to action that is designed to energize the will of those who just heard the sermon. I remember hearing William A. Jones, the great Baptist preacher from Brooklyn, New York, commenting on the need to preach with an eye toward persuading people to act. He said on one occasion, "When the ancient Greeks listened to a speech by Demosthenes they said to each other, 'How well he speaks.' However, when they heard a speech by Cicero, they said one to another, 'Let us go now and fight against the king.'" The ability to speak well is not fully exploited, so far as preaching is concerned, if it does not work on occasion to move people to take some challenging and difficult action.

c. Disturb the conscience

In the Gospel of Mark, the earliest of the Gospels to be written, both John the Baptist and Jesus begin their public ministries by calling people to repentance (Mark 1:4 and 1:15). There were attitudes and behaviors that needed to be abandoned. There were lifestyles that had to be renounced. There was oppression and exploitation of certain people, and it had to end. People whose lives are moving in a certain direction need to make a 180-degree turn in their conduct and behavior. Sometimes the preacher's goal is to so concentrate on some sin that the sermon unsettles and disturbs the conscience of the persons who are engaged in such actions. Having disturbed the conscience, the preacher then goes the next step and challenges people to repent.

There are innumerable biblical examples that support the importance of this kind of preaching. This is what the eighth-century prophets did when they challenged both Israel and Judah about turning away from Yahweh and following after other gods. This is what Nathan did in his confrontation with David following David's disgraceful behavior involving both Bathsheba and her husband Uriah. When Samuel confronted Saul concerning the king's disobedience to the commands of God, he was engaged in this kind of verbal encounter.

In the New Testament, John the Baptist set out to disturb the conscience not only of the people of Israel in general, but to disturb the conscience of Herod Antipas in particular, because of his illegal marriage to the wife of Philip, Herod's brother. In Acts 5 Peter confronts Ananias and Sapphira when they lie about holding back some money from the common treasury of the early Jerusalem church. In Galatians 2, Paul says that he had to disturb the conscience of Peter who was inconsistent in his views about how to incorporate Gentile converts in the Christian faith.

The God of the Bible is full of love and grace, but there are also commandments to be observed, disciplines to be practiced, and justice to be displayed by God's people. When God's people fall short of what God expects, God sends someone whose words serve to disturb the conscience of those whose conduct has become illicit and adulterous, whose salt has lost its savor, and whose light no longer shines.

This kind of preaching should be reserved for those areas of human conduct about which Scripture is genuinely concerned, and not simply about behaviors that are viewed as inappropriate according to some human standard of measurement. Many a churchgoer has been turned off by the preoccupation of the preacher with whether or not women wore lipstick or used makeup. It seemed that the greatest sins were not racism or sexism or environmental destruction. They seldom heard about the evils of war, the tragedy of homelessness, the poverty of the "working poor," or the loss of American jobs to Third World countries where neither fair wages nor safe working conditions were provided. Instead, the preacher's ire and the wrath of God were reserved for those who went to see motion pictures, or were seen dancing, or dared to smoke a cigarette, or were caught holding hands.

Too much Christian preaching is little more than nagging people over things concerning which the preacher or some ideological group does not approve. Is that because they do not have the courage to speak up about those things, clearly rooted in the Scriptures, that are the cause of so much pain and anguish in our society? Beyond that, too much preaching that seeks to disturb the conscience is highly selective concerning the sins about which it will and will not speak. I wonder about the faithfulness of that preacher who is quick to condemn homosexuality, but never says a word about those heterosexual adulterous relationships going on within his or her own congregation.

Even worse is the preacher who never sees that he or she is wrapped up in the dilemma of sin along with the people in the pews. "All have sinned," and that includes those of us who occupy the pulpit on Sunday morning. If we remember this, we stop preaching "at" our people, and start preaching "about" the sins that grip us all. We dare not allow ourselves to stray too far from the words that Paul spoke concerning himself in Romans 7:19,24 when he said, "For the good that I would I do not: but the evil which I would not, that I do . . . . O wretched man that I am! Who shall deliver me from the body of this death?"

d. Stir the heart

There are times when the preacher's task is to help people see through the storms that are presently raging in their lives, and remind them that "the Lord will make a way somehow." God is faithful. God's promises are secure. God's strength is sufficient for our heaviest burdens. "Greater is he that is in you, than he that is in the world" (1 John 4:4). As a pastor for the last twenty-five years, and after thirty years of ministry in general, I understand that sometimes the preacher's task is to present the love and power of God in such a way that the only appropriate response is, "Glory, Hallelujah!"

I remember the words of Samuel Johnson who said, "People do not so much need to be informed as to be reminded." They may have heard at some point in their lives about the miracle-working power of God. They may have been told in a time of "green pastures and still waters" that God is also able to keep us in "the valley of the shadow of death" and "in the presence of our enemies." However, when people find themselves brought face-to-face with crisis, sickness, mortality, or uncertainty, they may forget what they have heard about God. All they can see, feel, and consider is the problem at hand.

The job of the preacher is to help people break through those moments when they feel overwhelmed by the world, and remind them that they are still in the hands of God. Psalm 139 not only reminds us that we cannot hide our sins from God; it also reminds us that the love and grace of God can reach us wherever we find ourselves. God is able to comfort, sustain, encourage, and deliver us when we find ourselves in hospital wards, or inside courtrooms. God will not abandon us when we stand and gaze at all that remains of family or friends whose death has drawn us finally to their gravesides.

God can work to heal us after the disappointment of divorce, or after the sting of a racist comment or a sexist action by someone who was close enough to us to actually hurt our feelings. Life can be hard and cruel, but God . . . ! People may have heard before everything that we tell them on that day. But sometimes they just need to be reminded.

Kindle the mind, energize the will, disturb the conscience, or stir the heart. These are responses that a preacher can, and on occasion should, seek to evoke from those who have heard our sermons.

5. Emotional

One of the aspects of my own black preaching tradition that I value and treasure has been the level of enthusiasm and emotional investment so many black preachers have brought to the task. Sometimes that emotion has been scorned as nothing more than *"emotionalism."* There may be instances when that is true, and when preachers substitute emotionalism for serious consideration of the biblical text. That abuse of the preaching moment and the people is to be regretted. However, I hope that every preacher will come to value the importance of bringing some emotion to the preaching of the Gospel.

Most forms of preaching and public speaking can trace their roots to the statement of Aristotle that those who speak to others must possess *logos, ethos,* and *pathos.*[8] For Aristotle, logos meant the substance of the argument being made. Ethos meant the ethical character of the speaker, implying that the speaker's own conduct should not contradict the message that he or she is attempting to communicate. Pathos meant the necessary passion that the speaker must feel about the subject and the passion the speaker must bring to the delivery of the message if those who listen are to be expected to respond.

If it appears to our listeners that what we are saying does not matter to us, why do we think it will matter to them? All that has been said up to now has dealt with the logos portion of Aristotle's statement. The importance of the ethical dimensions of the preacher's own life will be dealt with later in this chapter. The issue at hand is the need for those who preach to allow themselves to demonstrate some passion, some emotion as a part of their presentation of the gospel.

Halford Luccock, who taught homiletics at Yale Divinity School for many years, raised a question with himself that every preacher needs to consider. He said, in his book, *Communicating the Gospel,*

> Eugene Ormandy once dislocated his shoulder while leading the Philadelphia Orchestra. I do not know what they were

playing, but he was giving all of himself to it. And I have asked myself sadly, did I ever dislocate anything, even a necktie?[9]

I am not urging people to preach themselves into a need for orthopedic care. However, I do believe that we ought to bring the same passion and enthusiasm to the interpretation and presentation of the gospel of Jesus Christ that a conductor brings to the interpretation and presentation of a concerto by Mozart or a symphony by Beethoven.

I have often wondered whether preachers should view their pulpit work under the lens of Paul's statement, "For I am not ashamed of the gospel of Christ: for it is the power of God unto salvation to every one that believeth" (Romans 1:16). At stake would not only be our willingness to speak about Jesus before a nonbelieving world, but to do so with a degree of enthusiasm and emotion that might give others the impression that we are not scholarly or logical or intellectual.

Somehow, I do not envision any of the prophets, or Paul, or Jesus being first and foremost concerned about whether they were being perceived as being too emotional. They spoke with urgency, with conviction, and with a sense of purpose that was so compelling that they evoked an almost immediate response from those who heard them. Sometimes the response was conversion and faith in Christ, sometimes the response was rejection and the need to flee the city to preserve their lives (Acts 19). But either way, it is easy to imagine that it was their obvious sense of conviction, of emotion, of passion (pathos), that moved the crowds who heard them. I sincerely doubt whether cold and dispassionate preaching would have resulted in "turning the world upside down" (Acts 17:6).

Henry Mitchell speaks persuasively about the use of emotion in preaching as being "the point of greatest divergence" between black and white preachers in America.[10] Writing in "African-American Preaching" in the October 1997 edition of *Interpretation*, Mitchell points out that this absence of emotion in preaching has not always been the case. Rather, the white preachers of the Great Awakening were noted for their use of emotion. In fact, they were commonly called "enthusiasts."[11] The use of that term by the clergy of the more sedate Anglican and Presbyterian churches was, of course, meant as something of a slur. However, the Baptists and Methodists who were identified with that term were the persons largely responsible for the Great Awakening.

Mitchell notes that it was during the Great Awakening that the forces of logos and pathos met and merged, and the result was a revival of religious enthusiasm that lasted well over one hundred years. More importantly, he observes that it was the emotional fervor of white preachers such as George Whitfield and Gilbert Tennent, along with the fervor and enthusiasm of traditional African religions, that ignited the flame of emotion that burns in the black church to this day. He says,

> The Great Awakening burst forth with shouting…under no less a preacher than Jonathan Edwards—though he was wary of it at first. The shouting really burst forth under Whitefield and the Tennents. Thus, in discussing emotion, if one goes back as far as the first and second Great Awakening, one finds the streams merged even here.[12]

Mitchell concludes by noting that it is a shame that even among those white Methodist groups once known for their zeal and enthusiasm, the pathos seems to have been lost. What is an ever greater form of historical amnesia is to see black Baptist and Methodist preachers and churches turning away from the use of pathos in both preaching and worship. When they do that, they are burning the bridge that brought us over!

6. Experiential

It is very possible that the best illustration of what it means to be "saved by grace," or to have been "delivered from the lions' den," or to have a joy and peace that "the world didn't give and the world can't take away," resides within the experience of the preacher himself or herself. In fact, part of the passion and enthusiasm that we bring to our preaching is due to the fact that the Good News of the gospel that we present to others was initially Good News in relation to our own sin and salvation saga. When approached this way, our preaching becomes infectious. The emotion that God's grace has stirred within us easily flows over into the way we share from the Scriptures.

Preachers will want to be highly selective in the ways they share their personal experiences in the context of their preaching. However, there is a general rule that might serve well in most instances. If the illustration or episode you are relating tends to place the preacher in a favorable light where it seems we are urging people to "be like us," we should probably not share that experience. Preaching is no time for us to hold ourselves up as moral examples. That speaks of both arrogance and ignorance. It is arrogant because our task is to help people see Jesus, not to focus on us (John 12:21). It is ignorant because it seems to ignore the fact that all have sinned and fallen short of the glory of God (Romans 3:23). Make no mistake about it, the preacher is a part of that *ALL!*

On the other hand, if the illustration or episode shows how God has worked for the good in the life of the preacher, if it shows how God has "brought us from a mighty long way," then that is a story worth sharing. If we are willing to allow the congregation to see that the sins abhorred by God have left their marks upon our own bodies, souls, and lives, our people might listen to us more willingly. We are often accused of "preaching at people," which implies that we are talking at them. The dynamics of preaching change considerably when we are willing to admit that "It ain't my mother, or my father, but it's me, O Lord, standing in the need of prayer."

Here again, the preacher can take a lesson from the ministry of the apostle Paul. He would frequently remind his listeners that he had not always been on the Lord's side. In his defense before Agrippa in Acts 26:11-15, Paul speaks about the time he had spent persecuting the followers of Christ before his conversion. He does the same thing in Galatians 1:13-16, when he notes that "I persecuted the church of God and wasted it." How much more powerful was the preaching and the testimony of Paul concerning the power of God to change and transform human lives when he could speak about that from personal experience. To the extent that we make our transformative experiences with God a part of our testimony when we preach, we aid and strengthen our sermons.

In his *Lectures on Preaching*, delivered as the Lyman Beecher

Lectures at Yale, Phillip Brooks states that the art of preaching involves the presentation of "truth through personality."[13] What is the personality of the preacher? Is it just his or her character traits, speech patterns, attitudes, and predisposition? Or does personality also include the full range of personal experiences that have helped to shape and mold the preacher's soul and spirit, thoughts and beliefs, hopes and fears? Not only should we not seek to preach without calling upon our experiences, but I very much doubt that we can preach without our collective experiences working to shape the message as they have already shaped the messenger.

7. Epigrammatical

In Chapter Four of this book I mention the value of a preaching style that appeals to the mind of the listener by appealing to all five senses of the human body. We experience and comprehend our world as a series of sensory encounters. We taste, feel, smell, hear, and see. It is impossible to fully communicate with people without some attempts to invite them to use one or more of their sensory receptors. As a preacher and teacher, I do not simply try to "tell" something to people. I try to present the Gospel story in as graphic and visual a manner as possible, appealing on every possible occasion to the use of their five senses. One of the most effective ways to accomplish this is to employ an epigrammatic preaching style. This means that the preacher makes use of word pictures, engages in storytelling, and makes the biblical text and the biblical world come alive in the mind of the listeners through character development and commentary on the actions being discussed in the text.

This is certainly the genius of the black preachers I have heard and most admired over the years. They do not simply read the words of a text and launch out into a three-point sermon and a conclusion. They take the listener on a walking tour of the world in which the text is set. Gardner Taylor, Samuel Proctor, William Jones, and Sandy Ray are the four preachers who have most influenced my love for preaching, even though I have never risen to their level of skill and power. When any one of them would tell the story of the passion of Christ, I was carried into the darkness of the Garden of Gethsemane. I was almost enabled to feel the pain and torture as Christ is beaten and flogged. I heard the mob cry out,

"Crucify him!" I could see the scowls on the faces of the Roman soldiers as they made sport of the Savior. I could smell the stench that must have hung in the air around Calvary as three men were crucified, hung up, and left to die beneath the baking sun of the Mediterranean region.

Of course, no one was better at the use of epigrams than Jesus himself. His use of parables, his references to things that could easily be visualized or imagined by his listeners was unparalleled. One could easily see a sower going forth to sow or a woman furiously searching her house in search of a lost coin. The challenge of the preacher is to follow that example when presenting the biblical story. Why talk about the fear that gripped the disciples when they were caught in a furious storm on the Sea of Galilee, without describing what they must have heard, seen, and felt at that moment? That is but one of a thousand instances where the sermon is strengthened if the preacher makes a conscious attempt to get the listeners to understand the text by focusing on the sights, sounds, and scents present in the story.

The epistles of Paul are somewhat less accessible at this level, but even that material can be presented with some attention to the human dramas that are present within his writings. Fortunately, the life of Paul can also be accessed through the use of the Acts of the Apostles, and there the opportunities for epigrammatic preaching abound. The preacher can then add to the sermon such illustrations, anecdotes, references to current events, and supporting Scripture references as will present the meaning and message of the primary text in the fullest and clearest way possible.

Very few preachers have the innate ability to preach with this level of attention to the details of the text, or create vivid word pictures that appeal to the five senses. This is, for most of us, an acquired skill. One of the best ways to acquire this ability, or to enhance what may come naturally, is to squeeze in the time to read an occasional novel. A novelist has to create the characters, the context, the plot, the steadily unfolding events, and the conclusion of the story. All of this is done through an appeal to our imagination, and through a masterful appeal to the five senses. Whether you prefer Tom Clancy or Toni Morrison, Stephen King or Alice Walker, you cannot help but learn how to be sensitive to the sounds of birds at night, the smell of the ocean, the taste of food or drink, or sweat or blood. You come away much more sensitive to the touch of human skin, especially when it is attached to a rough hewn wooden cross by large spiked nails driven through the wrists and ankles. Good preaching, like any other art, takes time and work. When we consider the weight and worth of the work we are called upon to do, the extra effort it takes to be truly effective as a preacher is not too much to ask.

8. Ethical

For those of us who preach the gospel, the only thing as important as the intellectual integrity with which we handle the Scriptures is the personal integrity with which we live our lives. Preaching is a very public act that requires that the preacher stand before an assembly of people and speak to them, sometimes about the flaws and failures of their lives. That can be hard to do when the sinful conduct and the immoral character of the preacher is the topic of conversation in the barber shops and beauty salons, and in the restaurants and recreational venues where people in the community and congregation meet and mingle.

As has been stated earlier, the preacher should never be presumed to be above sin, not by the congregation nor by the preacher himself or herself. However, when the sinful and immoral behavior of the preacher is blatant, persistent, and unrepentant, his or her authority and effectiveness in communicating the gospel to others will be greatly diminished. Preachers should seek to live their lives by the highest possible ethical standards, so that no aspect of their personal conduct prevents them from being able to preach any aspect of the gospel message with authority and sincerity. On too many occasions, I have heard gifted preachers attempt to deliver wonderfully crafted sermons. However, the congregation was more offended by their conduct out of the pulpit than they were interested in anything the preacher had to say while standing at the pulpit. Ethical conduct and personal integrity are two things that every preacher should work hard to establish and maintain. In short, it is difficult if not impossible to persuade people to receive *living water for thirsty souls* when the cup that brings them that water is dirty.

It bears repeating that no one, the preacher included, is beyond the upward reach and the downward pull of sin. Preachers struggle with failed marriages, alcoholism, sexual impropriety, financial mismanagement, reckless driving, racial prejudice, and gender bias. In the face of these issues, the gospel can be a healing balm as much for us as for anyone who occupies the pew. The words of Paul in 2 Corinthians 4:7 are true in this instance, "But we have this treasure in earthen vessels, that the excellency of the power may be of God, and not of us."

Nevertheless, God has called us to, and we have accepted leadership roles in, the body of Christ. The people of God have invited us, and we have agreed to break unto them, the bread of life. Most of this book has been devoted to the work of analyzing the Bible so that the preacher lives up to the challenge of 2 Timothy 2:15 which says, "Study to shew thyself approved unto God, a worker that needeth not to be ashamed, rightly dividing the word of truth." However, we can bring shame upon ourselves, our profession, and the cause of Christ not only by how we handle the Scriptures, but also by how we live our lives day by day.

Let this be the final note. When we stand to preach the word of God, may our logos, pathos, and ethos meet and merge in the pulpit. Let the truth and clarity of our message, the power and conviction of our delivery, and the ethical conduct of our lives work together in such a way that the people of God are nourished, the church of God is strengthened, and the name of God is glorified.

SERMON PREVIEW

I end this chapter and the book with a sermon based upon Galatians 3:26-29. In a sense, this sermon is offered as a model of all the steps mentioned earlier in the book. It seeks to focus on a specific passage of Scripture (*Limits*). It is an epistle written by Paul in an attempt to address issues that were of concern to a particular community of faith (*Literature* and *Location*). It makes use of some very important terms that are carefully reviewed in the sermon (*Language*). The sermon makes reference to numerous additional portions of Scripture (*Links*). The sermon attempts to identify the challenge that Paul was setting before the Galatian church

(*Lessons*). Finally, I attempt to offer some suggestions on how this passage speaks to the followers of Jesus Christ today (*Life Application*).

Finally, this sermon seeks to evoke a specific response from the hearers. While there are some aspects of kindling the mind, and some aspects of disturbing the conscience, my real intention is to energize the will of those who heard or will read this sermon to begin to address the issues that are being discussed. This sermon is a call to action for the church to begin to respond to "The Persistent Problem of Prejudice."

THE PERSISTENT PROBLEM OF PREJUDICE
GALATIANS 3:27-28

It would come as no surprise to any of you, that there are some diseases, pains, and afflictions that affect our health that are short-term and temporary in nature. Some infection flares up, some bone is broken, and some organ fails to function properly. The pain and discomfort may be intense, but the problem is short-lived because a solution, a remedy, a therapy is readily available. Most of us have been on an antibiotic for an infection that seemed unbearable when it was active within our system. But once we took the prescribed regimen of medications the pain was relieved, and the problem was removed. Some physical ailments are short-term and temporary.

On the other hand, doctors speak about certain physical problems that are chronic and persistent. They keep flaring up year after year. They seem to defy solutions. We might be able to relieve the pain, but we cannot make the pain go away once and for all. Heart disease, hypertension, diabetes, arthritis, and other such ailments fit into this category of chronic and persistent physical ailments. It is not that we have not tried to find a cure; it is simply that nothing we have tried so far has been able to solve these afflictions once and for all.

Let me use this as an analogy for sin and for the spiritual illnesses that afflict our souls. Some things are chronic and persistent. They defy easy solution. They not only persist throughout our lifetime, but they have been chronic and persistent problems from one generation to another. They have been problems within the souls of men and women almost from the dawn of time. That is what Paul is pointing to in Galatians 3:26-29. He is identifying three forms of chronic and persistent prejudice that are as entrenched in our twenty-first-century world as they were when Paul wrote these words almost two thousand years ago. Paul would have us to consider what we actually believe about the issues of race, class, and gender. And then he would say to us, that when we come to Christ we ought to never again allow those things to divide us one from another.

It is difficult for us to imagine how far Paul was attempting to move

---

This sermon was preached by the author on May 21, 2000, at Antioch Baptist Church in Cleveland, Ohio.

his first century listeners when he said that in Christ "there is neither Jew nor Gentile, neither bond nor free, neither male nor female." These divisions were so wide and deep that they must have seemed virtually impossible to close. The idea of a missionary outreach by Palestinian followers of Jesus to people in the Gentile regions was itself a tumultuous issue for the early church. Paul was going beyond that in this passage in Galatians 3:26-29. Here, he is making revolutionary suggestions that would have changed the social arrangement of the world at that time. Paul is calling for a community that is free, once and for all, of the chronic and persistent prejudices of race, class, and gender. And what Paul said to his own generation is no less relevant and no less difficult for us today.

As black people, we are well aware of the issue of chronic and persistent prejudice based upon racial differences. Just this week two men were indicted for a horrific act of violence. These men stand accused of participating in the Sunday morning bombing of the Sixteenth Street Baptist Church in Birmingham, Alabama, in September, 1963, when four little black girls were killed while sitting in their Sunday school classroom. Less than one month earlier, Martin Luther King Jr. spoke of his dream of a nation where "people would not be judged by the color of their skin, but by the content of their character." In a sense, the bombing that Sunday morning in Birmingham was a direct response to the future that Dr. King was attempting to set forth. Racial prejudice is a chronic and persistent problem.

Why were those four little girls killed that morning? Were they numbered among the leaders of the civil rights activities that had occurred in that city earlier that same year? No! Were they among a group of students preparing to integrate one of the formerly all-white schools of that Southern city? No! The only reason those four girls died in that deadly blast is that they were black. That was the only charge of which they were guilty. The events of this past week are a fresh reminder that human beings have been shooting, lynching, beating, burning, and otherwise brutalizing each other since the beginning of recorded time. Most of the time, the only thing of which the victim is guilty, as with the girls in Birmingham, is being different. We have never been very good at dealing with diversity.

Let me now remind you that black people have no corner on the market of suffering so far as racial, ethnic, tribal, and national prejudices are concerned. What has become of the people who once called this land their home? Where are the Native peoples, the Miami and the Seneca, the Mohican and the Huron, the Sioux and the Seminole and the Cheyenne? They were victims of our intolerance for difference. They were forced from their land and herded onto reservations. Those who resisted were imprisoned or killed. Those who complied now suffer the highest instances of depression, alcoholism, domestic violence, and suicide of any population group in this country.

Black people are just as efficient as white people are when it comes to targeting and terrorizing people who are different. Right now the continent of Africa is being drenched in blood as a result of tribal and ethnic conflicts. There are wars raging in Sierra Leone, where guerrilla soldiers were shown hacking off the arms and legs of the children of their ethnic rivals. Ethiopia and Eritrea are involved in a war that has already claimed 100,000 lives. The numbers are higher in the Congo, and higher still in the fighting between the Hutus and Tutsis in Burundi, Rwanda, and Uganda. Most of those people look exactly like the people they are shooting, maiming, and beating to death. But there is some difference, however minor. And that is enough to cause those terrible wars.

These examples to which I have pointed are just a few reminders of what I call *the persistent problem of prejudice.* Sometimes our prejudices lead us to terrible acts of violence. Other times, they lead us to cruel forms of segregation and social separation. It was just forty-six years ago last week, that the Supreme Court ruled in the case of *Brown v. the Board of Education*, ending segregation in public education throughout this country. Today, Central High School in Little Rock, Arkansas, and almost every school in the state of Kansas, where the Brown case originated, is overwhelmingly black. The white students have largely been withdrawn from public schools and enrolled in private schools. In the South, many of those schools are "Christian academies," opened between 1956 and 1960 for the express purpose of allowing white parents to continue to send their children to all-white schools.

What makes this problem of prejudice so frustrating is that Christian people continue to practice prejudice nearly two thousand years after the apostle Paul gave God's definitive ruling on this issue. In Galatians 3:27-29, Paul says, "There is neither Jew nor Gentile, neither slave nor free, neither male nor female, for all are one in Christ Jesus." God is no respecter of nationality, race, ethnic, or tribal group. God does not love some people more than he loves others. There is no aspect of our family tree that could possibly make God love us any more or any less.

There is a book that came out a few years ago, entitled *Our Kind of People*. It is about the black elite in America, a self-proclaimed black upper class largely defined by light skin color and straight as opposed to curly hair. This book goes on and on about how light-skinned black people are somehow smarter and more industrious than their darker skinned brothers and sisters. This, of course, goes back to the days of slavery and to the tensions between dark-skinned Booker T. Washington and fair-skinned W.E.B. Du Bois. Thanks be to God that in God's kingdom there is no color chart that we have to match, no social status that we have to achieve, no cotillions that we have to have appeared in, no family pedigree that we have to produce, and no professional career that we have to establish.

The prejudices discussed in that book are as far from the values of the kingdom of God as the east is from the west. There are no *our kind of people* in heaven. With God the only kind of people who matter are the sinners who are saved by grace, the pilgrims on their way to a city called heaven, and those who die in faith and look forward to moving into a house not made with hands. When you come into a saving knowledge of Jesus Christ, among the first things that happens to you is your willingness to abandon all prejudices based upon race and ethnicity. How different the world would appear if we could all give up this first persistent prejudice.

After Paul says, "there is neither Jew nor Gentile," he goes on to say, "there is neither slave nor free." This points not to ethnic background, but to social class. It continues to be true, that the best test of the character of any society is how it cares for its poorest citizens. If that is the case, then this is a tough place in which to be poor. Poor people in this country die sooner because they have no access to adequate medical care. They end up on death row faster because they cannot afford the best legal representation. They receive the least adequate education because per pupil spending in schools is less in the areas where they live.

It is a shame and a disgrace that we have people sleeping on the streets all across this country. We cut back the work force in a corporation. We end the livelihood of hundreds of workers who were earning enough money to support their families. Meanwhile, that same company gives a top executive it no longer needs a severance package of millions of dollars. Two weeks ago, the company that makes the Barbie doll fired its first female CEO. In order to get her to leave, company executives gave her $45 million. That number is exactly the number of people with no medical insurance in America.

So much of the violence, the drug addiction, the alcoholism, the domestic violence that we see in this country is a direct result of poverty and class distinctions. Paul says that in Christ there is neither slave nor free. There is no difference between Bill Gates and the poorest person in this county, so far as their worth and value in the eyes of God is concerned. We need to see the poor as God sees them, as people who deserve every opportunity that any one of us would want for ourselves. This is why issues such as living wage ordinances, universal health coverage, and fair sentencing guidelines in the court system are so important. When we are in Christ, we should hate poverty as much as we hate racism, and work just as hard to bring it to an end.

I heard an interesting comment last week from William Kennard, the director of the Federal Communications Commission. He is the first black head of that powerful agency in charge of telecommunications, radio and TV licenses, and the Internet. He said that one hundred years ago the great divide in American society was "the color line." In the twenty-first century, the great divide is "who is online." Who does and does not have access to a computer, to the Internet, to e-mail. People who are being left behind in terms of this technology may never be able to compete in this high-tech society.

What we must say as people of God is that no one should be left behind. No one should be left out. No one should be locked up and forgotten simply because he or she is guilty of the crime of being poor. But just as we make no room for ethnic or racial difference, so we make no provision for class and income difference. This is another form of the *persistent problem of prejudice.*

Then there is the problem of gender. There are still too many men who believe that women are second-class citizens, deserving of lower pay, lower promotions, and lower levels of respect. Next month, the Southern Baptist Convention will introduce a resolution to the delegates at its national meeting affirming the fact that the teaching and pastoral office of the church should be restricted to men (males). Women can use their gifts in other ways, even as assistant pastors and preachers. But the

197

office of pastor will be off limits to them, not because they are mentally or morally unfit for the position. The door to pastoral ministry will be closed to them simply because they are women!

This is the same Southern Baptist Convention that was created in 1845 because the American Baptist Convention called for an end to the slave trade. The Southern Baptist Churches opposed that idea, believing that slavery was acceptable in the eyes of God. Thus were born the Northern and Southern Baptist Convention. The Northern Baptists reclaimed the name of American Baptists, but the Southern Baptists refused to reunite. After 155 years, they still do not know what to do with difference. They are a living, breathing example of the *persistent problem of prejudice.*

However, the Southern Baptist Convention does not stand alone on this issue. I believe that many black Baptists across this country share in this view that the spiritual gifts of women ought to prohibited from being expressed in the pastoral office. They hold these views on the basis of 1 Corinthians 14:34-35 and 1 Timothy 2:12. They read those verses with no interest in doing serious biblical exegesis or hermeneutics, ignoring the fact that the status of women in the world at that time has been reversed 180 degrees in our world today. Yet, many of those who support limits on the gifts of women would be the first to protest any attempt to limit people because of race or class. Here is proof of how entrenched our prejudices can become.

What is the answer to this continuing problem of prejudice against people who are guilty of nothing more than being different in color, culture, class, or gender? I believe it can be found in 2 Thessalonians 3:5, which says, "May the Lord direct your hearts to the love of God and to the steadfastness of Christ." Prejudice will never end until the hearts of men and women have been changed. Prejudice will never leave the human heart until it has been replaced by the love of God. If you want to rid the world of the *persistent problem of prejudice,* pray that God will move in and work on the hearts of people and turn them toward each other in acceptance and affirmation. No law, no social policies, and no political protests will be able to accomplish the change that is needed. We need something that can treat a chronic and persistent problem, and only a change of heart can accomplish that kind of result.

Notice how specifically Paul speaks about what part of our lives it is that God needs to direct if there is to be any lasting effect. Paul does not say that God needs to direct our steps or our feet. It is a good thing that we allow the Lord to lead us into the places where God would have us to go. However, if God has not first changed our hearts, then when we get wherever we are going, we will be the same people that we were before, doing the same thing in a different place. So God does not want to direct our steps.

Notice also that Paul does not hope that God will direct our speech or our words. It certainly is important that "the words of our mouth be acceptable to God." But how can they be if God does not first have control of our hearts? The verse in Psalm 19:14 actually says, "Let the words of my mouth, *and the meditation of my heart,* be acceptable in thy sight." God does not control our words unless God first controls our hearts. That is why Proverbs 23:7 says, "As a man thinketh in his heart, so is he." Therefore, we urge God to take control not just of our feet or our words. Instead, we ask God to take control of our hearts. We ask God to direct our hearts. We ask God to move within our hearts. We ask God to have his way in our lives by having his way in our hearts.

I love the little song that says,

> *Into my heart, into my heart,*
> *Come into my heart, Lord Jesus,*
> *Come in today; come in to stay,*
> *Come into my heart, Lord Jesus.*

I do not know where God will lead us when he begins to direct our hearts. However, I believe that the only way we will overcome the grip of chronic and persistent prejudice in the areas of race, class, and gender will be as we allow the Lord to direct our hearts toward the love of God. And so my prayer shall always be, for me and for the church of Jesus Christ, *"Come into my heart, Lord Jesus!"*

End Notes

INTRODUCTION

1. Haddon Robinson, *Biblical Preaching* (Grand Rapids, Mich.: Baker Books, 1980), 77.

CHAPTER ONE

1. Edmund Holt Linn, *Preaching as Counseling: The Unique Method of Harry Emerson Fosdick* (Valley Forge, Pa.: Judson Press, 1966), 92.

2. Richard C. Borden, *Public Speaking as Listeners Like It* (New York: Harper & Row, 1935), 3–12.

3. Robert McCracken, *The Making of the Sermon* (New York: Harper & Brothers, 1956), 18.

4. Elizabeth Achtemeier, *Preaching from the Old Testament* (Louisville, Ky.: Westminster/John Knox Press, 1989), 39.

5. A comment offered by Dr. Gardner C. Taylor in a class on black preaching he taught at Union Theological Seminary of New York City in the spring of 1973.

CHAPTER TWO

1. James Cox, *A Guide to Biblical Preaching* (Nashville: Abingdon, 1976), 32–36.

2. Eugene L. Lowry, *Living with the Lectionary* (Nashville: Abingdon, 1997), 23.

3. Ibid., 26.

4. Merrill Abbey, "Crisis Preaching in the 70s," *Pulpit Digest* (February 1971), 7–12.

5. Ibid., 7.

6. Marvin A. McMickle, *Preaching to the Black Middle Class* (Valley Forge, Pa.: Judson Press, 2000).

7. Samuel D. Proctor, *The Certain Sound of the Trumpet* (Valley Forge, Pa.: Judson Press, 1994), 22.

8. Ibid., 25.

9. Ibid., 27.

10. Ibid., 5.

11. Merrill Abbey, 7.

12. Cleophus Larue, *The Heart of Black Preaching* (Louisville, Ky.: Westminster/John Knox Press, 2000), 22–25.

13. Haddon Robinson, *Biblical Sermons* (Grand Rapids, Mich.: Baker Books, 1989), 174.

CHAPTER THREE

1. James Cox, *A Guide to Biblical Preaching* (Nashville: Abingdon, 1976), 16.

2. S. G. De Vries, "Biblical Criticism," *The Interpreter's Dictionary of the Bible*, v. 1 (Nashville: Abingdon, 1962), 414–16.

3. Leander Keck, *The Bible in the Pulpit* (Nashville: Abingdon, 1978), 22.

4. Ibid., 22–23.

5. Haddon Robinson, *Biblical Preaching* (Grand Rapids, Mich.: Baker Books, 1980), 26.

6. Leonard L. Thompson, *Introducing Biblical Literature* (Englewood Cliffs, N.J.: Prentice Hall, 1978), 12.

7. William Thompson, *Preaching Biblically* (Nashville: Abingdon, 1981), 27.

8. Leander Keck, 106.

9. Ibid.

10. Thomas G. Long, *Preaching and the Literary Forms of the Bible* (Philadelphia: Fortress Press, 1989).

11. See Norman Porteous's *Daniel* (Philadelphia: Fortress Press, 1965), Leon Wood's *A Commentary on Daniel* (Grand Rapids, Mich.: Zondervan Publishers, 1973), and John E. Goldingay's *Daniel* (Dallas, Tex.: Word Books, 1989).

12. John Lovell, *Black Song: The Forge and the Flame* (New York: Macmillan, 1972), 329.

13. Ibid., 228.

14. James A. Sanders, "Hermeneutics," *The Interpreter's Dictionary of the Bible*, supplemental vol, (Nashville: Abingdon, 1976), 406.

15. See *Faces about the Cross, Meet These Men, Sermons on New Testament Characters,* and *More Sermons on Biblical Characters* by Clovis Chappell. Compare *Chariots of Fire, Great Interviews of Jesus, The Greatest Men of the Bible,* and *The Way of a Man with a Maid* by Clarence Macartney.

16. James Ward and Christine Ward, *Preaching from the Prophets* (Nashville: Abingdon, 1995), 11.

17. Elizabeth Achtemeier, *Preaching from the Minor Prophets* (Grand Rapids, Mich.: Eerdmans, 1998).

18. Warren Stewart, *Interpreting God's Word in Black Preaching* (Valley Forge, Pa.: Judson Press, 1984), 32–33.

19. Martin Luther King Jr., *Why We Can't Wait* (New York: Signet Books, 1963), 91.

20. Leander Keck, 106.

21. Merrill Abbey, 7.

22. Elizabeth Achtemeier, *Preaching from the Old Testament* (Louisville,

Ky.: Westminster/John Knox Press, 1989), 118–119.

23. Walter Brueggemann, *The Prophetic Imagination* (Philadelphia: Fortress Press, 1978), 44.

24. Ibid., 30–31.

CHAPTER FOUR

1. Reginald H. Fuller, *The Use of the Bible in Preaching* (Philadelphia: Fortress Press, 1981), 21.

2. *The Analytical Hebrew and Chaldee Lexicon* and *The Analytical Greek Lexicon* are both published by Zondervan Press.

3. Francis Brown, S.R. Driver, and C.A. Briggs, eds., *Hebrew and English Lexicon of the Old Testament* (New York: Oxford, 1968), Walter Bauer, *A Greek-English Lexicon of the New Testament and Other Early Christian Literature*, 2nd ed., rev. by William F. Arndt and F. Wilbur Gingrich (Chicago: The University of Chicago Press, 1979).

4. Gerhard Kittel, ed., *Theological Dictionary of the New Testament*, 10 vols. Geoffrey W. Bromly, trans. (Grand Rapids, Mich.: Eerdmans, 1977).

5. *The Laymen's Parallel Bible* (Grand Rapids, Mich.: Zondervan Bible Publishers, 1973).

6. The maps, column notes, and introductory statements in each of these books are very helpful.

7. Those interested in buying commentaries should understand that not every volume in a series is as helpful as others. This is a "buyer beware" area.

8. Alan Richardson, *A Theological Word Book of the Bible* (New York: Macmillan, 1950).

9. Ibid., 130.

10. Beth McMurtie, "Teaching Students Who Can't Tell Aristotle from Acquinas," *The Chronicle of Higher Education*, vol. XLVI, no. 31 (April 7, 2000): A18–20.

11. *The Interpreter's Dictionary of the Bible* by Abingdon is especially help-ful because of its supplemental volume. That makes this collection quite exhaustive.

12. *The New Harper's Bible Dictionary* was revised and updated in 1973 by Madeline S. and J. Lane Miller, eds. (Harper & Row).

CHAPTER FIVE

1. Marvin A. McMickle, "And He Called Them His Disciples," *Princeton Seminary Bulletin* (February 1984).

2. Herbert G. May, ed., *The Oxford Bible Atlas* (New York: Oxford, 1962).

3. Bernhard W. Anderson, *Understanding the Old Testament* (Englewood Cliffs, N.J.: Prentice Hall, 1966).

4. John Bright, *A History of Israel* (Philadelphia: Westminster, 1959).

5. Howard Kee, Franklin Young, and Karlfried Froehlich, *Understanding the New Testament* (Englewood Cliffs, N.J.: Prentice Hall,1965).

6. Willi Marxsen, *Introduction to the New Testament* (Philadelphia: Fortress Press, 1970).

7. Michael D. Coogan, ed., *The Oxford History of the Biblical World* (New York: Oxford, 1998).

8. Madeleine S. Miller and J. Lane Miller, *Harper's Encyclopedia of Bible Life* (New York: Harper & Row, 1978).

9. Pat Alexander, ed., *The Eerdmans Family Encyclopedia of the Bible* (Grand Rapids, Mich.: Eerdmans, 1980).

CHAPTER SIX

1. Harry Emerson Fosdick, "The Power to See It Through," *Riverside Sermons* (New York: Harper & Brothers, 1958), 28–37.

2. Leonard Greenspoon, "From Alexandria to Antioch," *The Oxford History of the Biblical World* (New York: Oxford, 1998), 459.

3. Ibid.

4. Ibid.

CHAPTER SEVEN

1. Burton H. Throckmorton, Jr., ed., *Gospel Parallels* (Toronto: Thomas Nelson & Sons, 1967).

CHAPTER EIGHT

1. See Alexander Maclaren's *The Exposition of the Holy Scriptures* (Grand Rapids, Mich.: Baker Books, 1982), C. H. Spurgeon's *The Life and Works of Our Lord*, 3 vols. (Grand Rapids, Mich.: Baker Books, 1979), and the multivolume series *The Words of Gardner Taylor* (Valley Forge, Pa.: Judson Press, 1999).

2. Clyde Fant and William Pinson, *20 Centuries of Great Preaching*, 13 vols. (Waco, Tex.: Word Books, 1981).

3. See Haddon Robinson's *Biblical Preaching* (Grand Rapids, Mich.: Baker Books, 1980) and *Biblical Sermons* (Grand Rapids, Mich.: Baker Books, 1989), and Dewitte Holland's *The Preaching Tradition* (Nashville: Abingdon, 1981).

4. James H. Cone, *God of the Oppressed* (New York: Seabury Press, 1975), 29.

5. The entire issue of *Christianity Today* (May 22, 2000) was devoted to this subject..

CHAPTER NINE

1. Haddon Robinson, *Biblical Sermons* (Grand Rapids, Mich.: Baker Books, 1989), 174.

2. Ibid.

3. Carl F. H. Henry, "Evangelical," *The New International Dictionary of the Christian Church*, J. D. Douglas, ed. (Grand Rapids, Mich.: Zondervan, 1978), 358–359.

4. F.L. Cross, *The Oxford Dictionary of the Christian Church* (New York: Oxford, 1983), 486.

5. Seward Hiltner, *Preface to Pastoral Theology* (Nashville: Abingdon, 1958).

6. Robert McCracken, *The Making of the Sermon* (New York: Harper & Brothers, 1956), 10.

7. William Sloane Coffin, "Iran," *The Twentieth Century Pulpit*, vol. 2, James Cox, ed. (Nashville: Abingdon, 1981), 34–39.

8. Aristotle, *Rhetoric and Poetics of Aristotle* (New York: The Modern Library, 1954), 24–25.

9. Halford Luccock, *Communicating the Gospel* (New York: Harper & Brothers, 1954), 145.

10. Henry Mitchell, "African-American Preaching," *Interpretation* (October 1997): 380–81.

11. Alan Heimert and Perry Miller, eds., *The Great Awakening* (New York: Bobbs-Merrill, 1967), 231.

12. Henry Mitchell, 381.

13. Phillip Brooks, *Lectures on Preaching* (Grand Rapids, Mich.: Baker Books, 1969), 8.

Glossary

ADVENT   The season of the Christian calendar that leads up to the observance of Christmas and the celebration of the coming of Christ into the world. It also serves as a time of spiritual preparation for the Second Coming of Christ at the end of history. The season extends over the four Sundays that precede Christmas Day.

ALLITERATION   A writing and speaking technique that places together words that begin with the same letter, as in the 8 Ls or the 8 Es used in this book. This technique also involves grouping words that begin or end with the same syllable sound, as with celebr*ation*, jubil*ation*, and exult*ation*. This practice is a pneumonic device that helps with memorization of certain rules or principles.

APOCALYPTIC   A form of biblical literature, typified by the Books of Daniel and Revelation and by lesser portions of other biblical books, that employs numerology, animal symbolism, and coded messages about the judgment that God is about to bring upon evildoers.

BIBLICAL AUTHORITY   The belief that the teachings and doctrines contained in the Bible should be the ultimate guide for believers in both faith and conduct. Other sources and persons can be consulted and considered, but where faith is concerned the Bible is the standard against which all other views and opinions must be considered. The authority of the Bible even extends over the authority of doctrines written by people, no matter what church office they hold.

BIBLICAL COMMENTARIES   These are scholarly research books that aid in the study of Scripture. Commentaries fall into several categories. (1) There are edited multivolume series covering the entire Bible that involve various authors who offer textual and theological insights into particular books of the Bible. (2) There are authored single-volume commentaries on the entire Bible, although these offer more general information and are far less thorough. (3) There are also commentaries on single books of the Bible that are not part of any larger series of books.

BIBLICAL CRITICISM   This is the process by which a portion of Scripture is analyzed with the goal of determining date, authorship, literary form and function, intended audience, and the message that was being communicated to that audience and to subsequent generations of readers and believers.

BIBLICAL SERMON   A homiletic method wherein the meaning and implications of biblical text serve as the central focus of the sermon. A biblical sermon occurs when the Scripture passage is not simply read but actually governs and determines the content of the sermon.

BIBLICAL THEOLOGY   An approach to the study of Scripture that concentrates on the Old and New Testament as being inseparably linked together, and that seeks to discover the large doctrinal and theological assertions that serve as the underlying message of the Bible. Biblical theology asserts that the Bible is not just a piece of literature to be read, but the expression of a community of faith that evolved over many hundreds of years and that seeks to communicate a message to the believing community at any future time and place.

CONTINUITY   This is the identification of those doctrines and practices required of the believing community in the Old Testament that remain true and valid in the New Testament as well. These would include such doctrines as salvation, sin, atonement, etc.

DISCONTINUITY   This involves those doctrines and practices taught and required in the Old Testament that are no longer held as vital or valid in the New Testament. These would include such doctrines as circumcision, animal sacrifice, dietary customs, the observance of special festivals (e.g., Passover, Pentecost, Tabernacles), and the continued expectation of the coming of the Messiah.

EISEGESIS   The practice of explaining the meaning of a biblical text so that the text is made to say what the reader or researcher wants it to say. It is reading into the text meanings and implications that would be found to be invalid or untrue if the text were properly analyzed. This occurs most commonly when someone wants to justify a pre-existing prejudice or practice by misusing a biblical text so that the attitude or behavior appears to have scriptural support.

EPIGRAMMATICAL   A style of preaching that employs stories, anecdotes, and other illustrations that appeal to the five senses of the listener or reader. People are urged to *hear, see, taste, feel,* and *smell* the events, emotions, and conversations being described.

EPIPHANY   From the Greek word for *manifestation* or *revelation,* this is the season on the Christian calendar that immediately follows Christmas. It refers to the Magi from countries beyond Israel who came to pay homage to the baby Jesus. When they returned to their respective homelands they became the first persons to spread the news about the birth of the Savior of the world. Thus, the work that God began in the obscure setting of Bethlehem was now being revealed to the wider world.

EVANGELICAL SERMON   Preaching that lifts up the salvation message of the gospel and that aggressively challenges people to respond by faith to that message. Romans 10:9 is the basis of this approach to preaching. It does not involve any special consideration of that set of social issues that have been identified by some conservative Christians, such as school vouchers, abortion, and other so-called family values issues.

EXEGESIS The process of drawing out from the biblical text the meaning that the original authors intended, and paying close attention to the language and textual issues that aid in establishing the clearest and most accurate understanding of what that text actually says.

EXPERIENTIAL SERMON Preaching that refers to experiences and events in the life of the preacher, some large cross-section of the congregation, or some other person who is well known, that aids in understanding the meaning of the text and the message of the sermon. This approach allows the preacher to share personal struggles with issues of faith, or illustrate how God has done in the preacher's life what the sermon suggests God can do in the lives of the hearers. This is not a license to celebrate one's own virtues, but to testify of what God has done in one's life.

EXPOSITOR The person who seeks, as preacher or teacher, to faithfully communicate the meaning of a biblical text, by considering the passage on a word by word and line by line basis. The emphasis is on what does the text *say* and what does the text *mean*.

HERMENEUTICS James Sanders calls this the process of "dynamic analogy," wherein the challenge of Scripture to an ancient community is directed in an appropriate way to become a similar challenge to the contemporary believing community. Hermeneutics also recognizes that the biblical text was shaped within a certain social and cultural setting, and must likewise be interpreted within a wide variety of other social and cultural settings. The interpreter needs to preserve the integrity of the biblical message during this shift from ancient community to various contemporary settings.

HOMILETICS The art and practice of sermon design and delivery. It involves the preacher in the decision of what text should be studied, what message should be developed, what type of argument should be employed, and what kind of response should be sought.

INERRANCY   The primary issue here is the truthfulness of the doctrines contained in the Bible, the observation of which will result in a true and lasting relationship with God. Inerrancy also involves the belief that the events, statements, and characters in the Bible reflect the actual truth so far as history is concerned. Those persons did exist, those events did occur, and those statements and their associated promises and warnings are to be taken literally.

LECTIONARY   A three-year cycle of Bible readings designed to lead the reader through the various liturgical seasons, major doctrines, and various literary types found within the Scriptures. Each week the reader is exposed to passages from the Old and New Testaments, with hints regarding how and why those texts should be considered together. The lectionary also includes suggested prayers and meditations that can be read during specific worship services over the course of the year.

LENT   The period of forty days, excluding weekends, before Easter when Christians go through a period of penitence and self-examination. Many Christians also include some form of fasting and making sacrificial gifts to alleviate poverty and human suffering. The season of Lent begins on what is called Ash Wednesday, so called because many Christians have ash marks placed on their foreheads as an outward sign that their time of penitence has begun.

LEXICON   A research tool used in the study of language. It offers suggestions regarding the form of speech in which a word is used (e.g., noun, verb, adjective), where else in the Bible a certain word may appear in that same form and, where Hebrew and Greek are involved, it indicates the root form of the word.

LITERARY GENRE   The Bible consists of sixty-six books that employ almost that many types of literature. The Bible contains law, history, biography, prophecy, poetry, wisdom, narrative, apocalyptic, Gospels, epistles, genealogy, and many other genres. The Bible student should always seek to understand what genre or type of literature is featured in any given text.

LITURGICAL CALENDAR Within the Christian church, the annual observance of events, centered on the Bible, that help to define the worship and study life of many congregations and denominations. The calendar flows from the seasons of Advent, Christmas, Epiphany, Lent, Easter, Pentecost, and back to Advent. This calendar annually rehearses the high points in the life of Christ and the formation of the early church. In some churches this rotation includes a change in the color of the vestments worn by the clergy and displayed in the sanctuary. Not every Christian community closely adheres to the liturgical calendar, but it is an excellent way to maintain a fresh and timely preaching schedule.

LITURGIST The worship leader who offers or leads in the prayers, reads the Scripture, and directs congregational involvement in the service. Typically, the title *liturgist* distinguishes other participants in the service from the person who preaches the sermon.

METHODOLOGY Used here to suggest the structured and regular process by which Scripture is studied, sermons are prepared and delivered, and a schedule of preaching is determined far in advance of the actual delivery.

PENTECOST From the Greek word for *fifty*, this originally referred to the Old Testament festival in honor of the grain harvests in ancient Israel that occurred fifty days after Passover. In the New Testament, it marks the birth of the church as described in Acts 2, when the Holy Spirit fell upon the apostles causing them to speak in tongues. On that day, Peter preached to a crowd that had gathered in Jerusalem from all over the world to observe the festival of Pentecost, and three thousand persons were converted to faith in Christ. Pentecost has also been called Whitsunday, because in some churches candidates are dressed in white gowns and baptized, thus reenacting the addition of new members to the body of Christ.

PERICOPE This refers to a passage of Scripture of varying length that can be studied as a self-contained unit. A sermon or a Bible study is usually done on the basis of such a unit of Scripture. A pericope is the beginning and ending point of a body of writing to be considered, without taking on more material than could honestly be handled in a sermon or study session.

PROPHETIC SERMON   A style of preaching in which the corrective and challenging message of the text is updated and directed to the contemporary congregation. The prophetic sermon is not necessarily based upon a portion of Scripture taken from one of the biblical books of prophecy. Rather, the content and authority reflected in the biblical prophets is present in the sermon. That authority does not reside in the opinions or person of the preacher, but in the courage of the preacher to stand up and say, "Thus says the Lord, . . ."

SITZ EM LEBEN   A German term that means situation in life, or the historical and cultural context in which a passage of Scripture was shaped, and in which it must be understood. It also refers to a preacher's understanding of the historical and cultural context of the people to whom that text is being directed in the sermon or Bible study. The preacher or teacher wants to be aware of and faithful to both settings, ancient and contemporary.

Bibliography

ABBEY, MERRILL. "Crisis Preaching in the 70s." *Pulpit Digest* (February 1971).

ACHTEMEIER, ELIZABETH. *Preaching from the Minor Prophets*. Grand Rapids, Mich.: Eerdmans, 1998.

————. *Preaching from the Old Testament*. Louisville, Ky.: Westminster/John Knox Press, 1989.

Alexander, Pat, ed. *The Eerdmans Family Encyclopedia of the Bible*. Grand Rapids, Mich.: Eerdmans, 1980.

ANDERSON, BERNHARD W. *Understanding the Old Testament*. Englewood Cliffs, N.J.: Prentice Hall, 1966.

ARISTOTLE. *Rhetoric and Poetics of Aristotle*. New York: The Modern Library, 1954.

BORDEN, RICHARD C. *Public Speaking as Listeners Like It*. New York: Harper & Row, 1935.

BRIGHT, JOHN. *A History of Israel*. Philadelphia: Westminster, 1959.

BROOKS, PHILLIP. *Lectures on Preaching*. Grand Rapids, Mich.: Baker Books, 1969.

Brown, Francis, S. R. Driver, and C. A. Briggs, eds. *Hebrew and English Lexicon of the Old Testament*. New York: Oxford, 1968.

BRUEGGEMANN, WALTER. *The Prophetic Imagination*. Philadelphia: Fortress Press, 1978.

COFFIN, WILLIAM SLOANE. "Iran." *The Twentieth Century Pulpit*, vol. 2. James Cox, ed. Nashville: Abingdon, 1981.

CONE, JAMES H. *God of the Oppressed*. New York: Seabury, 1975.

Coogan, Michael D., ed. *The Oxford History of the Biblical World*. New York: Oxford, 1998.

COX, JAMES. *A Guide to Biblical Preaching*. Nashville: Abingdon, 1976.

CROSS, F. L. *The Oxford Dictionary of the Christian Church*. New York: Oxford, 1983.

DE VRIES, S. G. "Biblical Criticism." *The Interpreter's Dictionary of the Bible*, vol. 1. Nashville: Abingdon, 1962.

FANT, CLYDE and WILLIAM PINSON. *20 Centuries of Great Preaching*. Waco, Tex.: Word Books, 1971.

FOSDICK, HARRY EMERSON. *Riverside Sermons*. New York: Harper & Brothers, 1958.

FULLER, REGINALD H. *The Use of the Bible in Preaching*. Philadelphia: Fortress Press, 1981.

GREENSPOON, LEONARD. "From Alexandria to Antioch." *The Oxford History of the Biblical World*. New York: Oxford, 1998.

Heimert, Alan and Perry Miller, eds. *The Great Awakening*. New York: Bobbs-Merrill, 1967.

HENRY, CARL F. H. "Evangelical." *The New International Dictionary of the*

Bible. J. D. Douglas, ed. Grand Rapids, Mich.: Zondervan, 1978.

HILTNER, SEWARD. *Preface to Pastoral Theology.* Nashville: Abingdon, 1958.

KECK, LEANDER. *The Bible in the Pulpit.* Nashville: Abingdon, 1978.

KEE, HOWARD, FRANKLIN YOUNG, and KARLFRIED FROEHLICH. *Understanding the New Testament.* Englewood Cliffs, N.J.: Prentice Hall, 1965.

KING, MARTIN LUTHER, JR. *Why We Can't Wait.* New York: Signet, 1963.

Kittell, Gerhard, ed. *Theological Dictionary of the New Testament.* Geoffrey W. Bromly, transl. Grand Rapids, Mich.: Eerdmans, 1977.

LANE, CLEOPHUS. *The Heart of Black Preaching.* Louisville, Ky.: Westminster/John Knox Press, 2000.

LINN, EDMUND HOLT. *Preaching as Counseling: The Unique Method of Harry Emerson Fosdick.* Valley Forge, Pa.: Judson Press, 1966.

LONG, THOMAS G. *Preaching and the Literary Forms of the Bible.* Philadelphia: Fortress Press, 1989.

LOVELL, JOHN. *Black Song: The Forge and the Flame.* New York: Macmillan, 1972.

LOWRY, EUGENE L. *Living with the Lectionary.* Nashville: Abingdon, 1997.

LUCCOCK, HALFORD. *Communicating the Gospel.* New York: Harper & Brothers, 1954.

MACLAREN, ALEXANDER. *The Exposition of the Holy Scriptures.* Grand Rapids, Mich.: Baker Books, 1982.

MARXSEN, WILLI. *Introduction to the New Testament.* Philadelphia: Fortress Press, 1970.

May, Herbert G., ed. *The Oxford Bible Atlas*. New York: Oxford, 1962.

MCCRACKEN, ROBERT. *The Making of the Sermon*. New York: Harper & Brothers, 1958.

MCMICKLE, MARVIN A. "And He Called Them His Disciples." *Princeton Seminary Bulletin* (February 1984).

————. *Preaching to the Black Middle Class*. Valley Forge, Pa.: Judson Press, 2000.

MCMURTIE, BETH. "Teaching Students Who Can't Tell Aristotle from Acquinas." *The Chronicle of Higher Education* (April 7, 2000).

MILLER, MADELEINE S. and J. LANE MILLER. *Harper's Encyclopedia of Bible Life*. New York: Harper & Row, 1978.

MITCHELL, HENRY. "African-American Preaching." *Interpretation* (October 1997).

PORTEOUS, NORMAN. *Daniel*. Philadelphia: Fortress Press, 1965.

PROCTOR, SAMUEL D. *The Certain Sound of the Trumpet*. Valley Forge, Pa.: Judson Press, 1994.

RICHARDSON, ALAN. *A Theological Word Book of the Bible*. New York: Macmillan, 1950.

ROBINSON, HADDON. *Biblical Preaching*. Grand Rapids, Mich.: Baker Books, 1980.

————. *Biblical Sermons*. Grand Rapids, Mich.: Baker Books, 1989.

SANDERS, JAMES A. "Hermeneutics." *The Interpreter's Dictionary of the Bible,* supplemental vol. Nashville: Abingdon, 1976.

STEWART, WARREN. *Interpreting God's Word in Black Preaching*. Valley

Forge, Pa.: Judson Press, 1984.

THOMPSON, LEONARD. *Introducing Biblical Literature.* Englewood Cliffs, N.J.: Prentice Hall, 1978.

Throckmorton, Burton H., Jr., ed. *Gospel Parallels.* Toronto: Thomas Nelson & Sons, 1967.

WARD, JAMES and CHRISTINE WARD. *Preaching from the Prophets.* Nashville: Abingdon, 1995.